RACE
FRANCE TO FRANCE
LEAVE ANTARCTICA TO STARBOARD

An American in the Vendée Globe, Racing Solo, Non-Stop, Around the World

—RICH WILSON—

Rich Wilson

sitesALIVE!

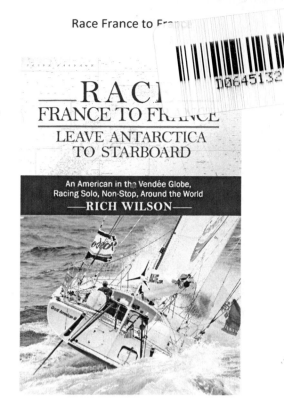

www.sitesalive.com
www.racefrancetofrance.com

ISBN-10: 0615666566
ISBN-13: 978-0615666563

Also by Author:
Racing a Ghost Ship
Walker & Co., 1996

To Mom,
the original adventurer of our family,
who went to Fairbanks in 1940
to host "Tundra Topics" at KFAR-660,
the first commercial radio station in the Alaskan Territory.

Dorothy Ann (Simpson) Wilson
1916 – 2010

Table of Contents

PART 1

PART 2

Appendices

Vendée Globe 2008-9

Solo, Non-Stop, Around-the-World, Without Assistance
~28,000 Miles, ~100 Days, 60' Sailboats, 30 Boats

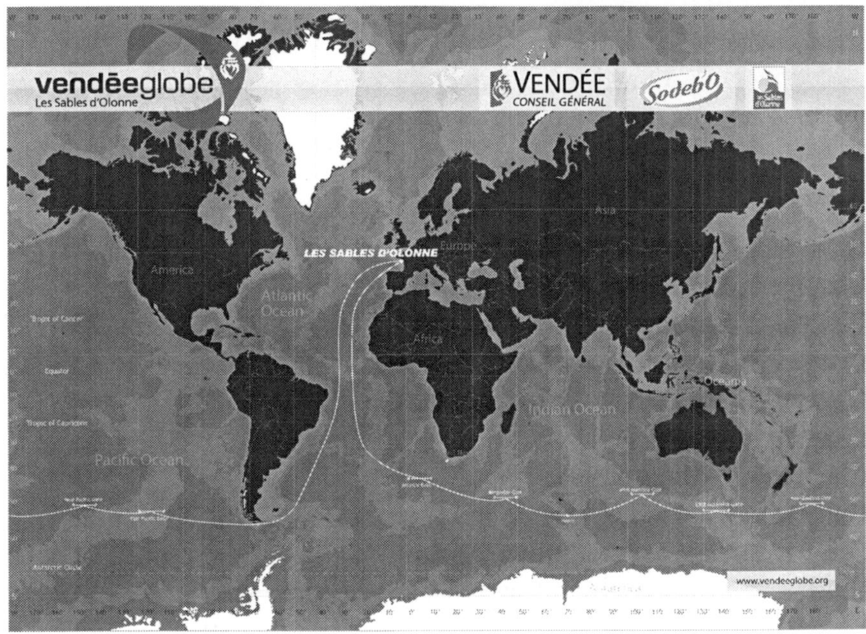

Vendée Globe 2008-9

30 Skippers

Back Row: Yann Eliès, Norbert Sedlacek, Vincent Riou, Derek Hatfield, Jean-Pierre Dick, Dominique Wavre, Brian Thompson, Jean-Baptiste Dejeanty, Rich Wilson, Armel Le Cléac'h, Unai Basurko, Jonny Malbon, Alex Thomson, Steve White

Front Row: Loïck Peyron, Jérémie Beyou, Sebastien Josse, Samantha Davies, Dee Caffari, Raphaël Dinelli, Marc Thiercelin, Mike Golding, Yannick Bestaven

Crouching: Bernard Stamm, Jean Le Cam, Marc Guillemot, Kito de Pavant, Arnaud Boissières, Roland Jourdain, Michel Desjoyeaux

Skipper	Nation	Boat Name
Unai Basurko	(ESP)	*Pakea Bizkaia*
Yannick Bestaven	(FRA)	*Aquarelle*
Jérémie Beyou	(FRA)	*Delta Dore*
Arnaud Boissières	(FRA)	*Akena Verandas*
Dee Caffari	(GBR)	*Aviva*
Jean Le Cam	(FRA)	*VM Matériaux*
Armel Le Cléac'h	(FRA)	*Brit Air*
Samantha Davies	(GBR)	*Roxy*
Jean-Baptiste Dejeanty	(FRA)	*Maisonneuve*
Michel Desjoyeaux	(FRA)	*Foncia*
Jean-Pierre Dick	(FRA)	*Paprec-Virbac*
Raphaël Dinelli	(FRA)	*Fondacion Ocean Vital*
Yann Eliès	(FRA)	*Generali Concorde*
Mike Golding	(GBR)	*Ecover*
Marc Guillemot	(FRA)	*Safran*
Derek Hatfield	(CAN)	*Spirit of Canada*
Sebastien Josse	(FRA)	*BT*
Roland Jourdain	(FRA)	*Veolia Environnement*
Jonny Malbon	(GBR)	*Artemis*
Kito de Pavant	(FRA)	*Groupe Bel*
Loïck Peyron	(FRA)	*Gitana*
Vincent Riou	(FRA)	*PRB*
Norbert Sedlacek	(AUT)	*NauticSport Kapsch*
Bernard Stamm	(CHE)	*Cheminées Poujoulat*
Marc Thiercelin	(FRA)	*DCNS*
Brian Thompson	(GBR)	*Pindar*
Alex Thomson	(GBR)	*Hugo Boss*
Dominique Wavre	(CHE)	*Temenos II*
Steve White	(GBR)	*Toe in the Water*
Rich Wilson	(USA)	*Great American III*

Great American III - **Hull**

Fibreglass cored hull
Carbon bulkheads support keel & mast
Carbon mast, boom, bowsprit
9 tons displacement (incl. 4 tons in Keel)
10 watertight compartments

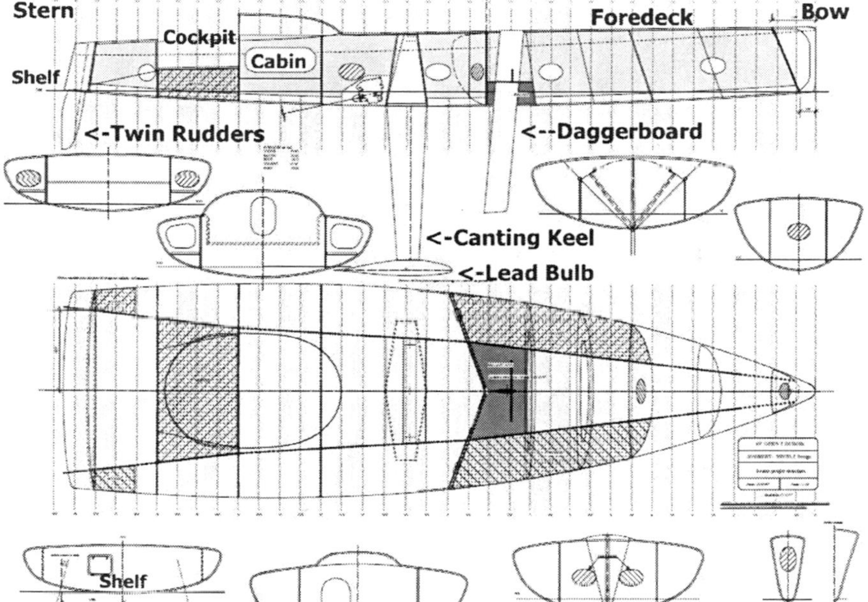

Great American III - Sailplan

60' Long, 60' Waterline, 6' Bowsprit, 18' Beam
90' Mast, 14.5' Deep Canting Keel
Two rudders, One daggerboard

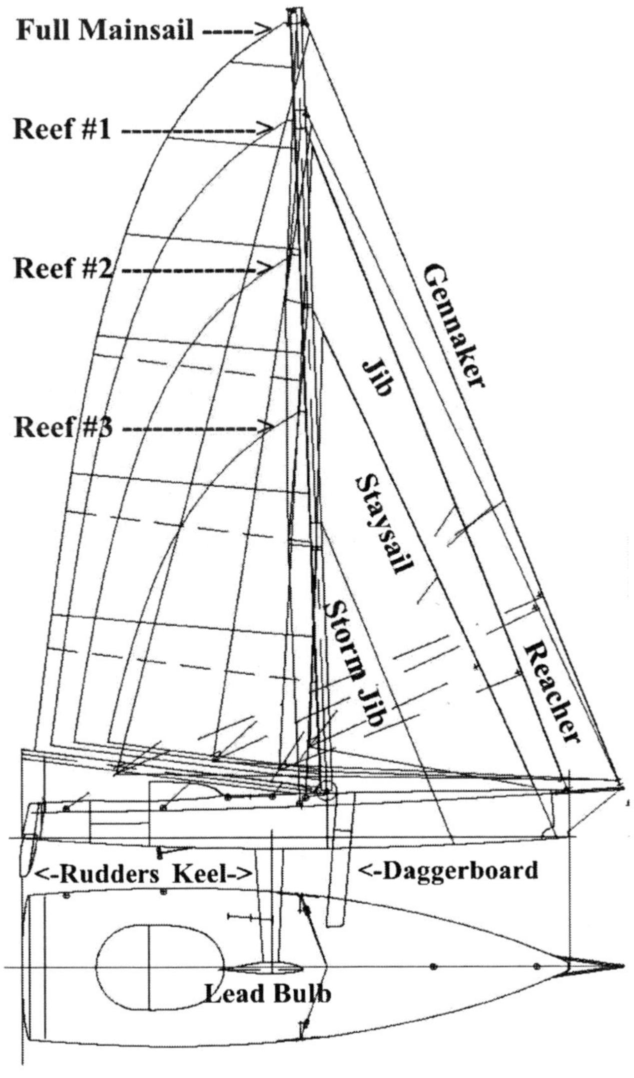

Great American III – Spinnaker

3500 square feet

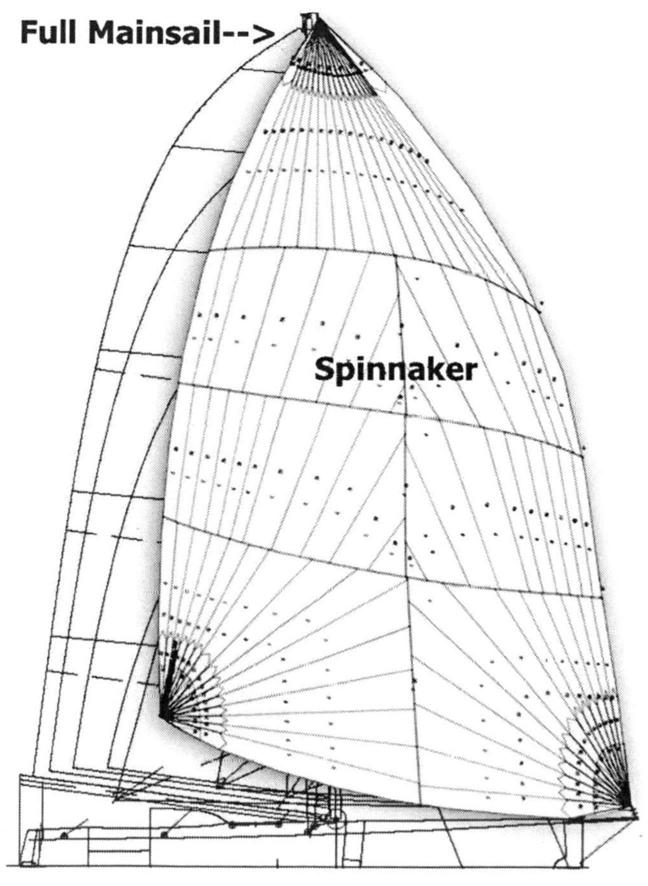

"They did not know it was impossible, so they did it."
...Mark Twain

Prologue

Everest of the Seas?
...Or the Other Way Around?

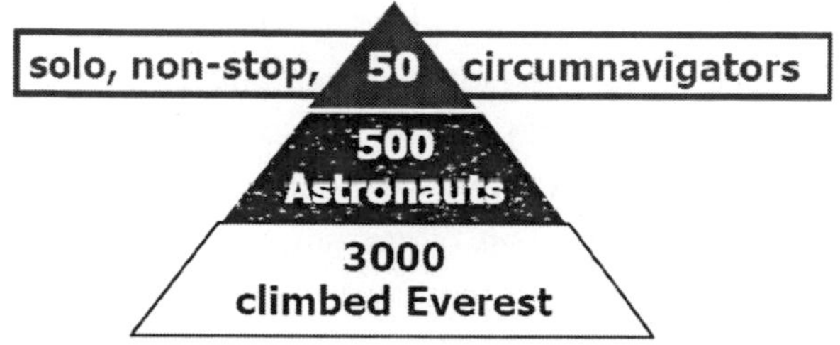

The Vendée Globe is the greatest sailing race in the world, and can more than hold its own against other great challenges. Often called the Everest of the Seas by the international media, it's arguably the other way around, Everest being the "Vendée Globe of Mountain Climbing." Whereas 3,000 climbers have summited Mt. Everest and 500 astronauts have been launched into space, fewer than 50 sailors have sailed solo, non-stop, around the world, without assistance – the terms of the Vendée Globe. Yet this epic race is virtually unknown in the U.S., by the public, the media, or the sailing community.

The race instructions are simple: depart Les Sables d'Olonne on France's west coast, leave Cape of Good Hope (Africa), Cape Leeuwin (Australia), and Cape Horn (South America) to port, leave Antarctica to starboard, finish at Les Sables d'Olonne.

The 28,000 nautical mile course (~32,000 land miles) will take ~100 days. The voyage will demand unimaginable physical endurance, sleep deprivation, problem-solving, and fear. In the five quadrennial runnings of the event, 75 boats had started and only 35 had finished, giving a greater than fifty percent average attrition rate. 8 boats had been lost at sea, including 2 skippers (with a 3rd lost en route to a start).

The boats are Open 60s, and huge for a solo sailor: 60' long, 6' bowsprit, 18' wide, 90' mast, 14.5' deep, weighing 9 tons with half of that in the keel. The mainsail is 1500 square feet (and weighs 450 pounds), the upwind jib is 1000 square feet, the balloon-like downwind spinnaker is 3500 square feet (dwarfing a doubles tennis court). Remember the 12 Meter class of boats from earlier America's Cup fame? Open 60s are slightly larger and more powerful in every dimension yet there are 10 fewer crew aboard, and you don't come home for lunch.

Coast Guards will tell you frankly: after day one, you're on your own, you'll be out of range of our ships, planes, and helicopters. You would have to sail your monster boat through the most remote and fierce seas on the planet, through the Southern Ocean. If you get into trouble, you'll have to rely on cargo ships in the area (if there are any), or your fellow competitors (and even if they can get to you, what are they going to do? They are alone too…) Mostly, you will have to rely on yourself.

There will be no timeouts when your game plan goes awry; no substitutes when exhaustion sets in or injury occurs; and no referees to keep the weather and seas fair. You may not use electricity to power the winches to control the huge sails. You may not receive advice on weather forecasting or routing. If you have to stop, you can anchor in a harbor (if you can get to one), but you can't tie up to a dock or buoy, and you can't go ashore above the high tide line. If you do any of these, or receive any physical assistance whatsoever, you will be disqualified.

§

There had been appalling episodes in past races: Bertrand de Broc sewing the tip of his tongue back on after he bit it off when his boat was knocked on its side in a storm, throwing him across the cabin; Thierry Dubois, after his boat had rolled upside down, rightside up, then upside down again in a horrible Indian Ocean gale that claimed four boats, jumping into the water in a survival suit to swim after a life raft, dropped by an Australian Navy patrol plane at the limit of its range, reaching the liferaft to find it damaged and deflating, and his boat now too far away for a return swim; Tony Bullimore living for four days on chocolate bars in the dark of his overturned hull after his keel broke off in a gale, not knowing if help would arrive soon enough; Gerry Roufs, disappearing without a trace in a violent storm on his final approach to Cape Horn.

And there were heroic stories: British sailor Pete Goss turning around and sailing 150 miles upwind into the teeth of an Indian Ocean gale to find and rescue Raphaël Dinelli from a liferaft after his boat had capsized and sunk; Italian sailor Giovanni Soldini rescuing Frenchwoman Isabelle Autissier whose cabintop had been swept off by an immense sea that crested aboard in the south; Loïck Peyron, finding Philippe Poupon sitting on the side of his boat, capsized with masts in the water, the boat unable to right itself, sailing past, getting a line to Poupon and towing the boat around to face the wind so that she could right herself, a feat of stunning boat-handling skill.

§

In the five previous events, only two Americans had entered. Mike Plant sailed the inaugural race in 1988-9, completing the course, but not finishing officially, as he had to stop for an assisted repair in New Zealand. Sailing transatlantic to the start of the second race in 1992, Mike was lost at sea when his keel broke off in mid-Atlantic and his boat immediately capsized. He was never found. In 2004, Bruce Schwab became the first American to officially finish the race, gaining 9th place. I would be America's third entrant, and the oldest skipper in the 2008-9 fleet.

"The Vendée Globe is a race that is almost beyond belief."
...Gary Jobson, ESPN Commentator

Chapter 1: Les Sables d'Olonne

I had heard about the crowds, and the channel procession, and had seen videos from previous race starts. Yet these could not prepare me for the overwhelming warmth, encouragement and pure humanity of the cheering French throng, 300,000 strong, that had trooped in the pre-dawn dark of a dreary November day to gain preferred positions on the channel banks. They wanted the best possible view to salute the thirty skippers and boats from seven countries one last time as they transited from the inner protected harbor of Les Sables d'Olonne to the wide open North Atlantic Ocean - and the Vendée Globe.

The Vendée Globe... As a sailor, I had followed the race since it began in 1988. Yet despite solid offshore credentials with three world records on 15,000 mile clipper ship routes and an overall win in the prestigious Newport-Bermuda Race, I had never had any interest in sailing it, though I admired those who did. It was too hard, too long, too dangerous, the boats were too big, the sails were too big, and you were too far from land or help for most of the race. Nevertheless, I was here, and I knew how and why it had come about. But still…

§

One has to have a very good reason to race the Vendée Globe, to justify both your own personal risk, and the emotional turmoil and anxiety that you will inflict on friends and family ashore. For two dozen of the thirty starters, fully sponsored professional yacht racers, like ocean-going NASCAR drivers, their goal was to win. For five more, it was to prove to a small sponsor that they should get a bigger sponsorship for a better boat next time. For me, it would be the culmination of my offshore voyages, a personal sailing challenge without equal, yet our true impetus for the effort was the creation of a global K12 school program via sitesALIVE!

How did I and we come to that?

My frontierswoman mother and entrepreneurial father had always sought far horizons. When they started sailing, I loved it. It was outdoors, active, in clean air (good for my bad asthma), and adventurous in its leaving safe land behind. Even as a kid sailing a little boat in a harbor, you were on your own, making decisions yourself, responsible for your boat and your own safe return. The boats and gear were endlessly interesting in their science and technology, as was the sea itself, with its currents, storms, wildlife and stars. At home, my parents had papered my bedroom walls with nautical charts that enticed my imagination. Books of the great captains inspired me, and those of the legendary solo circumnavigators - Slocum, Moitessier, Knox-Johnston, Chichester – piqued the personal question: could I ever be strong enough, smart enough, or brave enough to do anything like that?

Later, I taught high school math during the tumult of Boston's first year of school desegregation. Getting students to pay attention is the biggest challenge for a teacher, and I found that the students, even that year, if challenged with relevant, real-world problems from their own lives, perked up and paid attention, whereas textbooks put them to sleep. When two college-level, in-the-field science programs showed me the ultimate incarnation of that concept - send the students to the rainforest or to sea for their classes in those sciences – and when those students returned transformed by their experience, the seed of an idea sprouted.

My interest was K12, and since we couldn't send middle-school students to sea or to the rainforest, perhaps we could, with modern technology, bring those places, peoples, subjects and experiences to them in their classrooms and homes.

Our pilot project in 1990, a voyage from San Francisco to Boston aboard the 60' trimaran *Great American* challenging a California Gold Rush era clipper route record, ended in disaster at sea, with a double, somersaulting capsize off Cape Horn in 65' seas and 85 knots of wind, and a midnight rescue by the giant containership *New Zealand Pacific* that made Reader's Digest's "Drama in Real Life". Yet in our newsletter-fed classrooms, that failed and partial voyage nonetheless proved the concept as it succeeded in engrossing students in real world topics.

"Doc" Edgerton, a legendary MIT professor who had invented stroboscopic photography, once said: "The trick to teaching is to not let them know they're learning anything…until it's too late!" That was our philosophy. Hook 'em with a live, let 'er rip adventure, with drama, risk, and an uncertain outcome, then they'll come back tomorrow, to find out what happens next. Did you survive the storm? Have you been hit by flying fish? Did you repair that winch? It was real reality TV, not fake reality TV. With a daily audio report, ship's log data and journal, interactive Q&A, photos, videos, and teaching essays from sea tied to weekly classroom activities ashore (in a Teacher's Guide correlated to State and Federal curriculum standards), the students on land come to know the adventurer at sea. With knowing came caring, with caring came concern, with concern came the importance of understanding and learning the issues that were affecting the well-being of their new friend far away.

We tried that voyage again three years later, succeeding at sea with a world record aboard a smaller trimaran named *Great American II*, and in classrooms and homes via newly discovered distribution channels of Newspaper in Education (NIE – where newspapers would produce topical programs, market to teachers locally, and distribute newspapers to those who signed up) and Prodigy online that reached millions of readers and hundreds of thousands of students. Over the next two decades, we produced seventy-five live, interactive, semester-long programs, with content from accredited field school partners worldwide. We named our menu of programs sitesALIVE!, a *double entendre* on live foreign field sites and internet web sites.

The unique symbolism of the Vendée Globe is that it actually circles the world, and thus offers a unique chance to create a global school program. Oozing science, math, geography and history, with natural phenomena of stars, currents, weather and wildlife, infused with oceanic current affairs of shipping, climate change, pollution, and fisheries depletion, and with character challenges of perseverance, self-reliance, and problem-solving, this race would be our global teaching tool. Standard K12 curricular topics would be amplified and enlivened by exciting, real world, real-time input. Plus, with overseas schools participating, we could connect them to each other around these issues that affected all. A global interaction on fisheries between students in China, the U.S., Argentina, and Latvia? Now THAT would be COOL! That was our goal for this, our most ambitious sitesALIVE! program ever, and was the reason for racing the Vendée Globe.

To some, my commitment to deliver live daily content from a solo race at sea would seem a burden. To me it was the point of our race, and gave necessary purpose to my personal risk. I also knew that when times got tough, through exhaustion, gear failure, injury or fear, that writing for the students would motivate me. In those inevitable dark hours in the gales of the south, the students would help bring me home.

§

Our last dockline was cast off and a towboat carefully pulled us from our slip and toward the channel leading to the Atlantic Ocean. Hand on the tiller, I guided *Great American III* around the piling at the end of the finger pier, then turned back to look at the crowd jammed on the dock. They were cheering, clapping and shouting *"Bon Voyage! Bon Courage!"* Tears welled in my eyes, and I could see tears on the faces of friends, acquaintances, and others I didn't even know, as none of us could be certain that we'd ever see each other again.

Past our dock's end and through the jammed and cheering marina, with four close friends and crew aboard, we took our assigned slot in the single-file procession of boats and skippers being towed to the sea. Arcing slowly around the dogleg of the channel, the full brunt and enormity of the crowd was revealed in the mile long path that lay before us. To the far open end of this gauntlet, the shores were walls of people, walls of cheering, and the weight and sound of their emotion pressed on you and took your humbled breath away. They stood on the rocks, on the tops of cars, on balconies and buildings. They crowded ten deep on the pier, and under it too, some standing deep in the cold water, to be closer to us. They cheered and cheered and cheered, a mass of humanity wishing the fleet well with all their hearts.

On the starboard side, as we passed aboard *Great American III*, a few thousand people began loudly humming, almost shouting, the tune of the Star-Spangled Banner, in a gracious French salute to the lone American skipper in the fleet. A hundred yards further, on the port side, a 30' x 15' banner was unrolled down the side of the granite breakwater, proclaiming "YES U CAN!", a post-election take-off on President-Elect Barack Obama's campaign slogan. And further along yet, a new group of thousands struck up our national anthem again. In between, they simply cheered and waved, then cheered again.

Standing on the foredeck, per request of race management to showcase the skipper for photo-taking by the crowds and press, offered a welcome chance to salute the crowd with thanks of my own. In full ocean gear – long underwear top and bottom, wool socks and sweater, seaboots, and foul weather gear with safety harness ready to go - I bowed side-to-side, and pounded my hand over my heart, in gratitude to the amazing French, who had welcomed me, befriended me, and encouraged me without reservation during four months of final preparations before this start of their most daring, dangerous, and human sports event.

The French public had thought long and hard about this race, and what was about to be undertaken by these skippers. They knew where the Kerguelen Islands were, they knew which continent had Cape Horn, they knew about the gales and the icebergs and the cold in the south. They knew that half the fleet would likely not finish, and that a skipper might not return. They had their favorites in the race to be sure, but what they really wanted was for everyone to sail well, to the best of their ability, to report to them at home ashore what life was like at sea, and, most importantly, they wanted us to come home safely.

§

The fleet had been required to arrive in Les Sables d'Olonne three weeks before the start. A Race Village of 150,000 square feet had been built with tents for sponsors, press, public and private VIP functions, education exhibits, and a restaurant and bar. The indoor spaces were always jammed, with kids steering simulated sailboats around simulated icebergs, kids and parents looking through a bank of microscopes at plankton samples from the sea, radio interviews with skippers, designers, builders, sponsors, and politicians broadcast live throughout the village, and families honoring the event by diligently considering each and every exhibit.

Enormous Crowds on the Dock

Outside, huge crowds came to walk the docks and see the boats and skippers.

You haven't seen a sports event until you've seen the start of the Vendée Globe. That's a bold statement, and I'm from Boston, the sports hub of the universe! I'd been at Fenway Park for the 6th game of the 1975 World Series, but never got a chance to talk to Carlton Fisk. I'd been to Celtics-Lakers NBA Finals at the old Boston Garden, but never had a chance to talk to Larry Bird or Magic Johnson. In American professional sports, there is an athlete/fan divide, along physical, celebrity, and monetary lines.

Yet on the Vendée Globe dock in Les Sables d'Olonne, there was no such divide: the boats, skippers, families and shore crews were all mixed in with the public, press, and politicians. We were all in this together: the skippers had their role to play to sail the boats around the world; the public had its role to play to live and breathe every skipper's fears and joys, triumphs and travails as they dared to circle the world. A vast and continual flow of position data, skipper logs, photos and videos, wind and wave information from Météo France, live radio interviews daily with the skippers at sea, expert commentary from past racers, designers, and builders, and a massive online computer game permitting people ashore to race the sailors at sea, served to link the skippers to the public and the public to the skippers via newspapers, radio, TV, and the internet. We, humanity, together, would race around the world in the Vendée Globe.

35,000 people per day, 750,000 over the three weeks, jammed the docks. They wanted to see the boats, and to chat with a skipper, shore crew, or family member. A fence down the middle of the quarter mile long, twenty-foot wide dock, kept the people flow orderly: walk down the north side past fifteen boats, turn at the far end, walk back the south side past the other fifteen boats. The line to the dock stretched to an hour-long wait, yet courtesy, interest, patience, and friendliness were the order of the day. No torn jeans, no scruffy t-shirts, no bad language, no alcohol, the Vendée Globe was an event to be respected, and the crowd would comport themselves accordingly. They wished to shake your hand firmly and warmly, to pat you on the back, to ask their burning question. They wanted you to know that they were with you all the way. A photo with the skipper? *Un autographe pour mes enfants? Bien sur, Monsieur, c'est mon plaisir*.

The boats were incredible for sure, spectacular, huge, colorful, dramatic, shocking in their size, power and complexity, each one a

Starship Enterprise, but the people cared more about you. Are you scared? Is your mother scared? What about the gales? What about the big seas? What about the cold in the south? The best ocean sailors of the world, the Captain Cooks and Ferdinand Magellans and Joshua Slocums of their day, and anybody could talk to anybody. You could talk to Michel Desjoyeaux, or his family; you could talk to the young, blonde Brit Samantha Davies or her delightful parents, Paul and Jenny; you could talk to tall, handsome Armel Le Cléac'h and tickle his baby. It was pure humanity.

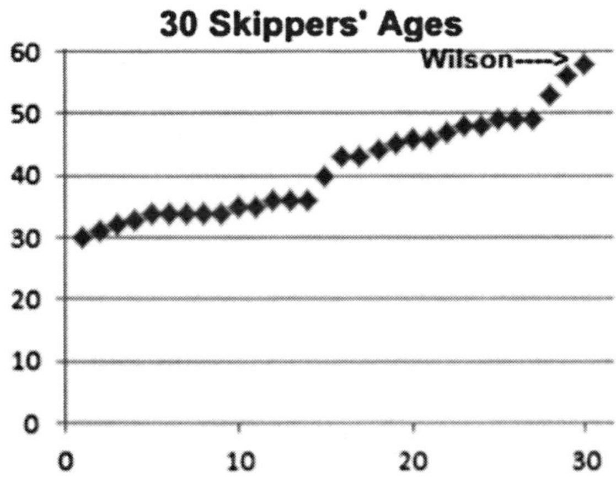

On the rare occasion of an interview with an American journalist, they would eventually ask me: "Are you going to win?" Had they done any homework, they would have known the answer: "Of course not!" My boat was three design generations old and had already raced around the world three times. I was the oldest skipper at 58, with fourteen in their 30s, thirteen in their 40s, and three of us in our 50s. I was American, and our country didn't offer the plethora of solo ocean races that fill the French calendar and act as the sport's minor league, where the best young sailors develop, prove themselves and move up in their sponsorships, all with the goal to race the Vendée Globe. I would push as hard as I could - one did that for self-respect, for respect for the race, and for those who had raced before - but there was no real chance of our winning. Then the American journalist would ask: "Then why are you doing it?" I'd explain about our massive K12 education program, but they never seemed to accept that rationale.

The French taught a different lesson, a better lesson. Neither their journalists, nor their public, ever asked about winning. They simply said: *"Si vous finissez la course, vous êtes un vainqueur."* And a young French boy on the dock had said to me, with wisdom beyond his years, the defining statement of entry into the Vendée Globe for all the skippers: *"L'important, c'est de participer."* This young philosopher and his countrymen hit the nail on the head, both for the Vendée Globe, and for life: it's important to participate; it's important to finish; if you do both, you're a winner.

The rolling waves of cheering went on and on as we proceeded slowly toward the mouth of the channel and the reality of the 2008 Vendée Globe. Three years in the making of our project, today was finally the day.

§

Emerging into the Atlantic Ocean, emotionally drained by the French send-off, we found an unsettled sea, larger than expected for the 20 knot southwest wind, rolling in from the west toward the coast. This sea train announced the distant and ominous storm that was forecast to arrive the next day from mid-Atlantic - 50 knots of wind, on the nose, in the shoaling Bay of Biscay. King Neptune wanted to get our blood flowing early, and was wryly suggesting that we make a rapid transition from the comfort and safety of a land world to the discomfort, rigor and risk of an ocean world.

We hoisted the mainsail to the first reef, giving 3/4 of the full mainsail area. No need for bravado at the start, ours was an older boat, I was the oldest skipper in the race, and had no big sponsors to impress by being exactly on the start line at the gun for front page photos for the French newspapers and TV. What would it matter if we were a bit late at the start of a race of 100 days? The most important task was to protect the boat, protect the skipper, not get into any trouble, nor make any mistakes in the excitement, anxiety and emotion of the moment.

As we struggled in the sloppy sea, hampered by a sudden uncertainty and tentativeness in anticipation of what was to come, *Foncia*, one of the race favorites, and a personal favorite to me, swept by going fast. I hustled to the leeward side of the cockpit, thrust both hands high overhead, and in a sweeping semaphore, waved goodbye and good luck to Michel Desjoyeaux. He was already alone, with one mainsail reef and his staysail, and making 14 knots toward the Committee boat, sailing his 60-footer as if he were sailing a dinghy. No uncertainty there, *Le Professeur*, nicknamed for his wide knowledge and willingness to share it, saw me, stood up, and returned the doublehanded wave high over his head. Perhaps the finest solo sailor in the world, he had helped me enormously with an extraordinary email exchange the winter before.

§

A solo transatlantic race is beyond the ken or imagining of almost all sailors, yet the Vendée Globe requires each skipper to finish one officially, on his or her boat, merely as a qualification for the main event. I had finished the solo Transat Ecover B2B (Bahia à Bretagne) from Brazil to France in late December 2007, to qualify. The next day, Michel was on the dock in Port la Foret, the finish port, and his hometown. Although I'd met him briefly thrice before, I still approached him tentatively, for he was the best of the best. In my high school French, worse than rusty after forty years, I asked if I could send him some questions about how to sail *"les soixante pieds."* He was pointedly appreciative that I was trying to speak in French, saying that they in Brittany liked it if foreigners made the effort, especially Americans since they rarely did, and said yes, it's OK to email some questions, and it's OK to write them in English, a leeway presumably granted due to my effort in French.

Michel Desjoyeaux

Yet upon my return to the U.S., out of respect for Michel, for the Vendée Globe, and for the French, I laboriously wrote ten detailed questions, in French. Twenty-four hours later, I received ten detailed answers...in English! His answers prompted clarification questions from me, which I again wrote in my labored French, dictionary and grammar book by my side, and 24 hours later yet again, I received detailed answers in English. This exchange continued through a half-dozen cycles totaling 4,000 words over three weeks. Topics ranged from sail construction, to caloric intake in the heat of the tropics vs. the cold of the south, to sleep management, to how to gybe the spinnaker at night, and many more. His technical information helped me enormously, yet his friendship and encouragement even more. If Michel thought I could do this, then maybe I could. Hoping that he'd be recognized in his homeland for his grace in helping a foreign competitor, I promoted the exchange to the French press; happily, the story was featured on national TV.

§

I turned the bow away from the wind to gain speed from the reefed mainsail, set the autopilot to steer, and then came the stark moment – the moment to say goodbye. In these last connecting minutes between a three-year preparation and the start, tears welled again, and the sloppy sea, further confused by the wakes of hundreds of spectator boats, churned already tense stomachs. I bid *au revoir*: to Hugues Riousse, who had sailed with my Dad thirty years before and had taken a leave of absence from his job to be my expert French *preparateur* - he had been a tower of knowledge and belief; to Rick Williams, a Marblehead friend and sailor, and degreed mechanical engineer who brought that logic and discipline to this highly complex and sophisticated boat; to Hugues' wife Flo, an organizer *extraordinaire*, computer and online wizard, always positive, always believing, especially in our onshore school program; and finally to my friend Ellen Stone, friends since high school, we'd been fortuitously re-connected after her husband's tragic death and my sad divorce, and she'd been a rock of Gibraltar to my sine curve of emotions through these years of planning and preparation. Nobody knew what to say. We hugged, shook hands, kissed, then all hugged again. Then they climbed over the lifelines, struggling to safely time their leaps into the erratically bouncing inflatable alongside.

I was alone.

At least most people would consider that I was alone. But I did have one shipmate still with me, our trusty *Great American III*, the Bernard Nivelt-designed, Thierry Dubois-built Open 60 that I'd acquired for the voyage. She was painted Cloud White, with her name discreet and tidy at the stern on both sides, and a big *37,* her sail number, on her bows per race rules. Her clean white topsides were elegant next to the sponsor-emblazoned topsides of the other boats. Under Thierry and another French skipper, she had raced solo around the world three times already. Hopefully, she had one more good one in her. She couldn't do it without me; and I couldn't do it without her. We, yes "we", *Great American III* and I, would team together to mount the effort.

With the start approaching soon, there was no time to indulge in the luxury of sadness or fear. We sailed slowly toward the French Naval Frigate *Le Tenace* which served as the Race Committee boat at one end of the starting line, and tried to identify the buoys marking the far end of the line and the spectator boat control areas. I tried to put out of my mind the enormity of what was to come, and to concentrate on the individual, sequential steps of boat maneuvers. I spoke out loud to myself, both to fill my ears with the comforting company of a human voice, and from hoping that if I was about to make a mistake, in sequence or step, some still logical and less emotionally distraught part of my brain would catch the error and make a correction.

"OK, let's steer over here into this empty space, then I'll go below and center the keel for the tack." "OK, we're in a pretty clear space here, so..., set the autopilot, last look around – are we clear? – yes, OK here goes for the keel." Rush below through the cabin door, down two steps to the cabin floor, past the chart table and tiny galley, through the door into the engine compartment to access the keel control winch, losing sight and contact with what is happening on deck in the milling about of raceboats and the spectator fleet, 10 seconds, 20 seconds, 30 seconds, get the 8,000 pound hinged keel centered vertically with the motorized keelwinch, rush back into the cockpit and take a fast look around. "OK, we're OK." "OK, let's stay clear of *Roxy* coming up ahead." "OK, there's the committee boat, and that must be the buoy at the other end of the line." "OK, let's not roll out the staysail until we've tacked for the start."

Only a few minutes to go; we kept our distance from the line and the fleet. My team, my friends, trailed behind in the inflatable, watching closely, and holding on tightly to not get bounced overboard into the cold November water. Trying to take photos, they imparted, by their presence and friendship, all of their heartfelt good wishes. I was the only one physically aboard, but they were aboard in spirit, and would ride the emotional roller coaster with me, through every storm and calm, breakdown and repair, fear and joy, injury and exhaustion, every sunrise and sunset, every day and every night, for the next four months. We would sail the world together, linked occasionally by satellite telephone or email, but constantly by concern, emotion, hope and friendship.

We tacked to head for the line. Three minutes to the greatest adventure and challenge of my life.

The Adventure Begins

I rolled out the staysail, grabbed the pedestal handles (think bicycle pedals driven by your hands), hunched over, and muscled in fifty revolutions to turn the leeward winch to trim the staysail, then disengaged the leeward winch clutch, engaged the windward winch clutch, and muscled in seventy grinds on that winch to trim the monster mainsail. Scanning the full 360 degrees of the horizon to be sure we were clear, I dashed below again to cant the keel to port to its full 40 degrees from the vertical. Swinging that ton of steel keelfin supporting three tons of streamlined lead bulb at the bottom to the windward side added counterbalance to the wind pressure on the sails. I rushed back to the cockpit, adjusted the autopilot to steer upwind toward the line, and…BOOM…the starting cannon on the French naval frigate fired, and we were off toward a physical, emotional, and mental unknown.

Ahead lay the great oceans of the world, the Atlantic, the Indian, the Pacific, and then the Atlantic again. Overlapping the three in the south was the awe-inspiring Southern Ocean, a dreaded expanse of gales and cold, of albatross, sleet, hail, and icebergs, of massive seas unchecked by obstructing land, and all the while a mostly un-rescue-able distance from any reasonable expectation of help.

But first, here and now, was the Bay of Biscay, a hollow in Europe's west coast, to the north of the Spanish peninsula, to the west of France, to the south of Ireland and the corner of England. A bay that shallows in its final 100 miles toward the coast, as if enticing North Atlantic storms to send their worst, so that the shoaling could add its own punch and loft and viciousness to the wave height and shape.

We heeled to 30 degrees, nine tons of *Great American III* and skipper, crashing up and down into the oncoming seas at 9 knots. I took off my foul weather gear jacket, an ill-advised action in those conditions, for if you take a wave over your head, then those unprotected clothes will be soaked with salt water and will never dry. Yet the jacket seemed hot and heavy and stifling. I needed to breathe. I needed the cold to keep me alert, for what I really wanted to do was to go below, curl up in the sleeping bag, and pull a stocking cap over my head and eyes to escape.

I was tired from the seemingly endless and detailed lists of final boat preparations of the last few weeks, and from the skippers' briefings, weather briefings, safety briefings, safety inspections, press interviews, communications checks, and PR sails for the race website. The details were continuous: our second liferaft's inspection certification would expire before I finished - ship it cross-country for re-inspection; swap out circuit boards in the Fleet 77 (a satellite telephone with high speed data) to offer a doubling of the 56k baud rate to 112k; have the storm jib deck bag re-sewn smaller; charge headlight rechargeable batteries; load fresh Granny Smith apples and navel oranges; sharpen deck knives.

I was drained by the constant anticipatory anxiety of the last three years since the decision had been made to enter the race. I hadn't slept well or much in the last days before the start. My stomach was upset. The previous three weeks had presented the fleet with glorious weather, warm, sunny, gentle breezes, lulling us to imagine that the race would continue in that vacation-like vein. Yet today was a slap in the face, arriving cold, cloudy, rainy, and windy, with a substantial sea running and a big storm forecast for tomorrow.

Looking around for other boats to see how we were sailing in comparison, a normal reflex of a racing sailor, was a conscious effort to bring me back from imagining the future to immediate reality. Besides, it was nice to see other boats around, since after a few hours we likely wouldn't see any again until we returned to France.

Glancing through the cabin door to make sure that our GPS position, denoted by a little red boat icon, was properly tracking on the computer screen, I thought back to my first transatlantic sail, completed with sextant, chronometer, trigonometric tables, a compass, and five shipmates hand-steering 24/7. How things had changed in the intervening three decades!

Now we were laden with technology.

We had four satellite telephone, two satellite text, and three position-tracking transmitters, plus four emergency satellite beacons (two boat and two personal). We had two liferafts, a radar, radar detector, and Automatic Identification System (AIS) that would place approaching ships on our computer screen with their name, course and speed. Redundant sets of wind direction, wind speed, and boatspeed sensors fed redundant autopilot systems of electronic compasses, computers and rudder-controlling hydraulic rams. We had spare rams and a spare rudder. Two computer networks and a router connected the sensors and communications systems to the main computer and its backup. A wind turbine and solar panels supplemented the diesel engine and alternator to generate electricity into our house battery bank of Absorbed Glass Mat (AGM) sealed batteries. A reverse osmosis desalinator made fresh water from seawater.

On deck, we had the latest PBO synthetic fibres in our rigging, sealed in a heat-resistant wrap of Technora, then an extra chafe wrap of Spectra, because the PBO fibres, featherweight, but immensely strong with no stretch, degrade if exposed to water or sunlight. Our mainsail panels were Vectran fibres laid along the load lines, then laminated between layers of Mylar and Dacron at 100 psi, and glued together. 51 sail control lines came into the cockpit to 25 line stoppers and 5 winches. Our hull was a fiberglass composite, but our bulkheads supporting the keel and mast were carbon fibre, as were the mast and boom.

Great American III, affectionately nicknamed *GA3,* was a complex system of advanced technologies that needed to function flawlessly for the next four months in a relentlessly hostile environment.

Her systems would need continual monitoring. If anything went down, it needed to be tended to immediately, or one could have a cascading series of failures, especially in the physically loaded systems of sails, rigging, keel, rudders, winches, and ropes, where if A breaks, it overloads B which breaks, which overloads C which breaks. Then, alone, you have a big problem. I would start checking the systems now; that would help bring me back to the moment. Just concentrate on the boat. The boat is everything. She will take you around the world. Focus on the boat.

Most of the fleet was to windward and ahead. The new boats, designed, built, prepared and trained with large sponsor budgets specifically for this race, the pinnacle of singlehanded ocean racing, were slowly pulling away. That was to be expected. Michel had told me that his new 2008 generation boat *Foncia* had 30% more righting moment, equating to stability, in turn equating to horsepower, than his 2000 generation winning boat *PRB*. *GA3* was of that 2000 generation, so Michel and the other new boats had 30% more horsepower than we did; there was nothing we could do about that, and no way that we could be as fast. He had told me that in a kind way, not to say, "Rich, you can't keep up", but meaning, "Rich, don't try to push beyond what your boat can do - sail your own race."

The top half of this fleet were the best ocean sailors in the world. The races and class lured the best skippers, designers, builders, electronics wizards, sailmakers, and *preparateurs*. The new boats were innovative, now with deck spreaders, curved asymmetric daggerboards, rotating wing masts, and sliding hatches to enclose the cockpits and protect the skippers. The fleet included twenty new boats for 2008, four boats from the still competitive 2004 vintage, plus six of us with boats from 2000 or before. What Michel had been saying more broadly was that one ought not have illusions that might get you into trouble. I didn't. The Vendée Globe is about nothing if not reality. Yet what an honor and privilege it was to be on that same starting line with that fleet of boats and that group of sailors!

§

GA3 sailed close to the wind on port tack, heading due west. Our desired course was southwest to Cape Finisterre at the northwest corner of Spain. Since that was where the wind was coming from, and a sailboat can't sail directly into the wind, but has to zig-zag, 45 degrees on either side of the wind direction, we, and the rest of the fleet, were heading west. When the storm's cold front, and its forecast windshift to northwest arrived, the fleet would tack, turning 90 degrees south to clear Cape Finisterre.

Large swells rolled in from the approaching storm, and although they had heft, there was no viciousness. That would come. The autopilot was steering. We were heeling to 30 degrees under staysail and one reef in the mainsail. The storm jib - tiny, tough, and International Orange for long-range visibility - was hooked onto the baby stay in front of the mast and furled in its bag, with halyard and sheets attached, ready to go when needed. The occasional wave swept the leeward deck. Soon we would be laboring and need to reduce sail.

In this first half hour, our team of friends bounced alongside *GA3* and me, not wanting to let go. And I didn't want them to leave. But we all knew they would have to turn around soon. A press helicopter, finished with filming the leaders, flew boat to boat through the fleet on its way back to land. It hovered loudly in front of us, then behind us, getting footage for the evening news. I waved and received a return wave and a thumbs-up *"Bonne Chance!"* when they banked and headed for the next boat.

An inflatable with the *Roxy* shore crew had left Samantha Davies and was headed back to port. They saw us and veered over for a final wave and cheer of *"Bon Voyage! Bon Courage!"*, then continued bashing and splashing their way toward land. This was the signal that it was time for our team, my team, to head back too. They bounced their way close alongside, we waved, blew kisses, shouted *"Au revoir!"*, and then they peeled off and headed in.

Of course it had to come, but it seemed unexpected. I watched them recede toward the horizon, until I could distinguish them no more. Abruptly, I was truly alone. Who knew when next I'd lay eyes directly on another human being? Who knew what challenges we would encounter, or whether we would overcome them, before we might sail these waters again, heading eastbound to finish at Les Sables d'Olonne?

"Dreams are only foolish to those who dare not go."
...Bob Dotson, NBC-TV, on Great American's 1990 Voyage

Chapter 2: Battling the Bay of Biscay

Toward the Approaching Gale

I was overly warm with the foul weather gear jacket or chilled without it. My stomach was upset, but that was normal. On our previous long voyages, doublehanded on the routes of the great clippers, I routinely got seasick the first night, from fatigue of preparation and anxiety about what lay ahead. Today's growing seaway added to my usual discomfort. Normally, a couple of good vomits or dry heaves over the side cleared it. But not today, and not tonight.

I hadn't eaten since a 5 am breakfast before driving in the dark to the boat. It was now late afternoon. The fleet spread out as it raced west. With each boat heading on a slightly different course at a slightly different speed, these small differences accumulated to disperse the thirty boats. I took a good look around, and, comfortable with our distance from the boats that I could still see, went below to study the chart on the computer, turn on the radar detector, and try to eat.

The last thing I wanted to do was not eat. You have to always keep something in the energy bank. Our nutrition goal was 6,000 calories per day, three times the normal intake, four full meals spaced every six hours, snack in between, hydrate constantly with Gatorade, Ensure and Nestlé's Nido Whole Milk. If I couldn't or didn't eat, that would lead to more fatigue and weakness and would invite the seasickness to linger. Plus, a momentarily weaker state might mean a mistake in a sail maneuver, a missed handhold, a trip and a fall, and rapidly the consequences could multiply. One could not be lax about anything, ever, in the Vendée Globe.

I heated some water on our one burner propane stove and mixed a cup of bouillon. Every movement in the cabin needed bracing and handholds. After a few sips my stomach rebelled. I tried a trusty Fig Newton, 55 calories, normally calming of an upset stomach. Like eating clay, my dry mouth couldn't get it down. Through the afternoon, the boat bashed upwind into a strengthening breeze, heeling more, and occasionally sending sheets of spray over the cockpit. I lay down at the chart table bench, but it took too much energy to brace myself and not get thrown off, so I tossed our specially sewn all-weather beanbag on the floor in the leeward corner of the cabin, and wedged myself there where I had to expend less energy protecting myself. Perhaps if I could completely relax my muscles, my stomach knots would diminish... Nausea, from the Greek word "naus" meaning ship. Now there is a properly derived word!

It was November 9, the days were getting shorter, and at 46° North latitude (about the latitude of Montreal), it would be dark by 6:30 pm. I watched the windspeed, wind direction, and boatspeed indicators. The radar detector alarm was silent. Every quarter hour I'd drag myself up to look at the computer screen, check the ink trace on the barograph to see if it had started its storm-indicating descent, climb the two steps into the cockpit, and pivot to sit in the windward seat under the sheltering cuddy. Sensing the boat's motion, I'd time my emergence to when a cold wave and spray was not coming my way, and stick my head up to take a comprehensive look around. On the windward, high side of the heeled boat, I could get a good view, on the leeward side, close to the water, my sight range was shorter, and obscured forward by the staysail.

The wind increased as we converged with the storm. Soon we'd need to reduce sail by lowering the mainsail to its 2nd reef, 60% of its full area. The next reduction would be either to the 3rd reef of the mainsail, or to roll up the staysail and set the storm jib, our smallest sail. Before the storm arrived, with 50 knots of wind, we'd likely have to do both.

§

Although the keel with its lead bulb is 14.5' deep, the hull is only 18" deep despite being 18' wide. Effectively, these Open 60s have shallow, nearly flat bottoms. So when they sail into the waves, like a surfer paddling seaward from the beach, they will rocket off a wave, go airborne, and come crashing down – BAM! Nine tons of boat landing flat on solid water is like dropping your house, with you in it, on concrete. If you're standing, the impact goes from your heels through your leg bones, to jar your teeth and concuss your brain in your skull. It gives you a headache. When it's really bad, you can't believe that the mast can stay up or that the keel can stay attached. At the chart table, crashing upwind, I've found myself reflexively throwing my arms over my head to protect myself from the mast, which will undoubtedly be breaking and crashing through the cabin top at any moment. How can the boat stay together? How could any structure survive this appalling beating?

If you eased the keel cant angle from 40 degrees to 30 degrees off-center, providing less counterweight so that the boat would heel more, when the boat rocketed off a wave it would crash down more on its side than on its bottom. The side is slightly curved, and this would cushion the impact slightly. But then, the daggerboard (a fin that slides up and down vertically in a slot through the hull and is intended to keep the boat from slipping sideways) would be even more angled in the water, its grip would be reduced, and the boat would slip sideways more. Every skipper made these types of trade-offs - for sail selection, steering course, boat maneuvers and weather-routing - every minute of every day: keep the boat going optimally; but keep the boat and skipper in one piece too. Both must survive the race to finish the race.

§

In a routine born long ago, I went on deck to inspect the boat at dusk. The jacket had a safety harness and tether permanently attached that could hook onto either the windward or leeward jacklines (safety lines on each side of the boat running bow to stern along the deck). Tethered to this jackline, I could go forward or aft always hooked to the boat. I hooked in to windward, took the two steps from cockpit to deck, and crouched as I went forward. My outboard left hand cupped the upper lifeline for guidance and steadying. Keeping my center of gravity low, I straddled the jackline and pulled up on the tether with my right hand to add stability.

The bow crashed into a wave and sent a sheet of spray back over me. I instinctively turned my head and hood to keep the deluge from going down my neck. I shuffled along crouched low, arrived at the mast, leaned on it, nestled my right eye next to the mainsail track running to the top, and sighted up it to ascertain straightness from left to right, and curvature from forward to aft. It was good, yet this sighting was a bit gratuitous. If it wasn't correct after the ten days we'd spent adjusting the ten individual shrouds by millimeters to get it perfect, there was nothing I could do about it now. With tension gained by hydraulically pumping the mast upward against these shrouds to 14 tons of pressure, the phrase "bar taut" doesn't begin to describe how tight they were. But if any of the rigging stretched over time, the 90' mast tube might begin to twist or bend one way or another. Even if only a trifle, it might dictate what sails to use or not use, given their different loadings on the mast, to protect the mast.

I worked my way carefully to the plunging bow, inspecting up close the stainless steel pieces and pins holding the forestay, then aft to the staysail stay, then aft to the baby stay with the storm jib nestled in its bag at the bottom. Were all the pins in firmly? Were there any cracks in the metal? I inspected the daggerboard and its control lines, then the lashings of the four stays alongside the mast, two on the windward side, two on the leeward side. I didn't expect to see anything amiss, but it needed to be done, not only to catch an actual problem, but also to give me the feeling that I was doing what I was supposed to be doing, that I was tending the boat and taking care of her. To do that was psychologically comforting.

§

It's easy to be brave in a warm, dry living room, imagining some future voyage. But will you be brave when the voyage arrives, you're scared and cold and tired in a storm, seas are coming aboard, and both you and the boat are taking a beating? Seasick and anxious, the first storm was coming, and I knew that soon I'd be scared.

Counterintuitively, this aspect of sailing is appealing. Whether you're an experienced skipper racing in the Bay of Biscay or a ten-year-old child sailing a dinghy in a harbor, the sea presents an abnormal environment whereby shoreside support systems to which we have become accustomed are not available. If you have a fire, there is no fire department; if the engine fails, there is no repair shop; if the sail tears, there is no sailmaker; if you're sleep tired, there is no one to spell you; if you're muscle tired, there is no one to help pull or grind; if you're hungry, you have to cook; if you can't decide, you alone must decide. You can get in almost as much trouble a mile from shore as a thousand miles out in the Indian Ocean. This aspect of sailing, and shorthanded sailing in particular, is what makes the sport such an appealing challenge: you alone are responsible for your boat and yourself. And when the boat calls for help, you must respond immediately, regardless of fatigue, nausea, or injury.

In my first big solo race, the 1988 C-STAR (Carlsberg Singlehanded Transatlantic Race – from England to the U.S. - aboard the 35' trimaran *Curtana*), six days in, a thousand miles out, pounding upwind at nine knots at midnight, I saw that the jib furling line at the bow had chafed. If I didn't fix it or replace it, it might break when I needed to roll up the sail. If it did, then the jib would unroll, I'd have too much sail up, it wouldn't be able to be controlled, and the boat could be capsized or the sail would thrash itself into a tattered mass of broken Kevlar threads and disintegrating Mylar. With thirty-eight infected cuts and nicks on my hands (I'd counted!), grabbing anything was agonizing. I knew what I was supposed to do - yet would I do it?

I, and most of my American generation, had hit the Homo Sapiens Lottery, the one in a million shot over millennia, of being born white, in the United States of America, in the second half of the twentieth century. If I'd been born in the northeast Congo, I'd have been dead long ago. So what to do or where to go to find out what you're made of? Going alone to sea was my testbed.

I had crawled to our bow with a headlight and a spare line to replace the chafed line. The bow was piercing every fourth wave. Every handhold was like holding a twisting knifeblade. A big wave bounced me up and off the deck, to land in an adjacent netting over the black water. If I'd gone another two feet sideways, I would have been past the netting and in the water, and it would have been impossible to get back aboard. I would have been dragged along by my harness until somebody found the boat and my drowned body alongside. I grabbed the bow pulpit and dragged myself back onto the deck, screaming with pain into the dark. There wasn't a boat within fifty miles to hear me.

Yet this was exactly why I was here, to find out, when things are going terribly wrong, when there is real risk, right here, right now, and you're hurting, tired and scared, will you do what you know you're supposed to do? On that occasion I did, and made the repair, yet every incident presents itself as a new challenge, and just because you answered the call the last time has no bearing on whether you will answer the call the next time. You will have to fight that internal mental fight all over again.

§

Into the night we thrashed upwind. Any warm, twinkling lights from Les Sables d'Olonne were long gone over the horizon. It was time for the second reef. We were sailing fast to the west, but with the increased wind and heel, the boat was slipping sideways to the north. The mainsail is a tall triangle, 90' on the vertical, 30' on the horizontal. It has control lines at each of the three corners, plus three additional pairs of control lines spaced along the vertical and diagonal edges which allow the sail to be lowered 20' to the first reef (1200 square feet), or an additional 20' to the second reef (900 square feet), or an additional 20' to the third reef (600 square feet). By setting the mainsail at one of its five settings - full (1500 square feet), first reef, second reef, third reef, or down all the way to the boom (zero square feet) - you can adjust the sail area to the wind velocity.

I made my way back along the lifeline to the cockpit and proceeded with our reefing protocol. Wrap the main halyard around the central winch of our cockpit's five winches, ease the mainsail out until the boom swings out over the water, and the sail is blowing back from the mast like a flag, and is therefore under no load. The boat is now sailing on the staysail alone.

Ease the 2:1 halyard out ten feet, so the sail comes down five feet. Then snug the new reeflines at the forward and aft edges of the sail down to the boom. Repeat three times until the sail is down to its new reef.

You could try to lower the sail the entire 20' increment between the reefs all at once, but then the lines for the third reef would go slack, with 40' of loose line (since it was also 2:1) blowing wildly in the dark, and likely to wrap itself around the end of the boom. Then you'd have to stop the whole procedure, crawl forward to the mast, climb on top of the sail on the boom, crawl on the slippery, wet, and loose folds of bunched sailcloth 30' to the end of the boom, which is now swinging over the seas in the dark night like George Clooney on the outrigger in The Perfect Storm, and by your LED headlight, untangle the mess that you'd created by trying to do everything too fast. Don't fall off or you'll be overboard and will die, don't get your fingers caught in the on-again/off-again loading of the main sheet block, don't get knocked unconscious by the flailing reefline.

No, much better to proceed incrementally, and keep everything under control. So down the sail came 5', then pull out the reefline, and pull down the downhaul, then let the sail down another 5', then pull out the reefline and pull down the downhaul, and repeat until the new reef is down to its marks. I snugged each of the three control lines, and ground another hundred revolutions on the pedestal to pull the mainsail back in so that it filled with wind and was contributing again. Off we went, heeling less with less sail area up, not slipping sideways as much, going just as fast, as always seems to be the case when you reef down. The first reef of hundreds that would be taken or let out in the Vendée Globe was successfully completed.

§

It felt good to get that first sail maneuver finished properly. I was being responsible, not being lured into pressing too much to keep up with the faster boats, and recognizing that I wasn't on top of my physical game. I went below to the beanbag and curled up. The boat is going up and down, twisting, turning, heeling more, then coming back up. It has the random motion of a mechanical bull, interspersed with occasional thunderous crashes, and if you are not on your toes, you're going to get hurt. In the beanbag for a while, my stomach suddenly rebelled. I dragged myself up, and leaned through the cabin door to the cockpit, not having enough time, nor the energy, to put on my jacket and get into the cockpit and properly throw up over the side. I tried to throw up on the cockpit floor. Heck, it would get cleaned up by the next dozen cold waves that poured into it. That was not a concern. But nothing came up, only retching, violent, dry heaves as if my stomach was trying to come up through my throat. I stuck fingers way down my throat, massive heaves, but nothing came up. Some people recoil at this description, yet it's simply a practical step to improve the situation, like bailing water from the cabin floor. My stomach is a mess, let's try to fix it, so stick your finger down your throat, throw up, and eject the acidic toxins in your stomach. But I couldn't throw anything up and so it didn't fix it.

When you're seasick, you just want to die, because it's so awful. A friend many years ago cruised with his girlfriend, a nurse, to the Caribbean. En route they encountered a storm that persisted for days. She was so sick that in a week she lost 20 pounds. He tied her down to the bunk for fear that she might just crawl on deck and flop overboard to end the overwhelming agony of the seasickness. On land, this story sounds ridiculous, but when you're badly seasick at sea, you will do anything, anything at all, to end it.

Into the night the wind strengthened and seas built. At 2 am, I went on deck to put in the 3rd reef. I managed it without incident, but with a big and cautious effort due to my weakness from seasickness and not eating.

Checking the barograph, its trace had begun to curve ominously downward.

A few hours later, with the wind past 30 knots, and seas at 15', it was time for the storm jib. I turned the boat ninety degrees to starboard, heading north and downwind away from our course, to ease the pressure on the staysail and the furling mechanism. The furling line wraps around a drum at the bottom of the staysail stay. Pulling the line from the cockpit rotates the drum on the foredeck which rotates the stay which has the sail's leading edge attached along its length, and the sail rolls up as if it were a 65' tall vertical window shade. 75 grinds on our central winch and the staysail was rolled.

Now for the storm jib. We're not even into the middle of the Bay of Biscay yet, let alone the gales awaiting us in the Indian Ocean, we're going to need this tiny, tough sail a lot in the next few months, so be super careful and don't trash it now. And in your seasickness, don't forget anything, don't make any mistakes, and don't make any mis-steps in the dark.

Thirty minutes and three round-trips (cockpit to bow) later, with focused caution exercised every step of the way, the storm jib was up and drawing.

Moving fore and aft on the deck in these conditions requires extraordinary care. It's not like casually walking down a sidewalk. I think of the final scene in the movie Grease, where John Travolta and Olivia Newton-John are on an amusement park ride that is a platform moving side to side, and up and down. That's only two of the three dimensions of motion that the boat exhibits, plus it's dark, plus it's blowing hard, plus random sheets of heavy spray, plus random solid water waves are sweeping the deck as if cresting on a beach, plus the boat is rolling, pitching, and yawing, plus the deck has tracks, padeyes, blocks, and a dozen ropes running mast to cockpit that roll like marbles underfoot if you step on them. The angry sea is trying to throw you off balance; the boat is crying to you for relief, you're tired, hungry and seasick, but you can't cower in the cockpit, you have to go, now.

§

You have to be in shape to sail the Vendée Globe, both for race regulations, with Doctors' permissions, and, if you're over 40 years old, a cardiac stress test, and for yourself, your friends and your family, because you want to come home.

Marti Shea

I had found an extraordinary trainer for my Vendée Globe effort, conveniently in my hometown of Marblehead. Marti Shea is a former All-American distance runner at Boston University. Coached by Joan Benoit Samuelson, the first woman to win the Olympic Gold Medal in the Marathon, Marti had turned to cycling mid-career. She was small, almost petite, but strong, relentless, fascinated by the Vendée Globe idea, tough as nails, and imaginative. Marti's husband Joe Tonon had been a sponsored professional cyclist, and now led cycling tours in Europe for serious riders. Weekly, I'd train two days with Marti, one day for cardiovascular with Joe, then swim two days at the YMCA, for flexibility and aerobic capacity.

When I first went to Marti on a friend's recommendation, she said, "I've trained sailors before, even Olympic sailors, but not long-distance solo sailors on big boats. Tell me what it will be like, what motions you'll need to do, what the challenges and loads are. I'll think about it, propose a training plan, we'll talk about my ideas, modify them with your ideas and as we go according to whether it's working for you." What a breath of fresh air! A trainer who didn't think he/she knew it all in the first meeting! My brief to her was simple: "I'm 6' tall, 160 pounds, and my asthmatic lungs work at 70% of normal. I'll never be the strongest nor have the most aerobic capacity. But I want you to be able to say when we're finished that nobody ever worked harder."

With a base level of fitness from boat preparation and three transatlantic passages in three months leading to race qualification, I gained leaps and bounds with Marti in sixty minute non-stop workouts, with two 30 second breaks if I just couldn't continue. We worked with nothing, with medicine and inflatable balls, with bungee, with free weights, with a skating slide, with overhead straps, with rollers, with the wall.

My mantra in training for offshore sailing has been how stupid it would be to die because you hadn't done the last chin-up in training. Marti had her own corollary: she didn't want to have it on her conscience that if I died at sea, an inadequate fitness level had contributed. So she worked me hard.

One day, I excused myself to go to the men's room, where I threw up like a high schooler. When I returned, Marti looked up at me quizzically: "Did you just throw up?"

"Yes, but I feel much better now, ready to go again."

"I'm so sorry, this hour is no charge."

"No, this is perfect, now we both know where the edge is." We continued.

For the solo sailor in the Vendée Globe the physical challenge is immense. The boat is huge, the sails are huge, you never stop, you're tired all the time, the boat is bouncing, you don't get enough sleep, moving through cramped interior compartments demands contortionist flexibility, there's nobody to help.

Pure physical power helps only a little, because if the systems go wrong in controlling the sails, there is nobody on Planet Earth, not even Francis Joyon, who holds the solo, non-stop record around the world in the 97' trimaran *IDEC* and is the strongest person I've ever seen, who can manually tame a few thousand square feet of out-of-control sail in a blow. Soft-spoken and modest, Francis looks like Arnold Schwarzenneger would like to have looked if Arnold could have ever gotten into shape.

Strength with endurance and contortion is the key. Spinnaker dragging overboard in the water through a muffed sail maneuver? It will take an hour to pull back aboard at your full power - slack off just once and every foot you've gained will be lost back overboard. Change from the biggest of the five jibs to the spinnaker when the wind changes? Like hammering for thirty minutes straight on every machine in the gym, and that's if everything goes right. If it doesn't, add another sixty minutes, full on, to fix the mess.

On long sea voyages, your upper-body gets stronger and stronger, from holding on, pulling lines, and grinding winches endlessly. Yet your leg muscles atrophy, as they are static in their job of bracing you in every orientation. So you have to be extra strong in your legs at the start, so that after degrading, they will have something left at the end of the race.

Marti devised an imaginative torture for this: hold two twenty-pound dumbbells at shoulder level to destabilize you up high, then do sets of one-legged deep knee bends – on a trampoline! Every muscle in my body came into play to keep my balance, and to slowly, slowly extend that leg and get my one-legged deep knee bend in. Don't put down that other foot now for stability or rest - do another! And another! And another! The trampoline was a stroke of genius, because it simulated the continually and erratically moving boat.

Marti got me into the best physical condition of my life, not simply relative to age, but absolutely, and compared to high school and college where I always played sports. I gained 10 pounds of muscle, flexibility, and aerobic and muscular endurance.

The requisite cardiac stress test (Bruce Protocol) is on an accelerating treadmill where the angle slowly elevates, so you're running faster up a steepening hill. With my lungs gasping for breath, and my Marti quads screaming agony, I mustered 14 minutes 52 seconds. I asked the attending nurse for what age was my finishing time the average. She looked it up - 29! So either I, asthmatic, at 58, was in incredible shape, or the 29 year olds of the world had some serious work to do!

When I left for France for final preparations and the race, she said "Well, you did it, nobody ever worked harder, you're ready." I took the inflatable balls, the bungees, the jump rope, and the webbing straps to continue training in France.

§

Dawn turned the black night into a dingy day, low gray clouds, churning and rushing overhead, gray water, gray spray. The barograph descended. By mid-day, the windspeed approached 40 knots, the seas had built toward 20' and were vicious. They crested onto the bow, and swept down the deck, they dealt body blows to the underside of the hull, exposed by our thirty degrees of heel, like a heavyweight connecting on a kidney punch. At noon it started to rain, torrential rain, as in the tropics, buckets and boatloads of rain, driven by 45 knots of wind. The radar was on, but it's transmitted signal would echo off the rain as well as a ship, thus camouflaging the latter. I turned it off and turned on the radar detector. If it received a radar signal from another vessel, it would flash a light and sound an alarm. On we crashed into the appalling, worsening, second afternoon.

Time to get our communications going. It didn't matter if I was still seasick, and regularly dry heaving out the door, we needed to communicate outbound from the vessel, and receive communications inbound. The race was on and our sitesALIVE! K12 program had started. Contracted deadlines loomed. I had to record my daily podcast, email ship's log data to our website, write an explanatory blog, and receive my first batch of student questions. I had to find out how the fleet was faring and let the race office know our status. We offshore, and they onshore, needed information.

Twenty-five newspapers had contracted to publish our fifteen week NIE feature series and deliver newspapers with this series to participating classrooms that had signed up with them. Our weekly reach was to 7 million readers at home and 200,000 students in classrooms. In another sitesALIVE! innovation, we'd assembled an astonishing Team of Experts who would write essays for this series alongside mine, and answer students' questions online. I was as proud of this as getting to the starting line – where else could students hear from such a diversity of accomplished people, and send them questions?!

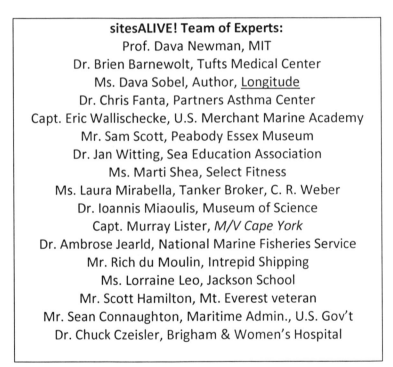

sitesALIVE! Team of Experts:
Prof. Dava Newman, MIT
Dr. Brien Barnewolt, Tufts Medical Center
Ms. Dava Sobel, Author, Longitude
Dr. Chris Fanta, Partners Asthma Center
Capt. Eric Wallischecke, U.S. Merchant Marine Academy
Mr. Sam Scott, Peabody Essex Museum
Dr. Jan Witting, Sea Education Association
Ms. Marti Shea, Select Fitness
Ms. Laura Mirabella, Tanker Broker, C. R. Weber
Dr. Ioannis Miaoulis, Museum of Science
Capt. Murray Lister, *M/V Cape York*
Dr. Ambrose Jearld, National Marine Fisheries Service
Mr. Rich du Moulin, Intrepid Shipping
Ms. Lorraine Leo, Jackson School
Mr. Scott Hamilton, Mt. Everest veteran
Mr. Sean Connaughton, Maritime Admin., U.S. Gov't
Dr. Chuck Czeisler, Brigham & Women's Hospital

The Inmarsat-C, an early generation satellite communications system with a slow, yet reliable, 600 baud text rate and costing only a penny per character, was permanently turned on per race rules. With a GPS chip inside, it would be "polled" automatically every 6 hours by our satellite service provider and our replied position would be emailed automatically to update our website. These satellites, at 23,000 miles high, orbited the earth at the same rate as the earth rotated, thus the satellites appeared steady above one point on earth, and were called geostationary. The area on the globe from which a transmitter could "see" a satellite was its coverage area. With four satellites spaced around the world above the equator, there were four coverage footprints overlapping globally called Ocean Regions. We were in AOR-E, for Atlantic Ocean Region - East.

From our own GPS input, our MaxSea software placed an icon of *GA3* on the digital nautical chart on our computer monitor. This icon traced our path accurately. The program could also receive specially formatted files from the Race Office via the Inmarsat-C of the identity, position, speed, and direction of each boat in the fleet. This data came from the three satellite GPS transmitters placed by race management on each boat. Out of sight over the horizon, the fleet showed vividly on our computer screen.

I clicked the tab to show the fleet's latest positions, then zoomed in, needing to stabilize my right index finger on the touchpad with my left hand, in the crashing, bouncing, and twisting of the boat in this Bay of Biscay gale. Hmmm, that's too bad, Dominique Wavre must have had a problem - he's back in port with his new *Temenos II*. And, what's that, *Foncia* and Michel Desjoyeaux are behind us? That's impossible. Either Michel has had a problem, or his position has not been updated from last night's position poll.

BEEP, BEEP, BEEP - the insistent tone of the radar alarm signaled a vessel within range and pierced my confusion and distress in reading the emails. I immediately swung my feet out from under the chart table, leaned against the center post as I struggled into my foul weather gear jacket (my seaboots and foul weather pants rarely came off), snugged my favorite sitesALIVE! baseball hat over my head underneath the hood, and closed the Velcro neck guard over my chin and mouth. Hopefully the hat's visor would protect my eyes in the lashing rain on deck.

Being severely near-sighted, I usually wore contact lenses at sea for 72 hours, then eyeglasses for 24 hours to give my eyes a rest, then repeated the cycle. I was in contact lens mode now, which was better than trying to see through glasses drenched with blowing rain and sea spray. On deck, though, I could see nothing. The torrential rain blowing at 50 knots was like trying to look into a hose being sprayed at your face, you just can't do it. Out there somewhere was a vessel of unknown size, direction, speed or distance from us. My eyeballs were lashed painfully by the rain. I tried to protect them with the visor, then with my hand, then gave up and looked only away from the wind to leeward to see if there was a ship down there. I could see a few hundred yards, to the tops of the next waves. A fishing vessel or a containership could be converging from a half mile away, and I'd see nothing because of the big waves between us. I saw nothing to leeward, and couldn't physically look to windward.

I rushed below, turned off the radar detector, turned on the radar (they couldn't both be on at the same time or the powerful active radar signal would fry the more delicate radar detector circuitry nearby), and waited impatiently for its two minute warm-up to complete. Nothing showed on the sweep, only a dense barrage of targets surrounding us for 360 degrees from the rain accompanying this cold front. The boat continued crashing upwind at 9 knots.

Then I remembered my construction goggles. Maybe they would work. Like ski goggles, but bigger and tougher, they might allow me to look directly into the rain. I pulled them out from their vinyl pouch on the wall, worked them onto my head, adjusted the strap, put the baseball cap back on top, then the hood over all of it, and went back on deck.

Well, those were a good idea. I could look directly into the fire hose of rain, so good call back there in the winter when I was looking for useful items online. I didn't see any ship, but at least I could seriously look. I watched for a solid twenty minutes, could find nothing anywhere around, then went below, turned off the active radar, turned on the radar detector - no flashing or beeping alarm. Whatever that vessel was, it was no longer in range. I sat momentarily on the inside cabin step to catch my breath, hanging on to the center post. Up and down over the waves, crash, crash, crash. I was beginning to feel a bit better in my stomach, so time to try to eat. But first, here's an idea, let's take a photo of these big goggles on my face for sitesALIVE!

On our 2001 New York to Melbourne clipper route voyage, it had been so cold for so long in the Indian Ocean, that eventually I asked my shipmate, Bill Biewenga, to take a series of photos of me getting out of the sleeping bag and putting on all of my clothes for going on deck for the midnight to 4 am watch, to try to give some perspective on the cold to our students. The series ran to 20 photos, the kids loved it, rave reviews came in online, it had engaged them in the voyage and to the sailors aboard. I could do the same with a self-portrait with these big construction goggles.

I took the digital camera out of its cubbyhole, removed my on-deck gloves to better manipulate the tiny switches, aimed the camera backward at my face, still holding firmly onto the post with my left hand, and took a picture. OK, did I aim it correctly? Let go with the left hand, turn the camera around, holding it with both hands to check that last image.

BAM! The boat was hit by a vicious uppercut wave, I felt myself airborne, flying and twisting across the cabin, back first. In mid-air, I knew what was about to happen but couldn't do anything to prevent it. BAM! My back hit a horizontal stainless steel grab bar above the bulkhead opening to the starboard bunk. In a one-point, full-body-weight impact after six feet in the air, it jack-knifed me, chest to knees, through that opening, rear end first, to slam against the inside surface of the hull. I crumpled in a heap underneath the bunk, with a sharp pain at the point of impact on the left side of my spine and near the bottom of my ribcage. My whole back cramped to protect the area. I'd hit so hard that I feared for paralysis. The boat was laying over 50 degrees on its side, my legs were trailing upward through the bulkhead opening into the cabin from my heap underneath the bunk. I tried to move extremities, fearful of the results, but my fingers worked, then wrists and elbows, I could scrunch my toes, rotate my ankles and bend my knees.

I scrambled out of the compartment in severe, breathless, agonizing pain, mostly to prove to myself that I could, and that my skeletal systems were functioning and my body wasn't paralyzed. I was scared at what I might have broken. Pulling myself up to the chart table bench to lean on it, I couldn't breathe, and didn't want to breathe, as moving my lungs and chest pulled and tore at the point of impact. My whole upper torso was in severe pain.

What do I do now? We're in a Bay of Biscay gale that is worsening. There is ship traffic around. What had I done? Had I ended my three year Vendée Globe effort and project on Day 2? Had I failed our students, our team, and my shipmate *GA3*?

I couldn't swing my legs onto the bench for the pain. I couldn't imagine that I could do anything on deck. Lucky we're already down to three reefs and the storm jib. The barograph is still going down. It's still raining torrentially and blowing 50 knots on the anemometer. The seas are 20' and building. I reached across the bench, a long reach for the satellite telephone, to call Dr. Brien Barnewolt, Chief of Emergency Medicine at Tufts Medical Center in Boston, one of our Experts, and our go-to guy for medical issues on our previous three long voyages. I'd never called him before, ever, for anything, and here it was, Day 2 of the Vendée Globe, and I was calling him with a serious problem. Only I wasn't, because the pain of moving and breathing prevented me from stretching that far to the telephone. I couldn't extend my arm, couldn't stretch across the bench and the table, couldn't get myself onto the bench to then swing my legs under the table to get closer to the satphone. I just couldn't do it for the pain.

I retreated to the beanbag, kicking it further into the corner for positioning, and underneath, in a puddle, lay the camera. I grabbed it and pushed a few buttons and levers, nothing, our only still camera aboard was finished.

For ten hours, the pain prevented me from getting to the telephone. Finally, in the early morning hours after midnight, with a prodigious effort, I got to the telephone and called the Emergency Room, leaving a message, then guiltily called his cell phone and left a message there too.

I carefully mixed a glass of powdered Nestlé's Nido Whole Milk and powdered Ensure, to force some bland fluids and calories into my stomach, hoping I wouldn't throw it up.

To distract me from my pain, and to re-engage with the race, I opened the EasyMail program on Inmarsat-C to check for messages from the race office, manned 24/7 by Race Director Denis Horeau and three assistants each standing 6 hour shifts for round-the-clock coverage. Ominously, there were many.

One by one I learned of the calamity that had struck the fleet. Dominique had electrical problems. Michel had a ballast tank leak that shorted his starting motor, preventing him from charging batteries. Swiss skipper Bernard Stamm aboard *Cheminées Poujoulat* had collided with a fishing vessel in the stormy night and broken his bowsprit. He was returning to Les Sables d'Olonne to rebuild it and restart in the ten-day window allowed by race rules. Jean-Baptiste Dejeanty returned with a crack amidships in his hull that reminded one of the America's Cup boat *OneAustralia* that broke in two and sank in sixty seconds off San Diego in 1995. It was an open question whether his boat could be fixed. Derek Hatfield returned with electrical problems.

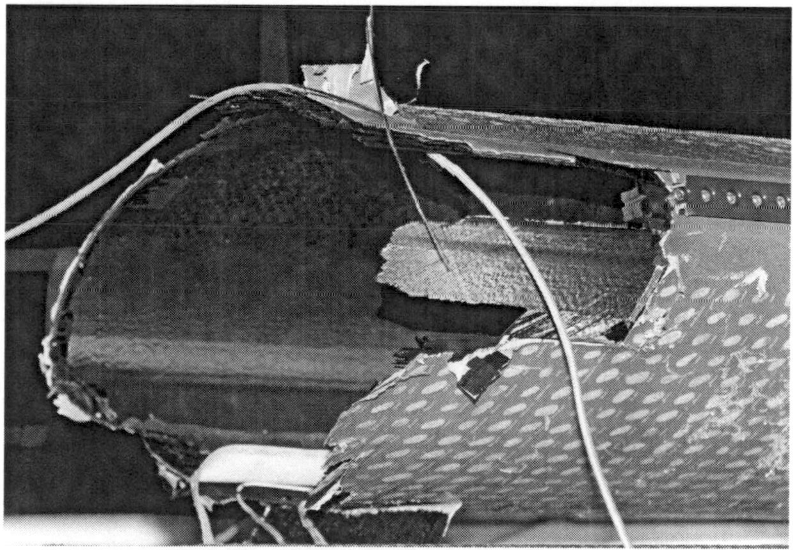

***Groupe Bel* – Kito de Pavant – broken mast**

Yet much worse for four others. In the shuddering crashes of sailing the flat-bottomed Open 60s hard upwind, Kito de Pavant on *Groupe Bel* had broken his mast, as had Marc Thiercelin aboard *DCNS* in his fourth Vendée Globe, as had Yannick Bestaven aboard

Aquarelle in his first. Alex Thomson on *Hugo Boss* retired after finding that his hull, two skins of carbon fibre sandwiching a rigid foam core, was cracking and peeling apart in the catastrophic pounding upwind.

Four had abandoned the race; five had returned for repairs; disaster for the Vendée Globe fleet.

I chastised myself, an older skipper in an older boat, for not having been more cautious. In the years of boat development, we'd taken every precaution we could think of, to make the race safer, incorporating every good idea from anyone or anywhere. The sea-going adage is: "One hand for yourself, and one for the ship." Had my instant of laxity thrown it all away?

A half hour later, BZZZ, BZZZ, the Iridium satellite telephone rang. I peeled myself carefully off the floor, grabbed the center post, worked my way onto the bench, swung my legs under the chart table, leaned painfully to the handset and answered "*Great American III*".

"Hi Rich, it's Brien, what's up?"

"The sea finds out everything you did wrong."
...Francis Stokes, American singlehander

Chapter 3: Respect in the North Atlantic

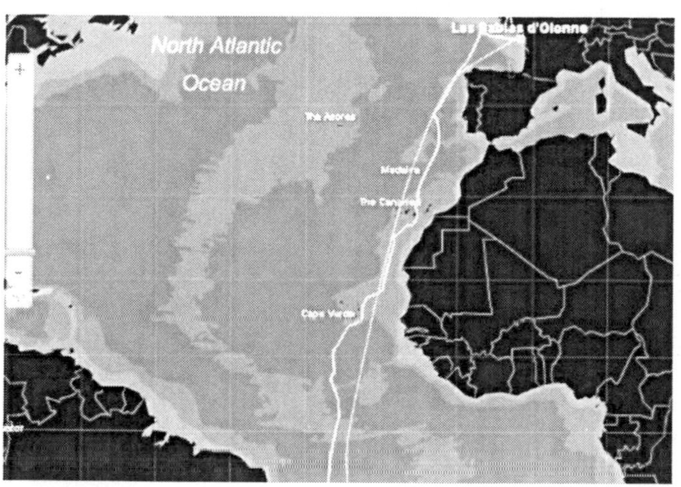

I thanked Dr. Barnewolt for calling back so promptly. He said "no problem, that's what we're here for", the royal "we" signaling that the expertise of the entire Emergency Room at Tufts Medical Center was on call for *GA3* offshore. I then detailed what had happened.

"How close to your spine was the point of impact?"

"Just to the left, an inch or two off, and 4 or 5 inches up from the bottom of my ribcage."

"Is there any tingling or numbness in your fingers, or down your arms?"

I checked again, flexing fingers, wrists, forearms. "No."

"How about tingling in your feet or toes?"

I wiggled toes, rotated ankles, bent my knees. "No."

"That's good. Now, how's your breathing?"

"It hurts like crazy to breathe, and when I have to grind the winches, or pull lines, or just hold on when the boat lurches, it's just agony, feels like there's a knife in my back and somebody's twisting it. I can't get into either bunk through the opening in the bulkhead, it's too painful to contort like that. And I can't lay on my back at the chart table bench to sleep, it hurts too much, so I'm resting on the beanbag on the floor. Somehow I tacked last night, and when the cold front went through, we started broad-reaching fast into the leftover sea. It was incredibly violent for the boat and me, so I rolled up the staysail to slow down and just went along with 3 reefs and no jib, to save us both."

"Good idea. It sounds as though you may have broken a rib or two, no way to tell for sure of course. There's nothing to do for broken ribs. We want to make sure that you haven't punctured a lung."

"With my asthma, I'm a pretty good observer of my lung function, and I think that's OK, it just hurts mechanically to breathe in and out."

"Sounds good. I'll call back on a schedule, maybe every eight hours for the next twenty-four, then every twelve for the next couple of days, and we'll see how it comes along. Take some ibuprofen every four hours, and try to minimize your physical activity for the next few days, if that's possible."

"Will do."

We signed off. I leaned against a big cushion on the bench and tried to relax.

Dr. Brien Barnewolt

What a relief to have Brien on our team. Ironically, his cautionary essay on Preventive Medicine for our NIE program was scheduled to be published the following week. Maybe if I'd had him write first, I would have read it and been doubly careful. Nevertheless, to have the Chief of Emergency Medicine of a major Boston hospital at the other end of a phone when I go flying across the cabin - amazing! I was so lucky.

My gratitude choked me up in the pain.

So many had helped us get to the start:

> Brian Harris, the only American to have worked on three Open 60s, all British, for solo ocean races around the world, he'd helped us hugely in preparing *GA2* for our New York-Melbourne voyage, then helping at the start of our 2003 Hong Kong-New York clipper route voyage; he had managed *GA3*'s massive re-fit with voluminous knowledge, infinite patience, and the ability to always muster a laugh and a smile when needed; he'd thought through problems I didn't know we had; his calm calmed me;
>
> Brian's team at Maine Yacht Center who performed the extensive, skilled, confidence-building re-fit of boat systems and re-building of certain boat structures;
>
> Mark Wylie, a British electronics wizard, who had installed, wired, tested, and calibrated the complex electronics of our sensors, displays, computers, telecoms, and networks; he was always available for a tweaking consultation with a skipper far at sea;
>
> Hugues and Rick who had installed our rigging so precisely, and had installed, refined and tested a multitude of equipment and boat systems too numerous to count, they had prepared us for sea;
>
> Hubert Desjoyeaux, Michel's brother, whose team at his CDK shipyard in Port la Foret, our home away from home, had dedicated themselves to *GA3* as if she were French.

All highly accomplished, they all had worked on her as if they were going to sea themselves aboard her. They were all with me every wave of the way.

As was Neal Skorka, sitesALIVE! veteran producer of dozens of our earlier programs, returning to manage this biggest and most complex one ever; as was Lorraine Leo, technology teacher extraordinaire and user of sitesALIVE! programs, connecting us to her worldwide teacher circle that she had gained one-by-one; as was my Mother in her believing and quiet way; as was Ellen, always willing to listen to me vent until calmer.

As were others behind the scenes.

Before buying the boat, I asked Clarke Smith, a friend and marine insurer, if he would insure it. He said, “I don’t insure sailboats anymore, and certainly not race boats.” My heart sank, knowing the prohibitive premiums of the European insurers, and expecting his next clause to be “and certainly not a solo, non-stop, round the world race”. Instead, “But I’ll insure you, because I know how conservative and experienced a mariner you are.”

I had asked Bob and Kate Niehaus, longtime sitesALIVE! supporters, if they would help yet again. Without a substantive initial pledge to know that we could fund the bulk of the school program, could we take the plunge? Bob had sighed, “Rich, we’re afraid that one of these voyages you’re not going to come home. You were born a century too late, after the great age of sail, but this is what you’re supposed to do, so, yes, we’ll support sitesALIVE! again.”

I had asked Michael and Dorothy Hintze, school friends whose London investment firm had helped us on two previous voyages, could they help fund boat operations again? In the middle of the Lehman Brothers collapse, and financial dominoes crashing globally, “Yes, we’re with you again. Sail safely, and write well for the students.”

The Vendée Globe is solo in race rules only, for every skipper depends on a wide network of people ashore. *GA3* and I, we sailed for all of them.

Hey! Snap out of your emotional reverie! Get back to the race! OK, OK...

At 58, I wasn't the oldest skipper to have ever raced the Vendée Globe. That honor went to Jose de Ugarte, a Spanish skipper, who had finished officially at age 64 in 134 days in the 1992-3 edition. Yet as the oldest skipper in this Vendée Globe, I wanted to make sure that nothing I did would give the organizers future pause in accepting older skippers into this toughest of all sailing events. There was a lower age limit of 21, but no upper age limit. I had to hold up my side. Breaking ribs early on was not a good start.

Others in the fleet had been seriously injured on these unforgiving, often violent, Open 60s. The tough-as-nails Swiss skipper Bernard Stamm had been forced to abandon a solo transatlantic race after a broken rib punctured his lung. Kito de Pavant, on a training session aboard his new *Groupe Bel*, had been thrown across his cockpit, breaking a leg so severely that it took 5 months to heal. Marc Guillemot had broken a rib aboard *Safran* during the solo Transat 2008, considered abandoning the race, then continued at a reduced level of effort to finish his qualifier.

Comforted by the conversation with Dr. Barnewolt, we continued, sailing conservatively even though the storm had departed, and worked back to race pace over the next painful days.

Other skippers' reports forwarded by Ellen comforted me that I wasn't the only one who thought that Bay of Biscay gale was tough:

> *Vincent Riou (defending champion from Vendée Globe 2004-5): Tired and bruised after two days of bad weather. Rarely been shaken up as much.*
>
> *Dee Caffari (first woman to sail solo, non-stop, around-the-world westbound): Those 48 hours were simply horrible, crashing about in the waves with absolutely no sleep.*
>
> Ellen went on:
>
> *It was so good to hear your voice today, albeit disturbing to learn that you feel somewhat disoriented, and hope it is only due to lack of sleep. So many people on shore are rooting for you, checking your progress at least twice daily. Read the following from Ralph Waldo Emerson and immediately thought of you: 'Do not go*

where the path may lead, go instead where there is no path and leave a trail.'

Her emails of support would bring tears to my eyes. Have to keep going and live up to everyone's encouragement.

Passing the Canary Islands a hundred miles off the southwest coast of Morocco, we saw the twinkling lights of their capital Los Palmas. Reminded of my first transatlantic passage, 30 years before, I called Jon Chorey, a friend and shipmate from that voyage, to reminisce. I reached him at home in Massachusetts and we had a nice talk, remembering shipmates and episodes in Gibraltar and the Canaries. This momentarily and usefully distracted me from shipboard challenges.

Later that night, with 15 knots of northerly wind, and forecast to stay at that strength, I considered setting the spinnaker. My ribs were only slightly better, and setting that largest and most unwieldy sail on the boat, a huge physical task that could get very out of control very quickly, especially in the dark, would be risky to do. And it would hurt. Yet this was the Vendée Globe and you had to respect and honor the race, by racing the race, forget the broken ribs. You had to respect your competitors and do your best always, so that if they beat you, their victory would have substance. You had to respect the sailors who had sailed before, whose feats had created the race's legend. You had to respect the French public who had welcomed and encouraged the skippers, and rooted for us all. And I had to respect my student audience, and show them my very best.

In the dark of midnight I started the task, focusing on every step and handhold and pull and grind of a winch, to minimize the strain on my ribs and to minimize the risk of the sail maneuver. A half hour later, this monster, twice as big as the mainsail, bigger than a doubles tennis court, was up and drawing in the moonlight. The boat took off at 14 knots average speed. Extensive morning communications with Mark and the autopilot manufacturers in England had fine-tuned our settings for multiple input variables: Deadband, RGAN, BLAG, BLEN, within the global PERF 1, AUTO NORM, RECOV MED mode. The adjustments and mutual interactions of these were hard to understand even if rested; the mental fatigue of the storm made that harder now. Yet the effort seemed worth it as we held our course better in the conflicting surges of wind, waves, sails and boat.

For a few hours we proceeded. I was happy with my decision, I was racing the race and doing what I was supposed to do. The stars and moon shone brightly. A stronger puff accelerated the boat to 18 knots, she heeled, slewed to port toward the wind, and broached, with mainsail and main boom dragging in the water. Laying over at 50 degrees of heel, the spinnaker luffed violently and likewise dragged in the water, the lightweight cloth at risk of explosion from air or sea. With the rudders completely overpowered, the autopilot's correction couldn't bring her back to course, and so the pilot alarmed insistently - BEEP - BEEP - BEEP. I ignored it while I desperately let out the spinnaker sheet and mainsheet so that the boat wouldn't get pinned on her side. Then I pushed the button to disengage the autopilot from the steering system, grabbed the tiller and pulled it hard over to try to wrestle the boat back to course. I hoped the spinnaker would fill gradually, and not with an instantaneous bang that could burst it. It did fill slowly, and eventually I got us sorted out and sailing smoothly again, autopilot re-engaged, boat upright, racing south at 15 knots. My ribs reminded me with every breath and movement of my accident a thousand miles ago. I knew why I'd put up the spinnaker, but really, why had I put up the spinnaker? Because this is the Vendée Globe.

Stable for a bit, another puff, another broach and autopilot alarm, another frantic effort to control everything. Over the next hour, the instruments showed the true wind speed increasing from 15 to 18 to 20 knots, another broach, then 22 knots, then 24 knots, another broach, then another. I kept hoping that the wind would retreat to the 15 knots forecast, but I also knew that hope has no role at sea. Blame the weather forecast? Never. I knew that forecasting weather precisely was an almost impossible task. Having worked with professional meteorologists for previous voyages, I knew their intelligence, competence, and dedication. The volume of weather information that we could receive at sea via satellite link to the internet was prodigious, and the technological improvements of satellite data collection and computer analyses were stunning advances compared to my first transatlantic passage three decades before.

In a stable moment, for curiosity sake, I checked at the chart table the graph of sail selection that Michel had drawn for *Foncia* for various wind strengths and angles to the boat. Likely a secret document, he'd emailed it to me in our exchange as I wasn't really a competitor to him. I was awed by one part of the graph, that Michel, while singlehanded, would set his 4500 square foot spinnaker in up to 27 knots of true wind! I had vowed to never be lured to match Michel on that graph, but now, here I was, close to it with the spinnaker up, blowing 24 knots true, dark of midnight, 500 miles offshore, broken ribs, and broaching regularly.

Well, at least I am racing the race.

In between broaches, *GA3* was flying in the moonlight, boatspeed 16-18-20 knots, surfing down the still gentle swells, shorts and t-shirt warmth off the coast of Africa, with harness and tether if I went forward, heading south toward the Cape Verde Islands, an incredible night. We must be making up on the boats ahead, and losing the boats behind. Keep going!

Yet these bursts of high speed also created bursts of high risk, and the arithmetic was that unless you could sustain these speeds for long periods of time, it wouldn't help much to increase your average speed over many months around the world. What it did do was increase the risk that something would go dramatically wrong dramatically rapidly that could quickly end your race. This sailing was undeniably exhilarating, yet far more important to improve an average speed of 10 knots to 11 knots over 3 months, than to go 22 knots for a few minutes or an hour and have something explode. So time to get the spinnaker down, a task more difficult and risky than setting it, with the now higher wind velocity.

A spinnaker is both the biggest and the least controlled sail on any boat. Open 60 sails are all triangles. Whereas the mainsail has two entire edges attached along mast and boom to provide control for the cloth in between, and the jibs have one entire edge attached to a stay to be roller-furled, the giant spinnaker is only attached by its three corners, and everything in between, three edges and body, can blow and twist and tangle wherever it can reach. They can wrap themselves around stays or spreaders, they can twist themselves into an undoable hourglass, they can wrap that hourglass around a stay, and you will NEVER get it down, until you somehow get yourself aloft with a knife and cut the sail away.

So how to control this monster, especially when alone? With a sock, hopefully. Before the race, the spinnaker is streamed from the top to the bottom and then a 90' long tube sock, 2' in diameter, is pulled down over it. The spinnaker has a halyard to hoist the sail, with this covering sock over it, to the top of the mast. The sock then has its own halyard. When the sock is hoisted, it releases the confined spinnaker inside to fill with wind. When it's time to take the sail down, you reverse the process, pulling the sock down over the spinnaker to snuff it. That's the theory. But if it's blowing too hard, you can't physically pull the sock down by hand over the highly pressured sail. The only solution is to let out the sail until it's luffing, violently in this instance, like a giant flag on a windy day, then wrap the sock downhaul line around a winch and grind it down to forcibly smother the raging acreage of cloth.

In the cockpit, I had avoided a few dangerous broaches by disengaging the autopilot and hand-steering the boat back to course in the nick of time. But if I left the cockpit to go forward to lead the sock downhaul through a block to the mast winch, and then try to grind the sock down from there, I would be leaving the cockpit for a perilously long time. Finally the lightbulb went off - lead the sock downhaul line through the block and back to the cockpit, then I can snuff the spinnaker with a cockpit winch, and grab the tiller in an emergency, simultaneously if need be. Eureka!

I waited for a lull, then, with a nine LED headlight to improve my odds, raced forward with a block, lashed it near the bow, squinted aloft into the dark to try to distinguish the sock's downhaul line from its uphaul line as the two disappeared high into the night, wrapping and unwrapping on each other as the mast swung back and forth on the boat going 18 knots, picked one with good confidence, led it through the block, then nearly ran with it back to the cockpit, led it to the off-duty running backstay winch, and breathed a premature sigh of relief. Now, the risky part. Ease out the spinnaker sheet, try to endure the horrible sounds of 3500 square feet of light nylon sailcloth snapping angrily in 20+ knots of wind, and grind smoothly on the downhaul. I pulled in 20', then ran to the mast to see how it was all doing up there in the dark, OK so far – I think - then run back, keep grinding until the noise of the luffing sail diminished to a virtual calm, OK, we've got the spinnaker under control.

Wow, do those ribs ever hurt.

Back to the mast and lower the sock with spinnaker inside to the deck. To the bowsprit to unclip the forward corner there, getting soaked and refreshed by the splashing bow wave in the process, remove the halyard and tie it off, stuff the huge pile of snaking sock with spinnaker inside, down the forward hatch, take a last look around for tidiness on the foredeck, then back to the cockpit for a sit under the protective cuddy, a fistful of Fig Newtons, a couple of Baby Bel cheeses, a tall glass of powdered Nestlé's Nido Whole Milk mixed with powdered Ensure, and a relax before unrolling the jib to get going again.

Well, that was exciting...and painful.

A few hours later, the sun rose, and a few hours after that, the wind backed off to 15 knots again, and I repeated the whole drill and hoisted the spinnaker. Then the wind diminished to 5 knots, the sail became unstable, and I had to snuff it and drop it, and then put up the huge light air gennaker jib, which would be more stable on its leading edge. Ah, sailboat racing across oceans, nothing ever stays the same for very long. But that's the beauty and challenge of the sport. How quickly, how accurately, how safely can you shift gears so that you are going optimally for as high a percentage of time as possible, while minimizing risk.

At a dinner in New York the winter before, I'd seen Ellen MacArthur, whom I'd met at the Transat 2004 solo race from England to Boston. A broken mainsail halyard an hour into that race had forced us back to the dock, and people came out of the woodwork to help replace it. Still at it at midnight, Ellen had come to the boat to ask if there was anything she could do. At age 24 in the 2000 Vendée Globe, the youngest entrant ever, she had finished 2nd to Michel, and in 2005 broke the solo round-the-world record in a 75' trimaran, for which she became Dame Ellen. I said I was honored to meet her, a bit embarrassed to meet her under these circumstances, thanks immensely for the emotional support, but that we were making progress, and no need for her to stay out in the cold, wind and rain. At that dinner, I'd introduced her to Bob Metcalfe, ethernet inventor, who asked her: "What is the key to success in the Vendée Globe?" She answered directly "Risk management." I vowed to never forget that exchange.

À propos of risk management, in adjusting the keel cant, something odd, then quite dire. The keel has a massive, 80 millimeter diameter stainless steel, hinge pin welded into the fabrication fore-to-aft. The protruding ends of this pin fit into two equally massive stainless steel slabs, each weighing 40 pounds, that are each bolted with eight 1" diameter, bronze bolts, to the bottom of two carbon bulkheads and hang the four ton keel by that pin. The keel hinge point is thus at the bottom of the boat. These two carbon bulkheads, plus a third supporting the mast, are the strongest parts of the boat. The keel extends 5 feet above the hinge pin into the space between these two bulkheads. The top of the keel has ten pulleys on it, five on each side. Forty degrees from the vertical on either side of the hinge pin, just underneath the deck, and bridging these two bulkheads, are two huge stainless steel tubes, each with five pulleys on them. Between these pulleys and the pulleys at the top of the keel are laced control ropes, each side having 10 parts to 1. The tail end of each side's control rope leads through a small hole in the aft of the two carbon bulkheads to a winch, and the keel can be pulled to one side or the other, pushing the 8,000 pound 14' deep keel forty degrees to the upwind side to counterbalance the load of the sails.

In the keel area, I noticed that the cosmetic cover over the port-side tube was askew. Not a big deal, but how did that happen? I took off the cover with a screwdriver, and noticed how it happened. And it was a big deal. This massive tube had twisted, and started to come out of its guide through the two bulkheads. It was 1/2" out already. If it came out another 1/2", it would come completely out of the forward bulkhead. If that tube was loaded, and the keel pulled the tube, it would crack the carbon bulkhead that held the keel in the boat.

A flurry of emails. To Brian, Subject: URGENT, saying I thought maybe one of the five sheaves was frozen and, under load, had rotated the tube. He consulted with his team who had serviced the tubes and sheaves. They suggested major lubrication of the sheaves, and possibly re-threading the line to bypass that sheave, go with 8:1 rather than 10:1. That idea needed an email to our French rigger: Is the keel control line strong enough for 8:1? Yes, the rope is Spectra, 9 mm diameter core, with 9 ton breaking strength and 4.5 tons Safe Working Load, so 8:1 would be 36 tons SWL and OK by us.

I went into the keel compartment and emptied most of a can of lubricant into the sheaves on both tubes, then got the biggest hammer that we had, and started pounding the tube back into place. Since the bulkheads weren't perfectly parallel, the tube's end wasn't cut square at 90 degrees. If twisted, it wouldn't completely bear on the bulkhead. To get full support of the loaded surface against the bulkhead, the tube had to be twisted back to its proper alignment. I tried with vice-grips, not a chance, I tried with the pipe wrench, nope. Finally, I tried with our gigantic, nearly two foot long, channel lock wrench. Jam one of the toothed forks into the tube, and twist - it worked! Then grab this long tool, and, although being a righty, with a lefty baseball swing because of the tube's portside location, both hands on the "bat", whale on the end of the tube to hammer it in.

With tacks and gybes, with canting and uncanting the keel, this batting practice with a 20" channel lock wrench would be used 2 or 3 or 4 times daily for the rest of the race to ensure that that tube stayed where it was supposed to stay. I got to be a pretty good lefty batter over the next months.

The boat is a complex piece of heavy equipment, operating in a working and hostile environment. The job list is short only at the start. Maintenance is key, and if I forgot that twisted tube just once, it could end our Vendée Globe.

An "additional thoughts" email arrived from Dr. Barnewolt:

Assuming you have a fracture of either a rib or even a vertebra, your caloric requirements have now increased. You should try to get 10-20% more calories in for healing purposes.

Regarding pain control, you may want to consider taking half a tablet of the narcotic pain medicine percocet or vicodin. I doubt it would alter your awareness much if you are reasonably rested. Perhaps try half a tablet upon waking up from a nap during the day and prior to going through some sail changes. It might help take the edge off and the effects only last 4 hours anyway.

Obviously, I would NOT advocate trying this for the first time at night with the spinnaker up and winds at 20 knots.

As if I wasn't already eating enough with my targeted 6,000 calory daily diet, now I had to push down more. Good to have the go-ahead on the stronger pain medication, but I'm going to grin and bear it with the ibuprofen for now.

I made my way aft and stretched painfully over the lifelines to untie yesterday's daily flag, and tie on today's. A tradition since our San Francisco to Boston voyage, every day we flew a new 12" x 18" U.S. Yacht Ensign, a seagoing version of the American flag, with an anchor and chain in a circle of thirteen stars in the blue area. I would write in the flag's margin the boat name, date, and latitude and longitude of the noon position. After the voyage, we gave these living mementos to staff, *preparateurs*, newspapers, donors, and special friends. If from a gale, the flag might be tattered and salt-encrusted, with green corroded brass grommets. If from a calm, it might be still pristine. Yet all had flown at sea in our voyages and proved emotionally popular among recipients. I had to be careful going back there and making the exchange, but it was a happy chore and done religiously daily. A small yet significant part of our voyage, every flag was living and unique.

Back into the cabin with yesterday's flag, solid handholds all the way, the Iridium phone rang.

"Great American III".

"Good morning Rich, it's Andi Robertson of *Radio Vacances*. How are your ribs today? And how is *Great American III* going?"

Andi Robertson

Radio Vacances was a fantastic French idea. Two radio broadcasters, one French-speaking and one English-speaking, would call seven or eight of the boats daily for live radio interviews. They didn't just call the leaders, they called everyone on a rotating basis, because everyone had a human story to tell. Through the race your broadcaster became your friend, wishing you well, remembering your and your boat's challenges, and your solutions. They were on your side and became great supporters.

In my first solo transatlantic race, aboard *Curtana*, I had spoken by ham radio with a friend working at NBC. Accustomed to dense news reports filed from the field, nonetheless, after the race she proclaimed astonishment at the breadth, depth and rapidity of my verbal data transfer of news from the boat. A good descriptor is that a solo ocean race is like a premium cable subscription, where all the channels are on and blaring simultaneously in your brain: the Weather Channel, the Food Channel, Discovery, History, NatGeo, News, Health, ESPN, Versus, Yoga, PBS, Tae Bo, the Motorcycle repair guys and Dr. Phil. Your brain is on high and full alert 24/7. Is the tube twisted? When is the next weather report? Analyze the MaxSea routing. I need to eat. Ease that mainsail. Need a backup lashing on the main boom block. Pump the forepeak leak. Check the autopilot linkages. Nap. Take the four asthma drugs. Re-charge the headlight batteries. Charge the house battery bank. Transfer diesel from the jerry cans to the main tank. Write the newspaper essay. Edit the video file. Call in your audio report. Desalinate some fresh water. Answer the kids' questions. Watch the horizon. Check the chafe on the jib tack. Replace the preventer fuse. On and on and on and on...and only 25,000 miles to go.

We crossed paths on the computer that morning with *Pakea Bizkeia,* sailed by my new Basque friend Unai Basurko. Unai was everyone's new friend. On the dock in Les Sables d'Olonne, he always wore a big, friendly smile on his face underneath his traditional Basque beret. Piercing blue eyes looked warmly at you, and he befriended everyone who had the good fortune to meet him. George Gibson, my closest friend since the 9th grade, had brought to the start an author-signed copy of a book that he'd published - The Basque History of the World. I presented it to Unai, for proud reading as he circled the globe. A smiling bearhug of thanks confirmed the gift as a good one.

A few days further south, faced with a Cape Verdean Island directly in our path, we forked to the east to go to the windward side so as not to be blanketed by the island were we to go to the west. A few more miles traversed, yet sailed in a stronger breeze. The memories of the cold and harsh Bay of Biscay faded as we ticked off degrees of latitude toward the tropics.

Though close to the Sahara, none of its fine sand, the consistency of talcum powder, had blown out from the desert to cover the boat's windward side. This Harmattan had covered *GA2* on the home stretch of our San Francisco-Boston voyage, even when 2,000 miles west of the desert. Despite its fascination, I was glad to miss it this time, as it had constricted my breathing and needed a deluge of rain to rinse it off the boat.

Huge Flying Fish Crashed Aboard

In the warming waters southbound, swarms of flying fish sporadically appeared. Averaging ten inches long, with a ten inch wingspan, with an occasional outsized monster, they escape predators by leaping out of the water to glide on wing fins for a hundred yards before splashing back into the sea. If near enough, they mistake the rushing *GA3* for a predator and leap out of the water to escape. Sometimes, seemingly more often at night, they get it wrong, and leap back at us, crashing on deck, or into sails or rigging. Sometimes they whiz dangerously through the cockpit at high speed – if you ever got hit in the eye... I'd been whacked hard in the chest by one on our San Francisco – Boston voyage; it had felt like a thrown baseball. And on our New York – Melbourne voyage, my shipmate Bill Biewenga had taken one off his forehead on a hockey-like deflection off the rounded cabintop. I'd seen them streak through the swept circle of our whirring wind turbine blades: usually they made it safely through, but sometimes not. So if I thought we were in a flying fish zone, I wore my construction goggles to protect my eyes.

The band of steadier trade winds provided a few days of fewer sail changes, a welcome respite for my ribs. Then a setback. If the boat pounded just so into a cross-sea with her bow, like a tuning fork the shock would reverberate down the monocoque structure of the hull. Laying on my back at the chart table bench one afternoon, we hit a sea and that harmonic wave rippled down the hull to crash upward at the chart table, as if a lumberjack had swung a sledgehammer into the bench from below. Arrrrgghh! The crushing blow wrenched my back and I felt the ribs tearing again. Massive pointed pain. Another conversation with Brien on finger or toe tingles: "OK, it won't be like going back to the beginning of your healing, it will be like going back to day 7, so you've got to re-heal a bit, but you're not starting over completely." That was a relief as we sailed south for the expected chaos of the equator.

I emailed the reverberation question to one of our Experts, Prof. Dava Newman at MIT. She replied that it would be fascinating to instrument the boat with sensors to detect and analyze this phenomenon, yet no way to model it now.

I remembered our first meeting and learning that she was from a small town in Montana. I asked "How did a young girl get from there to MIT?" She'd answered simply: "The Apollo program." Inspiration works. On that note, I'd asked her to write the first essay of our NIE series on our Teacher's Guide topic of "Follow Your Dreams". She did, entitling her piece "Love, Act, Discover and Innovate". Now THAT would get the kids off to a good start!

Scott Hamilton, another of our Team of Experts, and an Everest veteran, hearing of my re-injury, emailed of his breaking a rib when falling into a crevasse below the North Col on Everest, and asked if I had those shooting pains that felt like a bullet going through. I replied that I did. He then urged on me a Marine Corps quote: "Pain is weakness leaving the body." Emailing that to another friend who had come to the start, Lt. Col. Bill Griffen, USMC retired, for amplification, he replied:

> *Yes, a challenge to motivate recruits, but don't confuse the pain of exertion with the pain of injury. The messages are different and demand different care. Protect it, and visualize it healing as strong as a weld!*

One can simply not say enough good things about the people who surround a Vendée Globe skipper.

Southbound through the Atlantic, after the disastrous Bay of Biscay gale, ten of the new generation boats had surged to the front to form a lead pack fifty miles wide and a hundred miles front to back.

The pack's width came from each skipper's own analysis of the weather, the characteristics of his or her boat, and what route was thought optimal. Sailboat racing is not like car or ski racing where competitors are essentially funneled into the same confined track and only small decisions are needed on your path. In sailboat racing, you can choose widely where to go, where you think is best. So the fleet, heading south, also spreads east to west. The changing and uncertain weather then blesses or curses individual boats, with more or less wind, better or worse wind angles, bigger or smaller seas. A skipper in the lead may try to "cover" the other boats, to stay between the competition and the next mark, yet in this race, with thousands of miles between marks, "covering" is almost impossible. So the skippers sail their own best thought out course, trusting that Aeolus, the God of the Wind, and Neptune, the God of the Sea, will smile upon their choices.

This lead pack, comprised of great skippers, skilled, experienced, and tough, pushing themselves and their high tech boats hard, was sailing fast. The lead changed hands early on, with Marc Guillemot leading the first day, then Loïck Peyron, Jean-Pierre Dick, Roland Jourdain and Sebastien Josse each surging for a time. On day four, Peyron, nicknamed Yoda for his wisdom and calm, had taken the lead aboard his beautiful blue and silver *Gitana 80*. For the next 14 days and 3,000 miles he led at every position report, a breath-taking display of skill and tenacity. Yann Eliès, chasing from mid-lead-pack, wrote admiringly:

> *He's setting the pace and leading the way at the front. He never eases off in light or heavy weather. With his pace and his precision in the adjustments, he is truly impressive.*

Over that span of two weeks, the lead pack compressed and expanded like an accordion. This wasn't a 28,000 mile marathon, this was a 28,000 mile sprint.

A handful of new boats stretched out behind the lead pack into a disparate 2nd group. The third pack of older boats included us. Approaching the equator, the fleet ran headlong into the complexities of global atmospherics.

In physics, the Coriolis Effect states that things moving in the northern hemisphere will tend to bend to the right. If an area of lower barometric pressure builds, higher pressure around it will naturally flow toward that area, bending to the right as it goes. The lower pressure area thus starts to rotate counterclockwise, and the higher pressure area, away from which the flow is going, rotates clockwise. In the southern hemisphere, these forces and flows are reversed.

Manifested in the rotating weather systems, the forces collide at the ITCZ, the InterTropical Convergence Zone, where they try to sort themselves out. The ITCZ is a band of light winds, violent squalls, torrential downpours, spinning winds, flat calms, waterspouts (tornadoes at sea), brilliant sunshine, heat, and deadly looking clouds. The north-south span of this band of confusion varies from 100 miles to 300 miles, may overlap the equator or reside entirely north (as it did now) or south of it, and edges north or south seasonally with the sun.

Beautiful Double Rainbow

From France to the Cape of Good Hope, where the fleet would turn east into the Indian Ocean, the shortest route on a map would be the direct route in two legs: south to Senegal at the corner of western Africa, then straight southeast to the corner of South Africa. Yet this most direct route crosses a wide no-wind zone in the ITCZ at the Equator along the African coast. If you took a route bowing well to the west, all the way to the northeast corner of Brazil, you will have much stronger wind, and a narrower calm area in the ITCZ, thus making a faster, though longer, passage. What will be the correct longitude at which to cross the ITCZ and equator to answer optimally this wind versus distance dilemma? Every skipper spent hours, days, nights, and hours again, studying isobaric pressure maps, frontal system maps, sea surface temperature maps, plus satellite photos of cloud cover and real-time data buoy information, to try to get across and to the south as fast as possible. On our approach, analysis of these data suggested that at 26° West longitude we'd have only a tolerably small calm. We targeted that as our equator-crossing point.

For *GA3*, the ITCZ arrived suddenly. On port tack, moderate winds declining from the strong northeast trades, a gray day dawning slowly, we sailed toward the blackest cloud expanse, horizon to horizon, that I have ever seen. Though dawn was hours ago, it looked as though we were sailing into a wide, low-ceilinged cave of night. The black roof smothered us from above. When we got in there, would there be a way out? There was no light side to side, or here in the middle; there was not even a hint of light ahead. No discernible edge distinguished the black sea from the black cloud. There was no way around, we had to go in. I felt a tangible pang of dread. I'd sailed across the equator nine times before, but had never seen anything like this. It looked like the end of the world.

I hurriedly put the first reef in to be conservative. Then the wind increased as the blackness descended to envelope us. I rolled up the jib and unrolled the smaller staysail, cautiously, yet prematurely given the actual windspeed. On we went, tiptoeing our way into the cave at 8 knots, wind staying steady, and the blackness, like a night without stars, staying the same too. How could daytime be this black? On edge, I watched the barograph at the chart table and the wind instruments in the cockpit, hoping to catch any blip in data that might signal a calamitous squall about to crush us into the sea.

Hour after hour we sailed, hair up on the back of my neck, scanning side to side for any sign of anything. Ordinarily, in difficult conditions of seas or storm or wind, one gains confidence over time, in the boat, in your sail selection, in your decisions. No such confidence was gained that morning. I stood still in the cockpit, holding my breath, *GA3* sailing comfortably and eerily quietly at 8 knots, no physical exertion being expended, but with my heart pounding in the ominous, unrelenting, inexplicable blackness.

After several tense hours, ahead lay a break in the clouds. An hour later we emerged into a more normal overcast day with lightening winds. Further still, a flat calm stopped us, its imperceptible swell gently rocking the boat. The mainsail and jib slatted back and forth, the mainsail against the running backstays - WHACK - the jib against the staysail stay and baby stay - WHACK - WHACK. Back and forth, back and forth, back and forth - WHACK - WHACK - WHACK. You know it's bad for the sails, all that abrasion and chafe and shock load for zero forward miles, but if a zephyr of wind came up, if a catspaw brushed the mirror surface, we'd need the sails instantly to get us out of this. Somehow we have to cross this desert. The autopilot tries to steer - ERRRR - ERRRR- ERRRR - but we have no steerage way so I turn it off. Then the boat drifts slowly to head wherever she wants.

Acute frustration, exacerbated by fatigue and stress. Everybody else is sailing fast, in good winds, you just know it, and here we are going NOWHERE. The second guessing began. I should have crossed further west, where the two sets of trade winds, northeast in the northern hemisphere, and southeast in the southern hemisphere, have had more time and distance to merge almost together, to eliminate this gap. I'd watched Michel, after he restarted the race, press hard to catch the fleet. He'd caught us and the 3rd group early on, then picked off the second group one by one, then closed on the lead pack. Might he be tempted to cut the corner at the Equator, to edge to the east to shave distance? No, he'd gone to 30° West, a full 240 miles further west than us, and sailed straight through, as if he knew there was a wall at the Equator, and instead of trying to struggle over it or break through it, he just decided to walk around the end of it. Why didn't I do that? Why didn't I follow *Le Professeur*? Because I thought we had a good shot here, and we'd save some miles. But you can't save miles if you're stopped! Internal debate and recrimination raged. I rolled up the jib to save it from thrashing against the staysail stay. The boat drifted in circles, the ultimate ignominy, the bow pointing at Morocco, then Greenland, then Boston, then Florida, when all we wanted was south.

In a flat calm there is nothing you can do except wait for a weather system with wind to move over your position. Should I use this time to try to sleep? Not possible, the slatting mainsail is worse than dripping water. Besides, it's a hundred degrees in the cabin. If we could make even one or two knots, we'd make progress toward getting out of this. Keep working.

Dolphins Patiently Await a Bow Wave

Seven hours later, a puff of wind on the horizon as a local weather system drifted past us. Roll out that jib! I teased the boat to head south, after the several circles we'd done in the flat calm. We moved a bit. Off to the southwest, in the direction of Venezuela, was a bigger cloud. We turned toward it, it slowly moved away, we hung onto it, making about 2 knots, then slowly a bit more breeze came, we were up to 4 knots and gaining on that cloud. For 90 minutes we chased that cloud. Other clouds joined the vicinity. Now making 6 knots I eased our direction more south, gradually we slowed as we diverged from the cloud - can't do that! I headed back for the cloud and our speed improved again. Into the late afternoon we inched our way southwest.

Despite the virtual non-existence of wind, we'd been sailing with one reef in the mainsail, for fear of a sudden ITCZ squall, and because when the wind puffs drifted off, the sail would not slat so much. It seemed more stable to have less sail in the very light wind. This proved fortuitous.

Something in the distance, on the water, it looks like a dark line, a mile away. It moved toward us, then it was darker - a squall! I always sail with seaboots on, to protect my feet, but in the stifling, sweaty heat, I'd been caught barefoot, with just running shorts, no t-shirt, no foul weather gear, injury just waiting to happen. I hurriedly rolled up the jib, and then went to put another reef in. The dark line was now 1/4 mile away, I watched it as I reefed in a desperate sprint, grinding the pedestal, wrenching the half-healed ribs, now the dark blue line was a hundred yards away, and angry. The reef was in, BAM, the squall hit, 40 knots of wind, into the back of the mainsail, BANG, the fuse line on the preventer holding the boom broke, and the boom crashed backwards across the boat into the running backstays, laying the boat over at 50 degrees in the wrong direction, BEEP - BEEP - BEEP the autopilot alarm screeched its torture of trying to push the hydraulic ram beyond its stops to bring us back on course, torrential rain lashing the boat and me. I disengaged the pilot and grabbed the tiller, squinting through the rain at the instruments and the masthead windvane. I couldn't let the boat crash-gybe back until we were ready. With the mainsail aback, we were being pushed mostly sideways, the deck dug in and pushing the water like a shovel plowing snow, but a little bit forward too, enough to steer to keep the wind at the same angle to the boat so we wouldn't crash-gybe back and shock load the sails, mast and rigging again. 5 minutes, 10 minutes, 15 minutes, I followed that squall's wind around in a circle, the boat laying over on its side, lashed by wind and rain, turning for Africa, now France, now Canada, now Venezuela, now Africa again as the viciously rotating ITCZ squall passed slowly over us. After 20 minutes of onslaught, the wind began to relent, the boat stood up straighter, the waterfall of rain draining off the mainsail slowing to a trickle.

I gybed back and sorted out the mainsail. No damage done to this strong boat, her strong sails and rigging. I replaced the preventer fuse, a small loop of dacron rope cover, which is intended to absorb the initial force of a shock load, then break so that the boom or padeye that holds the preventer doesn't break. I rolled out the staysail to get us going south again, conservatively. Spent, I went below to towel off, then stretch out on the chart table bench. Instantly I was asleep. Dr. Claudio Stampi, a sleep expert, had told me in sleep training for the Transat 2004, "When the sleep door opens, walk through it." I did, and knocked off a refreshing 30 minute nap before returning to the fight ring on deck.

We could take extra sail, so I rolled the staysail and unrolled the jib, then laboriously hoisted the mainsail to its first reef. If we had broken through to the south side of the ITCZ we had to make miles fast, now, to ensure that we stayed on that side of it, and that if it whimsically decided to move south again, it wouldn't overtake us. If we were out, we had to stay out. The full mainsail shortly followed, and we increased speed in the steadying wind to 10 knots. This was better!

Through the night and into the next day - had we escaped? No. The wind diminished, then turned squally again. The ITCZ had crept back over us.

Through that day and night I made 13 sail changes in 15 hours, a beyond exhausting, maximum effort. I longed for the simplicity and brevity of land sports: give me a football game, with 10 minutes of actual action in three hours. That black cloud coming up - will it be a squall? Better put a reef in, then nothing in the cloud. OK, roll out the reef, another 500 loaded revolutions on the pedestal. OK, how about that next black cloud, well maybe we'll just wait and see, give the ribs a break, after all there wasn't anything calamitous in that last one, and BAM, another 35 knots of wind and reef in the tumult. OK, now that's gone, well maybe I won't roll out the reef for a while, then you know you must, you roll it out, another 500 revolutions, and then "oh, brother, here comes another black cloud - what should I do with this one?"

The three biggest winches of the five in the cockpit each have three gears, low, medium, and high and are driven independently or by the pedestal. The low gear means more revolutions with less load. The high gear means a big load with fewer revolutions. Most tasks on the boat cannot be done in high gear, because the loads are too big, and I don't mean they can't be done by me, they can't be done by anybody who is alone.

To hoist the mainsail from one reef to the next required 375 revolutions on the pedestal in the low gear. If impatient, I could reduce the revolutions by switching to the medium gear, where it would only take 175 revolutions between reefs, but the load was double. This power vs. endurance trade-off was front and center. Certain tasks, i.e., hoisting from the first reef in the mainsail to the full mainsail, when the total weight of the 450 pound sail was bearing, could not physically be done in the medium gear even with the 2:1 main halyard cutting the load in half. Going up a reef, I would need to grind 40' with the winch to raise the sail the 20' needed. If in the low gear, I would count 100 revolutions, then stop, catch a breath, check all the lines to makes sure none was fouled and contributing friction and drag to my load, then continue and do another hundred. If in the heavier medium gear for the second or third reef, I'd do 50 revolutions before catching my breath and checking the lines, then continuing. From my qualification race, I knew my average to be 3,000 to 5,000 loaded revolutions to make each day's 5 to 7 major sail changes, plus normal trimming. Thus the 6,000 calories per day nutrition target!

Sails up and down, wind up and down, rain and no rain, moonlight and sunlight, it didn't matter, I worked the boat and the weather as best as I could, and we made our way south until we were finally, firmly, definitely out of the ITCZ and into the southeast trades of the southern hemisphere.

A friend and competitor, Raphaël Dinelli aboard *Fondation Océan Vital*, appeared on the horizon to the east. He had fitted his boat with a plethora of solar panels, and a large vertical axis wind turbine at the stern, to sail the world using only renewable electricity. One jerry can of diesel provided backup for electricity generation from his engine's alternator. With our course being slightly to the east of south, and his to the west of south, he crossed us just ahead. Later he kindly telephoned and we spoke a bit, but as it was hard for both of us to understand the other with the language barrier, we hung up after a few minutes.

On Day 16 we counted down Northern latitude minutes to the equator.

For the occasion, I flew the prayer flags, blessed by the Nepalese monks, that Scott had given me - they are slowly blown apart in the wind and bring good luck. I flew a flag hand painted by Lorraine Leo's 6th grade class in Massachusetts. Finally, I flew Cindy Collins' favorite Chanel scarf. Cindy had been a stalwart sitesALIVE! believer and veteran, representing us for seven years at K12 conferences and schools with enthusiasm, professionalism, and presence. Tragically, she had succumbed the year before to brain cancer. Her devoted husband Larry had asked me to fly Cindy's favorite scarf on our voyage around the world. I cried as I tied it onto our stern lifeline as we entered King Neptune's new domain.

Cindy's Favorite Chanel Scarf

"Well, how did I get here?"
...Once in a Lifetime, Talking Heads

Chapter 4: My Path to the Vendée Globe

Entranced at an Early Age

My father, John, grew up in Dorchester, a working class section of Boston, in a triple-decker, three families for three floors. Guided by a diligent mother, he received a full scholarship to MIT, where he studied Engineering Management. Launched on a successful business career, he worked quality control in a Pittsburgh steel mill, sold textile machinery in the south, and managed production at Waltham Watch Company. During World War II, too old to serve in uniform, he became General Purchasing Agent for Sperry Corporation in New York, a defense contractor specializing in bomb sights and gyroscopes. With each company change, he smartly changed job function, so that when ready to run his own company, he had gained broad operational experience.

My mother, Dorothy Ann, grew up in Tacoma, Washington, the oldest of six siblings. After college, she moved to Fairbanks to help build KFAR-660, the first commercial radio station in the Alaskan Territory. She hosted a show called "Tundra Topics." What an adventure! A single woman, in the Alaskan Territory, in the early 1940s! She flew with the bush pilots landing on snow, ice, water or terra firma, and reported from the mailboat *Kusko* on its first voyage up the Yukon after the ice broke in the spring. A photo shows her swimming in Harding Lake, east of Fairbanks, with a friend from KFAR. The lake is a mile across to the trees, and yes, all that white stuff between her and the far shore is...ice! Mom was the original adventurer in our family.

When Japan invaded Kiska in the Aleutian Islands in 1942, she returned to Seattle to work at Todd Shipyard. She read blueprints to determine what grade of steel should be used in various parts of the ships. When the Japanese were pushed out of the Aleutians, she returned to Fairbanks. After the war, she came out from the territory with a vacation trip through the east to visit relatives. Dad was working in New York for Sperry. Buying an airplane ticket at Grand Central Station to fly New York to Washington DC, he spotted a distinguished woman in line ahead of him, but social mores of the day made it inappropriate to introduce himself. Initially taking the wrong bus to LaGuardia Aiport, he eventually arrived as they were pulling the stairway from the closed plane, but he, being Dad, persuaded them to open it again. There was one open seat left and it was next to...the beautiful woman! They conversed en route. Mutually drawn to each other, they corresponded diligently when she returned to the Pacific Northwest, then went on to Canada, near Hudson Bay, for a research job with a British writer and his wife. Meeting again eight months later in wintertime New York, they were engaged and married early that summer, then moved to Boston, where Dad had managed to acquire a Sperry subcontractor in high technology.

Daughter Anne arrived the next year, I arrived two years later, and Sarah three years after me. An earlier marriage of Dad's had given him my half-sister Eleanor. Dad's company Doelcam prospered after the war, and a decade later he sold it to Honeywell. Taking on volunteer positions at his beloved MIT, first as President of the Alumni Association, next as Chairman of the Second Century Fund drive, then as Secretary of the Corporation for two decades, his freed up time allowed the family to try new activities, sailing among them.

§

We sailed as a family on a small day-sailing boat. I took lessons at Pleon Yacht Club, a junior sailing club in Marblehead, 20 miles north of Boston. Mom and Dad bought us a little boat, a Sprite, and we kids sailed and raced it together. One day, alone in the tiny boat, our class had a short race around two buoys and back, about 1/2 mile in all. It was high adventure! I concentrated hard to trim the sails properly, to steer straight without a "snake wake" that would slow us in the little waves, and to gybe and tack carefully at the marks. I won! Ten years old, I remember it a half century later with utter clarity. For me, it was less about beating the other boats than that if I had arrived first, I must have sailed well. That was my gratification.

Dad commissioned his dream offshore cruising boat, designed by a Dane, Aage Neilsen, and built in Denmark. Loving the country and her people, he named her *Holger Danske*, to honor Denmark's hero, who had fought with and against Charlemagne, and briefly been King of England. Commemorated by a statue in Kronborg Castle, of Hamlet fame, Holger sits sleeping, with Curtana, his Sword of Mercy, across his knees. By legend, he awakes to save Denmark when she is in trouble.

In the next decade I advanced to bigger boats, crewing for others rather than skippering. If I steered, I'd finish in the middle of the fleet. If I crewed for better skippers, we finished higher and I learned more. I sailed one-design day races, then overnight, coastal races, and then to the pinnacle of U.S. ocean racing, the mythical Newport-Bermuda Race, 650 miles over four days with ten crew with my Dad skippering aboard *Holger Danske*. With a handicap rule favoring pure racing boats rather than traditional cruisers, we finished poorly; yet it was a great adventure to go that far to sea, for that long.

Dad then ventured into longer ocean passages aboard *Holger Danske*, completing five transatlantic voyages with crews of friends over the next decade. Before the sixth passage home, he had a heart attack and couldn't go offshore again. I offered to take a leave of absence from my job in Washington to sail the boat back to our side of the Atlantic. Dad said OK, and at age 28 I went with four crew. I hadn't sailed with Dad on any of his crossings, due to my commitments, so this was my first, and it was fascinating: Sardinia to Gibraltar to the Canaries to Barbados. The passage prompted an idea - let's race Newport to Bermuda again. The boat is fast, we have a core of ocean sailors and can get skilled, small boat, racing helmsmen from Marblehead, the handicap rule has been changed to evaluate boats from first principles of aero- and hydro-dynamics so now we'd have a fair chance. We raced, and to everybody's astonishment, except perhaps our own, we won the St. David's Lighthouse Trophy as Overall Winner of the 1980 Newport-Bermuda Race in a fleet of 162 boats.

Holger Danske

Confidence gained from that victory encouraged me that boat preparation, crew selection, and weather analysis, mixed with the requisite luck, could have positive results despite my not having the ability to make a sailboat go as fast as the best skippers. It's the Roger Federer problem. No matter how much you might love tennis, nor who your coach might be, you could practice until the end of time and you would never be or beat Roger Federer. He is supernatural in his tennis play. It's the same for sailing: some people can just make a sailboat go fast, and others don't have those last few percentage points of speed. So I would be a "work and worry" guy, in the wonderful words of the great American singlehander Francis Stokes, and hopefully that would gain success at sea.

In my late teens, I read the books of four inspiring solo circumnavigators: Joshua Slocum, Francis Chichester, Robin Knox-Johnston, and Bernard Moitessier. Slocum, an American, was the first aboard his rebuilt *Spray* in 1895, sailing three years with multiple stops. Chichester, an Englishman, stopped once in *Gipsy Moth IV* in 1966-7, and his countryman Knox-Johnston, aboard his 32' ketch *Suhaili,* was the only finisher of the 1968 Golden Globe race, the first solo race around the world. This one-time English event was the pre-cursor in course concept to the French Vendée Globe, established twenty years later. Moitessier, aboard his 42' double-ended steel ketch *Joshua*, respectfully named after Slocum, became the romantic inspiration for the French maritime culture when, after five and a half months at sea, steadily catching Knox-Johnston in the final ocean of that race, he decided he wanted neither the celebrity nor glory of winning, abandoned the race, sailed halfway around the world again, and dropped anchor in Tahiti. He felt that his true spirit was alive and at peace at sea, not in front of TV cameras and microphones.

Reading of these great adventures and sailors, I was inspired and in awe. I wondered if I could ever be brave enough, strong enough, or smart enough to sail a significant singlehanded voyage, not like theirs, of course, because theirs were around the world, and that was beyond imagination, but a shorter one, an overnight, or maybe a few days alone over a few hundred miles, if I really got up my nerve. The lure of singlehanded sailing is that you have to learn everything about the boat. If you sail with a big crew, you might be cook or navigator or helmsman or sail trimmer or foredeck man. It would be "Here is your winch, learn to love it." Almost never would you get to be, or have to be, all of the above. But the singlehanded sailor has to do all those tasks and many more, and that would make it supremely challenging.

§

Nobody goes solo ocean racing without mentors. Even Michel Desjoyeaux had his in apprenticing with the legendary Eric Tabarly. My two mentors were Phil Steggall and Walter Greene.

I met Phil in the early 1980s. A New Zealander, he had come to America at age 17 as a crewmember aboard Ted Turner's ocean-racing boat *Tenacious*. Later, Phil came third in the 1980 OSTAR (Observer Singlehanded Trans-Atlantic Race) in a 37' trimaran only hours behind Phil Weld's winning 50' trimaran *Moxie*. I admired him from afar and was honored that he invited me, after our Bermuda Race win, to navigate a boat he was managing for the 1983 Southern Ocean Racing Circuit in Florida. We became fast friends.

In 1986, he invited me to Newport to help a Kiwi countryman in final preparations for the BOC Race, a solo race around the world in four legs. The morning of the start, lashing down an anchor in the forepeak, Phil turned to me and said, "We should be doing this ourselves." I agreed, and the next morning I called the Royal Western Yacht Club in Plymouth, England, to get an entry form for the 1988 Carlsberg Singlehanded Transatlantic Race (C-STAR). This would be my grand solo adventure.

Thinking that if you were going to sail that race once, you should really race the race, not cruise the race, and since the multihulls (trimarans and catamarans) always beat the monohulls, I decided to race a trimaran. But the stories of them capsizing, and not being able to be righted, frightened me. I spoke endlessly with Phil about this until one evening, in exasperation, he said, "Richie, if you want ultimate safety, you want a multihull, because even if it's upside down, it won't sink because it has no lead keel." I acquired a small 35' wooden trimaran that had sailed two transatlantic round trips, named her *Curtana* in honor of Holger's sword, and was on my way.

That BOC Race that triggered my C-STAR adventure was won by Frenchman Philippe Jeantot, his second straight BOC victory. Jeantot, a world record holding deep sea diver, had begun to sail after reading Moitessier's book *The Long Way*, on his Golden Globe circumnavigation. Yet he now felt that port stops disrupted the beauty and spirit of a sea-going circumnavigation and mused: why not race around the world without stopping? Like the Golden Globe twenty years before? The Vendée Globe was born.

Via Phil, I met Walter Greene of Yarmouth, Maine. Walter designed, built, and raced multihulls, both trimarans and catamarans. Greene Marine was the *de facto* headquarters for U.S. multihulls. Driving over the top of the hill, you see an extremely weathered building, and multihulls scattered everywhere on the grounds, half on land, half overhanging the marsh of the Cousins River, all packed together like pieces of a spilled jigsaw puzzle, and you think, whoa, what's going on here? But then you go inside the shed and see the detailed design, the loving care of construction, thin strips of various woods, cut, assembled, and glued together in beautiful curves, all yielding immense strength, by shape and construction, to withstand the ocean's onslaughts. Greene Marine is a studio, and Walter is the artist.

Walter believed that boats should be strong. That strength could derive from exquisitely engineered carbon fibre (strong, light, and expensive) or exquisitely shaped two by sixes of mahogany (strong, heavy, and less expensive). Walter could build it either way, it just had to be strong. Having competed in the demanding French and English short-handed ocean-racing circuits, he had vast, practical seagoing experience. At the start of the transatlantic race, he came aboard for a final inspection in Plymouth, pronounced the boat fit, and then gave me eternally valuable advice:

Richie, make the easy miles, there will be plenty of tough miles, so when you can go, go as fast as you can for as long as you can, and make the easy miles.

§

I successfully completed that solo transatlantic race to Newport, in fact winning my Class V. Frightened much of the time, I endured three distinct episodes of sleep deprivation induced hallucinations. In the first, a week into the race, eight people came aboard in my mind, and sat in shorts and jerseys in the nets between the three hulls, enjoying crackers and cheese. Worried that when I let the boom out to reef, that someone would get hit in the head, I modified my maneuver for their safety, heading up into the wind to keep the boom away from them. This mistake tacked the boat. She stopped and started going backward in the middle of the night. Kindly, the people stopped talking so that I could focus without distraction on sorting the mess. I didn't speak to them, because some part of my mind knew they weren't real, and that if I spoke to them, my mind would have to erase the image, and I liked having them there.

The second and third episodes were similar, yet involved expert sailors who showed up when I had specific worries about the boat and my sailing. Was I pushing the boat too hard at fourteen knots across the Grand Banks in thick fog? Jan and Meade Gougeon, standing at the mast and inspecting the panel layout of the jib, seemed not to think so. Down to storm jib in a Gulf Stream gale and steep seas, did I have the little boat set up properly to survive the tumult? As I sat below at the chart table, Jean-Yves Terlain and Titouan Lamazou, who had each sailed Southern Ocean gales in the BOC and were in our race ahead of me, chatted amiably in French in my cockpit and seemed not to be concerned. I gained confidence from their presence and calm.

§

I loved the challenge of short-handed sailing. There was so much to learn! There was the aero- and hydro-dynamics of sail and hull shapes, different materials for sails, ropes and rigging that had different characteristics of stretch, strength, durability, stiffness, UV-resistance. There was the pre-GPS challenge of celestial navigation and detailed log-keeping of direction, speed, and time for Dead Reckoning to find buoys intentionally, rather than rocks accidentally, in dense fog. Later came the GPS generation of technology, of satellite communications replacing long-range radio, of wind sensors and electronic autopilots replacing windsocks and helmsmen, of desalinators and freeze-dried food replacing water tanks and canned food, of learning meteorology and storm tactics by book and by experience, of software simulations to suggest the fastest route for your particular boat in the forecast wind conditions.

And would the sport be physical? Oh yes... And not the hour-long games of football, hockey or basketball, followed by a nice dinner and a quiet bed, but races of days, weeks, or months, with nothing quiet about them whatsoever!

It was by far the most complex, interesting, and challenging sport I'd ever played. There were so many ways to enjoy sailing: cruise or race; little boats or big boats; multihulls or monohulls; salt water oceans or freshwater rivers or lakes; alone or with crew. Think of the adventures you could have on that vast playground of oceans! Cruise overnight in your 13' Bluejay with a little bobbing fleet of your friends. Grow up, expand your skills and experience, and race across the Gulf Stream to Bermuda. Expand yourself further, and sail across the North Atlantic Ocean to Europe, arriving not through airports with "take off your shoes and belt" security, but in an ancient port where Customs & Immigration officials row out to greet you and check your Ship's Papers and Passport in your cockpit, then share a cup of tea with you before you sleep at anchor in your bunk for the night. You've arrived the way travelers had for half a millenium before. Stretch yourself again, and sail to Patrick O'Brien's <u>Far Side of the World</u>. If you were looking for adventure, the sport of sailing offered the biggest ones globally.

§

Well aware that I was extremely fortunate, indeed privileged, in having smart, curious, adventurous, and successful parents, a good education and opportunities, my obligation then was to work hard and try to find my most productive niche to make a contribution. My early career entailed a variety of jobs and returns to school.

While studying math at Harvard, I enjoyed immensely a summer job teaching kids at Upward Bound. After college, gaining a Massachusetts Teaching Certificate at Brandeis University summer school, I signed up as a substitute teacher in Brookline, Belmont, and Newton. I was called every day. Yet those wealthy suburbs were easy street; the real test was - did I have the nerve to sign up in Boston? After two weeks, I took the plunge.

Called the next morning to teach sheet metal shop at Boston Technical High School, a mid-day query arrived from the School Department, “We have a math opening at Hyde Park High School, grades 9 and 10, for the rest of the school year, do you want it?” Hyde Park was 99% white, and one of two epicenters, the other being South Boston, for the earthquake that was the first year of forced busing in Boston, ordered by Federal Judge Arthur Garrity to integrate the Boston Public Schools. “Yes, I’ll take it.”

One quarter of the tenured white teachers had quit, rather than teach the bused-in blacks from Mattapan. The student body would be 50/50 black/white. Morning convoys of school buses, escorted by Boston Police on motorcycles, brought the Mattapan students into Hyde Park. Afternoon convoys took them out. The second half of the year, two Police officers sat outside every classroom throughout the day. Six class periods in a row, no recess, no lunch, no sports, no clubs, the administration didn’t dare put all the students together.

Among the many things I learned that year, two stood out: first, if you took all the parents and shipped them to Nevada, the kids would figure out just fine how to get along; second, when I brought real-world problems into my math classes, rather than the textbook problem sets, the kids paid closer attention.

At year’s end, though, despite amazing and fond experiences of wonderful kids of all colors, I felt that being in front of a class was not the optimal use of me. I imagined some role, unknown at that time, where I could impact a wider group.

§

Accepted into MIT for a Master’s program, I studied Ocean Resources Management. Good fortune occurred in writing my thesis on the Antarctic Krill Fishery. Submitting a draft to my adviser, Dr. Ray Pariser of MIT Sea Grant, he thrashed it, questioning every word: “Why is that there? Why is this here? What do you mean by this sentence? That word doesn’t mean what you think it does. ‘But’ doesn’t mean ‘but’, it means ‘and’.” Two hours later, he had taught me the elements of writing.

I got a job in Washington, DC, for Analytic Services, Inc., a quasi-governmental entity contracted to the Office of the Secretary of the Air Force. Twelve such companies, categorized as FCRCs (Federal Contract Research Centers), were funded by line items in the Federal budget and didn't compete for contracts. ANSER knew this status wouldn't last, so they experimented with me to see if an analyst with a different background could do their core work, and perhaps open new research areas.

Working on range versus payload trade-offs for B-52s flying to cold war targets in the Soviet Union, and radar detection of cruise missiles in various terrains, I was challenged to my limits. In college during the Vietnam War, sweating through the lottery to a high draft number of 334, working now with these smart, diligent, hard-working analysts, many ex-military, yet none warmongers, was eye-opening. Given a chance to brief a two-star General in charge of Operations & Plans at the Strategic Air Command in Omaha, and a panel of Lt. Colonels at the Pentagon, I learned that you didn't open your mouth unless you knew absolutely what you were talking about.

I wanted to hear a Congressional Hearing, and when the Merchant Marine & Fisheries Committee announced one on a proposed Antarctic Conservation Treaty, my boss approved my request to go. In the hearing, Congressman Forsythe of New Jersey was upset that the Treaty didn't include krill, the essential link in the Antarctic food chain. I wrote to him offering to send him a copy of my MIT thesis. He invited me to do so, and to brief the Sub-Committee staff directly. I did. They decided to write a bill, The Polar Living Marine Resources Conservation Act of 1978, to build an Antarctic capable oceanographic research vessel.

Afterward, the senior counsel thanked me, saying, "I'm a lawyer, and I've been doing this job for ten years now, and yours is the first scientific paper that I've read that I could understand." All hail Dr. Pariser!

I was invited to explain the bill to various Departments of the government. ANSER approved of this effort. I was impressed by the smart, dedicated government workers that I met. Any could have gained higher pay in the private sector, but they were committed to working for our country. So often derided as "bureaucrats", I thought otherwise and admired them immensely. I submitted written testimony for the Committee's hearing on the "The Krill Bill." The Act passed the full House, then died in the Senate.

Later that year, after sailing Dad's boat home, I return to Boston, to be closer to the family and for new opportunities. While working for a company that consulted on power and desalination plants in Saudi Arabia, another fascinating job appeared.

A small company had been formed during the OPEC oil embargo, and its resultant high oil prices, to study putting sails on ships to reduce fuel consumption. Most would have thought this a hippy's fool's errand. Yet the founder was the most experienced shipbuilder in the U.S., Lloyd Bergeson, MIT alumnus, General Manager at Electric Boat when they built the *Nautilus*, the world's first nuclear-powered submarine, and at General Dynamics shipyard in Quincy when they built eleven LNG tankers. Lloyd was also an accomplished transoceanic sailor who understood empirically the potential of wind energy. Wind Ship Development Corporation was taken seriously.

Wind Ship built a giant sailing rig for the Greek freighter *Mini-Lace.* It worked well mechanically and reduced fuel costs by a quarter. Yet, the oil embargo soon ended, and the elevated price of oil plummeted, eliminating the rig's cost advantage and clouding Wind Ship's future. Wondering how to corral my evident wide interests, I applied to Harvard Business School, thinking that general management training would prove applicable across multiple fields.

Indoctrinated by Dad's lifelong mantra that one needed to work in science and technology, in a small company, and be the owner, upon HBS graduation I asked Dr. Pariser what opportunities he saw in the marine environment. From his several suggestions, I picked one: to start a small company to make limulus amoebocyte lysate, a refined extract from horseshoe crab blood. The FDA required medical devices and intravenous solutions to be tested for endotoxins. LAL proved superior to the decades old rabbit test in its sensitivity, reproducibility, and ease of testing for such endotoxins. This rabbit test was to be phased out and replaced by LAL.

While friends went to Wall Street, I went to a basement lab. Years into it, when our hired PhD consultant hadn't solved the problem, I and a lab technician set up a new facility, and through brute strength and ignorance, we figured out how to make LAL. Much to our satisfaction, our product's sensitivity and consistency was superior even to that of the huge pharma Baxter Travenol. Much to our chagrin, however, it became clear that another small company, that had been making LAL since it was discovered, had come to dominate the market, so that our road to profit would be unsustainably long and expensive. For me, confidence was lost in the business failure, yet confidence was gained in persevering to our technical solution.

§

Earlier, our winning Bermuda Race had triggered an invitation to join the Overseers, and later the Board of Trustees, of Sea Education Association in Woods Hole. SEA was a college-level deep sea oceanography program. The students spent six weeks studying on land, then six weeks at sea aboard SEA's sailing oceanographic research vessel *Westward*. Via SEA I met a similar organization, The School for Field Studies, a land-based version of SEA, and was similarly invited to join their Board. Expanding from a single summer program of wildlife management in Kenya, SFS grew to six permanent field research stations worldwide.

SEA and SFS students returned utterly transformed by these academically rigorous, hands-on, team-oriented semesters, far from society's normal land-based support systems. Bored in your four-walled classroom? Go to sea on a ship, or trek into the rainforest, to learn your science in the real world. You will work within teams, overcome physical hardship, adapt to foreign cultures, and do serious real world academics.

The closing of our LAL effort had occurred coincident with my grand adventure in the solo transatlantic race. During that 1988 race, I was interviewed at sea live by Bill Smith, a radio host at WZLX, a popular radio station in Boston. At first, he understood this event only as a lark, some guy sailing around somewhere. Yet for our second live interview, during drive-time Boston, I was in my Gulf Stream gale, down to storm jib only, and in my survival suit fearing capsize. Hearing the fear and fatigue in my voice, he "got it" - there is a guy out there alone, a thousand miles from land, he's tired, cold, scared, and in a storm...and we're not sure what's going to happen next.

After the race, I met Bill. He said:

You could hear your voice going up and down with the radio waves, you could hear the wind and sea in the background - it was the theater of the mind.

For years thereafter, I met people who had heard those few broadcasts. They might not remember the details, but the drama of "that guy alone in the Atlantic" had stayed with them. This proved the critical point that even though sailing was relatively unknown to the public, if you kept the communications on a human, non-technical, level, you could excite and engage that public with a dramatic adventure - which happened to be at sea.

Real world problem sets in the Boston Public Schools, the transformational real world experiences of the SEA and SFS students, the "theater of the mind" of live, interactive broadcasts – could these be combined into new and potent school programs? This seed of an idea sprouted.

"The trick to teaching is to not let them know they're learning anything - until it's too late!"
Prof. Harold "Doc" Edgerton, MIT

Chapter 5: sitesALIVE!

My interest lay in K12, before final decisions on college majors and careers were decided, and more narrowly still on elementary and middle school students, where wonderment and adventure still reigned, and where teacher were still teaching multiple subjects, offering congruency with the multiple interacting disciplines inherent in adventures and expeditions. If you could excite kids early, about science, geography, math, and history, you could have an important impact.

I imagined a great voyage, since sailing was what I knew something about: long enough to include many classroom topics, dramatic enough to garner media coverage and hopefully sponsors, and offering uncertainty of outcome, plus the competition of a race against history, to grab and keep the kids' attention.

In 1990, mortgaging my Boston condo, I acquired *Great American*, a 60' trimaran, lying San Francisco. She was an older boat, immensely strong, and had just broken the clipper *Flying Cloud*'s record time from New York, by way of Cape Horn, set in 1853 during the California Gold Rush. I'd sail doublehanded with Steve Pettengill, who had crewed on the trimaran's voyage around the Horn and knew the boat well. We'd try to break a return record of 76 days 6 hours to Boston, set in 1853 by the clipper *Northern Light*, Captain Freeman Hatch in command.

The voyage and program would last 11 weeks, race history on an important American trade route, and risk the peril of Cape Horn. It would overflow with science, math, and geography. Audio reports would provide our "theater of the mind", daily ship's logs would provide data for math problems, our journals, written at sea, would enliven the classroom activities in a Teacher's Guide. We would piggyback our written information on a newsletter going to classrooms. Bob Dotson sent us off from San Francisco with a wonderful story aired on NBC Nightly News.

That pilot program voyage failed disastrously at sea, with our terrifying, somersaulting double capsize, and subsequent rescue, off Cape Horn; yet it succeeded marvelously in our classrooms.

Returning to Boston, I visited schools that had participated in our abbreviated voyage program, bringing the survival suit that I'd worn at the Horn. Enticed to dream beyond the four walls of their classrooms, the students had been mesmerized by the adventure. Encouraged by the students' and teachers' enthusiasm, I began to think about trying again.

I incorporated a new company, Ocean Challenge, Inc., and raised money from a dozen investors, including classmates from HBS, toward a bigger, more elaborate school program, and toward another older trimaran, 50' long, that we named *Great American II* in honor of the vessel whose massive strength had saved our lives by not breaking up off the Horn.

Meeting with The Boston Globe to ask them for ten weeks of column space for our next attempt, we discovered Newspaper in Education. Nearly every newspaper nationwide, and many globally, did NIE. Yet NIE produced static programs – a topical activity guide to accompany a classroom set of newspapers - with no certainty that any published article would relate to the program topic. We proposed a voyage activity guide for teachers, plus writing a weekly column live from sea, tied thematically to that weekly classroom activity, to be published in the full run of their newspaper. We argued that our voyage would be current news and therefore worthy of publication. A century before, the Globe had published letters from Joshua Slocum from his solo circumnavigation: ships met randomly at sea carried his stories circuitously home; satellites would deliver our essays directly. These would link our voyage live to students in classrooms and families at home, and would help teachers with exciting content.

The Globe thought this was a great idea, committed to it, and introduced us nationwide to other newspapers' NIE departments. Our home-grown NIE syndicate snowballed until 12 major market newspapers (including the Los Angeles Times, Detroit News, Minneapolis Star-Tribune and Philadelphia Inquirer) contracted to publish our series and distribute papers and Teacher's Guides to classrooms. The San Francisco Chronicle set a goal of 350 teachers; 2,000 applied. Teachers were clearly clamoring for something to help them excite and engage their kids. Ultimately, we reached 13 million weekly readers, and 250,000 students on that ten-week voyage.

Our second breakthrough was with Prodigy, then the fledgling online community's largest service, with 2 million members (50% of the entire U.S. online community, with Compuserve at 1.4 million and AOL at 600,000). After months of discussion, we persuaded them that a live ocean adventure, with daily ship's log, journals, Q&A, map-tracking, and graphic activities (online digital photos didn't exist yet), would excite and engage their members. An "unprecedented success" ensued with 10% of their membership, 100,000 adults and 100,000 children, logging on regularly to follow our voyage. They had to hire extra people to handle the volume of questions sent to their Q&A feature "Send Note to Boat!" Parents loved this family activity that they could do with their children, and where they both learned, together.

With an eye toward our school program, I had tasked our Board of Directors to interview and select the best communicator, without my input, from sailors that I pre-qualified for their sailing skill. They chose Bill Biewenga, a veteran of the round-the-world fully-crewed Whitbread Race, a prolific author for sailing magazines, and a former Marine whose Vietnam War experience had given him a view of the world that emphasized education and trying to understand other's perspectives. Together, Bill and I succeeded at sea, arriving Boston in 69 days 20 hours to break the record, and, more importantly, breaking through educationally with our NIE and Prodigy partnerships.

Gaining the front pages of both the Boston Globe and Boston Herald at our finish, a live interview from the dock with Katie Couric on NBC's Today Show brought our success nationwide. Later, Ken Brecker, head of The Children's Museum in Boston, told me that the best lesson we gave the kids was to fail the first time...and then try again.

§

PACT95, an America's Cup syndicate from Maine, noticed our success and contracted with our little company to create a science and technology program for their 1995 *Young America* campaign. Properly funded, with a Teacher's Guide from Scott-Foresman, the big textbook company, and an online presence via News Corporation's fledgling Delphi, it succeeded magnificently. We gained 27 NIE programs, reaching 21 million weekly readers and 300,000 students for an 11 week series. Our Scott-Foresman contact told me afterward:

> *I didn't think you could get inner city kids to follow a bunch of rich old white men sailing around San Diego in no wind - but you did!*

Concurrently, the American Sail Advancement Program, an industry promotion group, funded us to produce another new program. West Island College, a secondary school in Montreal, operated Class Afloat, wherein 45 high school juniors and seniors would spend one or two semesters aboard the 188' barkentine *Concordia.* Visiting 25 countries per year, while studying the rigorous academia of the Canadian provincial curriculum, their graduates had seen more of the world than 99% of the world's population, all by the age of 18! We hired teachers to write a Teacher's Guide, then produced Class Afloat Live! and distributed it via NIE and on our new website, connecting those students offshore with K12 students onshore in the U.S. For the next nine years, eighteen semesters in all, Class Afloat Live! became our core program.

Thus launched to other partnerships, over the next dozen years we produced 75 live, interactive, full semester programs distributed to schools via NIE and online. We partnered with accredited field schools: The School for Field Studies, The Island School, and Ocean Classroom Foundation. Their live content input our new series of programs: Rainforest Live!, Oceans Live!, U.S. History Live!, Wetlands and Fisheries Live! and Islands Live! We even produced Bluegrass Live! with the New England Conservatory of Music. Our goal was to offer a menu of programs to K12, so that a teacher could do their science, geography, math, and history with live, real world content to excite their students. Our users were mostly in the U.S.

***Great American II* Departs New York for Melbourne**

Our original plan had detailed three clipper voyages as content sources for programs, including challenging the records on the two other great American routes, New York - Melbourne (Australian Gold Rush, clipper *Mandarin*, 69 days in 1855, Captain John Parritt) and Hong Kong – New York (China Tea Trade, clipper *Sea Witch*, 74 days 14 hours in 1853, Captain Robert "Bully" Waterman). Yet by the time we went to sea to tackle these in 2001 and 2003 (setting records of 68 and 72 days respectively), we had produced 46 other full semester, live, interactive programs with our content partners over the intervening 8 years.

Neal Skorka

One year, our wonderful staff of eight believers, led by Neal Skorka and Cindy Collins, produced and marketed 17 live semesters of programs, over 200 weeks worth of programming. Urged by a distribution partner to choose an umbrella name for our product line, we trademarked sitesALIVE!®.

My notion after Hyde Park High School, that there would be some education role for me, not connecting face-to-face with students, yet attaining a wider impact, was fulfilled with sitesALIVE!

§

Although our programs worked educationally, we couldn't figure out how to make them profitable, or to break even. Newspapers paid little for our NIE content, if anything. And for our online offerings, schools were behind in computer labs, connectivity, and teacher capabilities to use such programs.

A reality check came at the National Education Computing Conference in Chicago in 2002 at McCormick Place, with 15,000 self-selected teachers attending and 600 companies exhibiting, of which we were the only one with live online content. In this year of our 17 simultaneous programs, at the height of the dot-com boom, a teacher visited our booth and asked "www.sitesalive.com, does that mean I need a computer?"

The fear was front and center that we were a decade, or more, ahead of our time.

Bob Niehaus, HBS friend and investor in Ocean Challenge, Inc., urged me to turn us into a non-profit 501c3, saying that it would be easier for many to support our innovative idea as donors, rather than as traditional for-profit investors. We formed Sites Alive Foundation, Inc.

A few years further on, as funding again ran low, we had to reduce our program offerings, until in 2004, we produced just one program, a final fourth voyage, the solo Transat, with our trusty trimaran *Great American II*. After that program she was sold and we were forced to lay off our already reduced staff. Was there a future for sitesALIVE!?

§

Unburdened by the sale of *GA2*, I followed the Vendée Globe 2004, interested as a sailor. As the fleet circled the world, with one adventurous episode after another, and with the first three boats finishing only days apart, it occurred to me that the Vendée Globe could provide an opportunity to produce the next generation program for sitesALIVE! Perhaps we could, with the unique symbolism of this globe-circling event, create a truly global school program and move beyond our U.S.-only constituency. Perhaps elsewhere, in cultures where education was truly revered and where technology's benefits had been seen and adopted, would offer more fertile markets for our idea.

I consulted with Lorraine Leo, a wizard technology teacher at the Jackson School in Newton, Massachusetts, who was connected to teachers worldwide. She had used our programs in her classroom. Could this work globally? Yes, there is a small but growing band of technology pioneers in K12 and she could connect us with many of them. There were networks forming, individual teachers were producing their own content, not willing to wait for the ponderous textbook publishers to get on board the digital revolution. There were kids connected to kids across countries and oceans. Excited again, I plunged in, and started down the parallel paths of boat development for the offshore race as our program vehicle, and NIE and website development for our onshore program.

I exhibited at the World Association of Newspapers' Young Readers' Conference. Newspapers from 74 countries attended. Oceans, although 70% of our planet's surface, had long been ignored in the social and political discourse, but now, due to climate change, fisheries depletion, and dramatic events of marine pollution, gradually they were breaking through as a legitimate topic of global concern. Our program was billed not as a French yacht race, but as a "Live Ocean Expedition" with a 15 part series to be published in newspapers worldwide and backed by a comprehensive website to link schools globally. I personally spoke with newspapers from 37 countries. They had never seen anything like this before. From China to Colombia, Lebanon to Taiwan, South Africa to Switzerland, Pakistan to Poland, they got the point and were interested to publish our series for their students and families. Exhibiting at the U.S. NIE conference in Phoenix re-connected us with American NIE programs that we'd worked with before, as well as a wide array of potential new partners. I was exhilarated.

We programmed a new website with our hosting company, and re-engaged Neal to manage our program ashore. Per an idea from our singlehanded Transat 2004 program, we formed our new Team of Experts, both to ease my writing load at sea, and to showcase a diversity of accomplished professionals to students. As one of the greatest challenges for education is to match a student's natural curiosity to a topic which will become a passionate interest, our Team of Experts offered a broad range of expertise, and increased the chance that some topic would click and a student would run with it.

Relentless pursuit of both foreign and domestic distribution began to bear fruit on the home front. The overseas market proved difficult to pin down. The southern hemisphere papers, though fascinated, were nervous about publishing a school program in summer that would only reach students at home. I focused hard on The China Daily, the English language paper in Beijing, thinking that if we had them, many others would follow as all would want to be connected to the Chinese. As the start approached, after months and a multitude of phone calls and emails, we had twenty-five U.S. Newspapers, some big like the San Francisco Chronicle and some small like the Cherokee Sun in southwestern North Carolina. Whether dailies or weeklies, coastal or landlocked, they committed to market, publish and deliver our series. Despite the expressed international interest, we hadn't cracked that market yet with a contract.

A new online partner emerged in the American Association for the Advancement of Science. Their K12 teacher website Thinkfinity.org received 400,000 visitors monthly, with 30% overseas. They programmed a special Ocean Challenge section of their website. Lorraine brought in her network of schools in China, Taiwan, Australia, Scotland, Romania, Argentina, Italy, the Phillipines, and more.

We were advancing toward our goal of making a global school program out of this uniquely global event. And to the original question "Why race the Vendée Globe?", what better answer could there be than "To excite, engage, connect and teach schoolchildren around the world!"

"For Life Without Limits"
...Asthma & Allergy Foundation of America motto

Chapter 6: Asthma at Sea

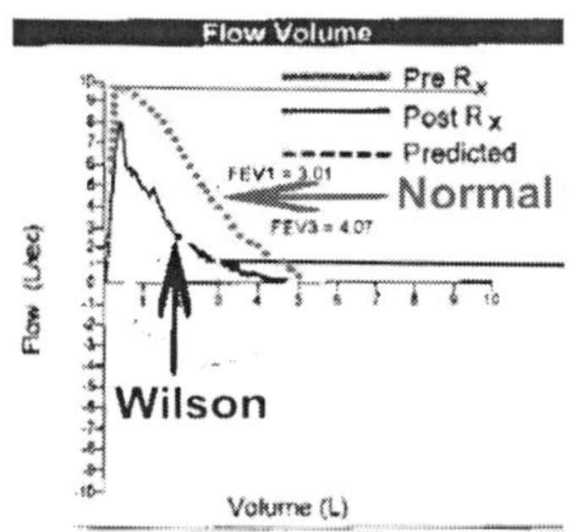

My Pulmonary Function Test

At age one I was diagnosed with severe asthma.

This chronic disease has two major symptoms: spasmodic constriction of the muscles around the bronchial tubes, which thus make the air passageways smaller; and inflammation of the bronchial surface, which then generate mucus to try to soothe itself, which in turn clogs the airways. It's not understood why certain lungs react and others don't. Genetics and environmental allergic triggers are deemed the fundamental problems.

Regardless of cause, the result is the same, gasping for breath, a tightening of the chest that feels as though André the Giant is sitting on you, increased pulse rate in trying to make up for less oxygenated blood by pushing more of it through your body, and a desperate feeling of suffocation as if you're slowly drowning. An earlier American Lung Association motto was on point: "If you can't breathe, nothing else matters."

In the Vendée Globe, the big loaded Open 60 sails, the thousands of daily revolutions on the pedestal winch, constant stress and sleep deprivation, all with chronically defective lungs, would present a huge challenge that had to be managed well to survive and succeed. Ironically, within the context, I've also pondered the curious question: if I hadn't had asthma since I was young, and thus hadn't been challenged to develop the perseverance and determination that it demanded, would I be out here racing the Vendée Globe? Having only lived my asthmatic life, I can't, and thus don't, know the answer.

§

When young, tests had revealed that I was allergic to cats, dogs, grass, trees, flowers, smoke, dust, wool, dust mites, fumes, perfume, as well as peanuts, nuts, grapes, chocolate, peas, and eggs. Essentially, I was allergic to land. When sailing, the air on the water didn't contain the usual airborne allergens, and my labored breathing was somewhat relieved. This plus was offset now by the fact that stress, an obvious constant when alone at sea, was also an asthma trigger for me.

As I grew, I received allergy de-sensitizing injections, two every two weeks. I could never tell if these made any difference. When we moved to a new house, my sister got a cat. Dr. Hill, my pediatrician, and a kind man, was nonetheless direct with my mother: "Mrs. Wilson, either the cat goes, or I go." The cat went.

Asthma is especially difficult for kids. If you can't run around outside with your friends, you won't have friends for long. For me, it forced perseverance. No matter how hard it was to breathe, I would keep going. Playing high school soccer, I would run myself nearly unconscious. That determination stood me in good stead a half century later at sea. Likely all asthmatics in that era endured the same thing. Unless willing to withdraw from life, you would continue to antagonize your asthma by living.

It was also difficult because there were no asthma role models. It would have been hugely helpful to have seen someone, anyone, doing something, anything, who had asthma, thus showing that you could still pursue your dreams, whatever they might be, even if you had asthma. Yet I never saw on TV or in the sports section anyone identified as asthmatic.

In that era, there were no asthma drugs for daily home use. Hospitals used epinephrine in emergency rooms for acute, life-threatening asthma attacks. Occasionally I had to be rushed to the hospital for that injection, and once endured an overnight stay in a stifling oxygen tent. Eventually my mother was trained to give me the injections at home. Decades before EpiPens, and with acute attacks usually coming after midnight, she would get up, boil (to sterilize) a re-usable (pre-disposable) hypodermic syringe in a saucepan in the kitchen, draw in the epinephrine, and give me the injections.

Then at age 10, the first asthma inhaler for daily home use arrived: a plastic tube like a turkey baster, with chambers in the middle into which you eye-dropped medication and then squeezed the bulb at one end to blow an aerosol out the other end. It helped!

My bedroom in our new house had a hardwood floor, for easy dusting, and an early generation air filtration machine, a metal structure about 2' x 2' square x 4' high, that sucked air in from the bottom, through a filter, and blew it out through the top. Home from school, I would lean on the top, face to the grate, and breathe as deeply as I could of the cleaner air. I slept leaning against four pillows, because a more vertical posture was preferable to horizontal. One night in the spring, the worst of the seasons, I leaned against the wall all night, wide awake before a math exam, and not because of the exam, but because every plant had decided to bloom at the same time, offering a buffet of allergens to my welcoming lungs.

By college years, there was now a short-term bronchodilator in a pressurized canister – no more turkey basters! Yet visiting a friend over Christmas, I discovered to my fright that they had long-haired cats. Within hours I was in the emergency room and given epinephrine, then a 10-day prescription for prednisone, a miracle drug that opened my airways as if my asthma was gone!

Of the allergen triggers, peanuts were the worst. Driving once with a friend in the winter, car windows rolled up, he began eating a peanut butter sandwich. Within minutes, my lips had swollen from the fumes. And years later, at a wedding of two who had met in the Peace Corps in Africa, I sensed that something was wrong after a sumptuous and spicy feast. I went directly to the chef and asked if any of the food had been cooked in peanut oil: "Yes, most of it, since the dishes are African." I told a friend I had a problem and needed to go the hospital immediately, then went to the parking lot, and stuck my finger down my throat to throw up dinner. My friend found her sister and husband, we climbed into his car, and headed for the hospital. I asked him to call ahead to have the epinephrine waiting; he did. By the highway, my eyes were swollen tightly shut, my nasal passages were swollen shut, and my throat was closing. The husband, a former Navy Seal, was calm and deliberate: "Can you estimate the progression rate of the anaphylactic reaction? How much time do you have?" "About fifteen minutes." "Good, we're eight minutes away." We made it.

Through the years, new drugs were developed. For the spasmodic muscular constriction of the airways, addressed by the short-term bronchodilator, a longer-term, 12 hour, version was developed. Corticosteroids were developed to counter the inflammation of the airways. These two drugs were cleverly combined by Glaxo into the Advair Diskus, the now ubiquitous purple hockey puck. As asthma triggering blood components were identified, specifically leukotrienes and Immunoglobulin E (IgE), which both could trigger mast cell explosion and thus set off a chain allergic reaction, targeted drugs were developed (Singulair from Merck for leukotrienes, and Xolair from Genentech and Novartis for IgE) which helped to neutralize those molecules.

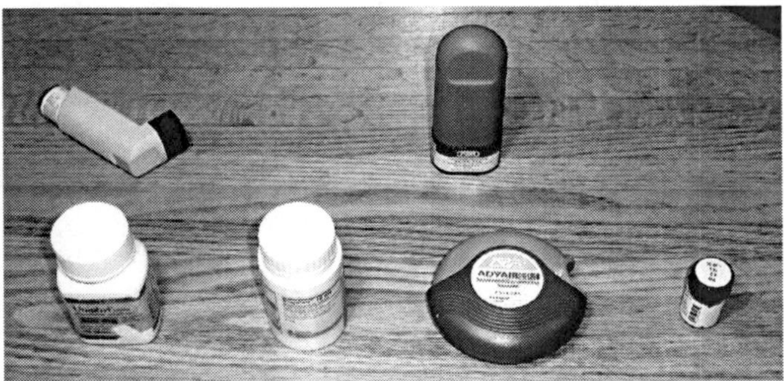

Albuterol, Fluticasone
Theophylline, Singulair, Advair Diskus, Xolair

Although taking these four drugs, my core medication continued to be theophylline, whose molecule is similar to caffeine. As caffeine inhibits the natural breakdown of the extra adrenalin that your body makes to be sure you have enough, thus energizing you, so does theophylline serve the same purpose, by allowing a low level of extra adrenalin/epinephrine in my system. My body could tolerate occasionally forgetting a dose of the other drugs, but not forgetting my theophylline. A 24 hour theophylline was later developed, with a half-life of 17 hours. Ashore, I tried to take it in the early morning so that it would be mostly out of my system by bedtime. A dilemma: do you impair your sleep by keeping a caffeine equivalent in your system to allow better breathing but which will keep you awake like a cup of coffee? Or do you eliminate the caffeine equivalent, but then make your breathing worse, which impairs your sleeping? Pick your poison! This was exacerbated alone at sea, because one would be sleeping, optimally, in single 90 minute naps, specifically to match the length of a biological sleep cycle, and these naps were taken, per demands of the boat, randomly around the clock. Thus I would never have the theophylline entirely out of my system. Asthma medication programs, on land or sea, are a balancing challenge.

Medications are a necessary but not sufficient condition for successful asthma treatment. You need an excellent doctor who can tailor a medication program for you. Yet you the patient must do your part too, by being an accurate and detailed scientist about your own body, and how it reacts both to asthma triggers and to medications so that you can give that information to your doctor. After all, you spend 365 days with your asthma in a year, your doctor perhaps three or four hours. In my early 30s, I was the patient of a nationally known allergist. Yet my asthma was a mess. Desperate, I started running to try to strengthen my lungs. It felt horrible. The first time, I ran 1/4-mile before having to stop and walk slowly home, gasping for breath.

My medication routine made me vomit in the morning. When I asked the doctor about this he replied, "You can take the theophylline, throw up in the morning and breathe, or not take the theophylline, not throw up and not breathe." Could that possibly be my only choice? I kept hammering on the running, and after several years eventually worked up to 10K road races and several years later, the Boston Marathon. It would take about 6-8 miles before my lungs settled down. Before my fourth Boston, when I was in my most excellent condition ever, my doctor backed off his support for the effort one week before the start. I ran anyway, finishing in my best time of 3:30, and vowed not to return to that doctor.

I asked a cardiologist friend to find the best asthma doctor in Boston. Two months later, he called back. Three sources had each given him a list, each list had only one name on it, and the name was the same on each list - Dr. Chris Fanta at Brigham & Women's Hospital, and I was in luck, he was taking new patients.

Dr. Chris Fanta

Was I ever in luck! I switched doctors, not an easy decision in our society where doctors are revered for knowing everything, and you, the layman, know nothing. Eight months of experimentation later, with no new medications in the asthma toolkit, but simply by paying attention to dosages, time of delivery, blood monitoring, and balancing between multiple options, Dr. Fanta had my asthma stabilized and under control for the first time in my then 35 years. By paying attention to every detail of my asthma, he changed my life. Years later, when we formed our Vendée Globe Team of Experts, Dr. Fanta joined immediately.

My detailed medication plan of five drugs resulted in my pulmonary function test improving to where it shows in the graph at this chapter's start, about 70% of normal for my age and height. Without this plan, it would be far worse.

Just as never wanting to be behind in food consumption, and therefore risking a momentary physical weakness, I had to always be on top of my asthma game, which required strict adherence to my medication routine. As with all systems aboard, I had to constantly make my best effort at asthma management, since who knew when we might encounter some massive boat problem that would require a beyond massive physical effort a thousand miles at sea?

"You must STRETCH your mind!"
...Dr. Ray Pariser, MIT

Chapter 7: The South Atlantic in Missouri

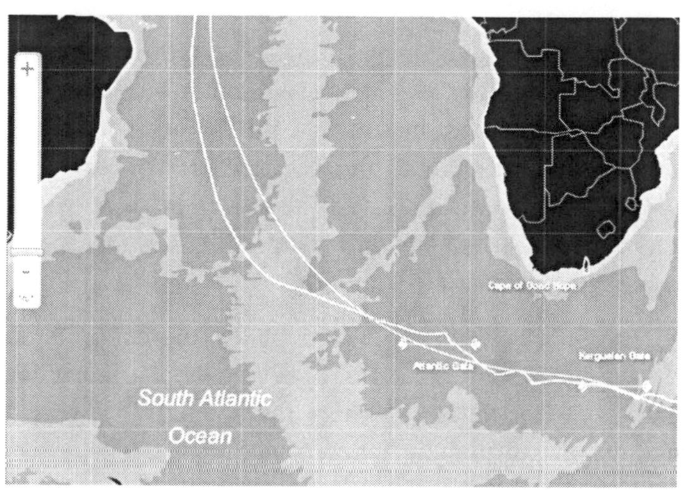

Equator crossings are major milestones for any mariner. First-timers must be initiated by an onboard ceremony. A shipmate who has previously crossed dresses as King Neptune, with crown, beard, and trident, then humiliates the initiate with bilge water or dirty dishwater or worse rubbed through his (or her) hair, as he questions disparagingly whether the initiate is worthy to make the crossing. This centuries old tradition is taken seriously by all mariners. Even aboard *New Zealand Pacific*, our rescuing ship off Cape Horn, the first-timers were initiated with merchant ship bilge water, a disgusting blend of dirt, oil, grease, and bunker fuel, when we crossed the Line in the Atlantic sailing north for Holland.

In the South China Sea, on our Hong Kong to New York passage, I initiated my shipmate Rich du Moulin. Although a shipowner and experienced offshore sailor, Rich had never crossed the equator under sail. I made an aluminum foil crown, used a white washcloth for a beard, and molded aluminum foil onto the bristles of the deck brush to make a trident, pounded the trident on the deck as Rich slept, waking him and demanding his presence on deck, whereupon I questioned his worthiness to cross the Line while slathering granola and milk into his hair. Ultimately, King Neptune deemed him worthy. We crossed the Line and sailed on.

This being my ninth crossing, I needed no initiation, yet did salute Neptune by pouring a nip of rum over the side for him. Appropriate to the occasion, our Expert Dava Sobel, author of the best-seller Longitude, about John Harrison's invention of the chronometer to allow sailors to find accurate positions at sea, wrote her NIE essay on Dead Reckoning (DR), a less certain solution for finding where you were. Having used both DR, sextant and chronometer on my first transatlantic, I knew those techniques. Yet accuracy in them needs mental acuity which needs sleep. I hadn't been doing the sleep part very well and so was glad we had GPS aboard.

Hand-steering for the occasion, I dashed below momentarily to videotape the N turning to S on the GPS, and wondered soberly, as every skipper did, what lay ahead for us in the south. What would happen between now and two months hence when, after passing south of the three Great Capes and circling Antarctica, we would next cross this line racing north? If we made it that far... The gales and cold and seas of the south, that's where the race would be won or lost for the leaders, and where the most challenging tests of boat, skipper, preparation, skill, endurance and courage would be for all. The south - for the three years of preparation for the Vendée Globe it was always a distant dread, a fear in the future, that chilled me. The south, aboard a sixty-footer, alone. We would get there soon, but first, the South Atlantic.

Released by the ITCZ, we crashed upwind into the steady southeast trades. 70 miles off Recife, at the northeast corner of Brazil, the faint loom of the city's midnight lights glowed over the horizon as we passed. Paralleling the Brazilian coast, we pinched our path to the east. The days were hot as we chased the sun south. Not until December 21 would it turn around at the Tropic of Capricorn, at 23.5° South, to head north again.

Despite the complexities of the ITCZ, despite the rib pain and the physical fatigue of sleep deprivation and the daily multitude of arduous sail changes, an equator crossing is a time for wonderment. Descending through the North Atlantic, I'd nightly watched Polaris, the North Star, sink toward the horizon in our wake. At 10° North latitude, Polaris is 10° above the horizon, visible only on the clearest of clear nights. At the equator, that familiar signpost, that celestial anchor for Northern Hemisphere inhabitants, is gone.

To fill that vacuum and lift one's spirits, a new art gallery rises ahead, a gala *"grande fête"* opening of the southern sky. New stars, new constellations, new stories in the mythology. With no star bright and precisely centered as the counterpart to Polaris in the north, the Southern Cross makes do, with two long-axis stars pointing at the south celestial pole. Different from perfect Polaris, nonetheless, this Southern Cross reassures with its nightly circling.

Despite the precision offered by our technology to accurately steer on our intended route, sometimes at night I'd turn off the autopilot, take the tiller in hand, and revert to when I was young and sailing with my Dad and simply "sailed for that star". My favorite in the south was Alpha Centauri - say it aloud, it just rolls off your tongue melodiously - Alpha Centauri, four light years away, double star neighbor to Beta Centauri, 350 light-years away, in the constellation of The Horseman.

Since bringing Dad's boat back from Europe, our Ship's Library has always shelved a copy of "The Star Book", by H. A. Rey. Wait, wasn't he the creator of "Curious George"?! Yes! That's him! His book is the absolute best for finding the constellations and stars, guiding you sky region to sky region, and explaining the mythology underlying their names and shapes. On that return voyage long ago, we'd hung a flashlight in the stern rigging, covered the bulb in red plastic from a cheese wrapper to maintain our night vision, and studied the stars. On a clear night at sea, with no clouds, buildings, hills, mountains, or trees to obstruct the view to the horizon, nor light pollution to obscure dimmer stars, you will be overwhelmed by the immensity of the universe above you, and by the uncountable stars visible. You feel alone on the planet. And in your specific, personal hemisphere, tangential to the globe at your position, you are.

How small are we in the universe? On a starry night at sea, the answer is clear: smaller than a nano pixel, we are nothing in this immensity. Yet since we are here, we'd better make a lifetime contribution while we can, right now. A clear night sky at sea will make anyone a philosopher.

By the Star Book, I identified further constellations and read their mythologies. To recognize these landmarks in the sky lent comfort in familiarity, and any speck of comfort available would be gladly embraced in the south.

Passing Salvador, Brazil, where our qualification race had started exactly a year before, we celebrated Thanksgiving Day. I had much to be thankful for: we were racing the Vendée Globe; we had a great school program, a great Team of Experts and a great group of friends encouraging from afar. *GA3* was holding up; and my ribs were feeling better. I called Winston Flowers in Boston by satphone to deliver a dozen roses to Ellen on her birthday. Onward.

300 miles off Rio de Janeiro, we arced gradually to the southeast, toward the first of seven "ice gates", virtual marks set by the Race Office across the south. The ice gates were pairs of waypoints defining an east-west line between them. By race rules, a skipper had to be north of that line at some point along it. These served to keep the fleet north of iceberg areas. An ice gate location could be changed by Race Management before the lead boat reached the previous ice gate if new or moving icebergs were shown by photographs from French satellites or reports from shipping. The shortest route around the mark of Antarctica was to sail as close to it as possible. Without the ice gates, skippers would be tempted to sail past the Roaring Forties, into the Furious Fifties and Screaming Sixties. The gales and cold and isolation were bad enough, but the ice could be catastrophic. Hitting an iceberg at Open 60 speed would be like sailing into a concrete wall - it would crush the bow. Like everyone else, I kept our forward two watertight doors closed and dogged, always.

The previous summer, I had studied for a week, one-on-one, eight hours daily, homework at night, with Jean-Yves Bernot, the guru of the great French weather routers. On our previous clipper voyages, we had worked with skilled American meteorologists, yet what distinguished Jean-Yves was that he had raced around the world twice, and so could bring personal, at-sea experience to his teaching and analysis. He had been there.

In our studies, we tracked the race route, ocean segment by ocean segment, and considered the two, three, or four most probable weather scenarios in each, how they would develop, and how to respond to them. I took copious notes. We practiced with the MaxSea program that would analyze a route by applying the boat's sailing parameters, its "polars", to digitized weather forecasts called GRIB files (GRIdded Binary), and then suggest optimal routes. As with any simulation, it's only as good as the data input, and both polars and weather forecasts were known to be imperfect. Thus a skipper had to apply his own judgment to the computer's suggestions.

Jean-Yves Bernot

I used to think that I was pretty good at weather analysis and forecasting. After all, I had used well a Gulf Stream eddy and meander for speed boosts in navigating our 1980 Bermuda Race win. That route selection supported the superb helmsmanship and sail trimming of our ace crew to give us victory.

But Jean-Yves had answers to questions that I would have never thought to ask! How far, specifically, per differing situations of wind strength and direction - off the volcanic Canaries or Cape Verde Islands should you sail to escape their wind shadows? He had high resolution satellite photos of the sea state around the islands for different wind velocities and directions; the resultant varying sea heights displayed in slightly different colors and defined the wind shadow limits!

Jean-Yves mixed words of advice and warning into his technical lessons:

Try to put yourself into a position to get lucky.

Going south, the cold will come upon you fast. You'll go from shorts and tee-shirts, to full Southern Ocean gear in 24 hours, and you'd better be ready.

Do not take lightly the frontal systems of the Indian Ocean.

Beware the bomb in the deep south Pacific. If two highs squeeze a low out between them, and a low from the hot interior of Australia merges with it, it will explode.

Some races permit onshore "weather routers" to guide the racers offshore. We used routers on our clipper passages. It's much easier to have an experienced and rested meteorologist thoughtfully analyze weather map after weather map from a warm, dry office, with a hot cup of coffee and a fresh croissant, versus trying to do it yourself, offshore, cold, wet, sleep-deprived, and apprehensive. Such guidance is expressly forbidden by the race rules of the Vendée Globe, on pain of disqualification, and worse, dishonor. This is a solo race around the world, analyze the weather and pick your route by yourself.

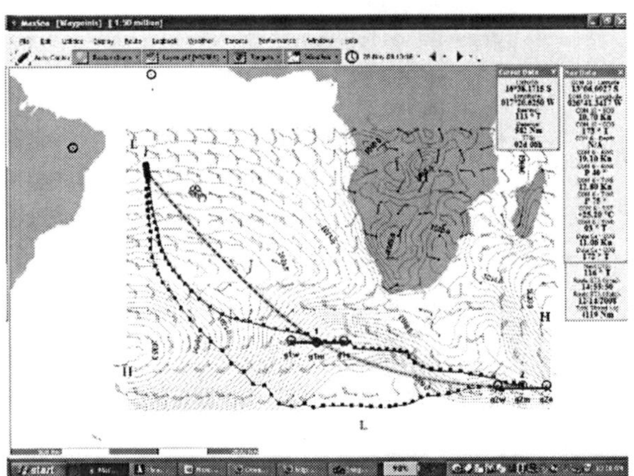

MaxSea Routing Analysis

Watching the fleet and weather up ahead, the South Atlantic High, normally centered near the African side, had moved abnormally to the southwest. Since highs in the south rotate counter-clockwise, the lead pack was forced to sail further south than usual to wrap around that misplaced high before turning east.

Remembering Jean-Yves' urging to put ourselves in a position to get lucky, I thought that if we edged our southerly route to the east, then if the high moved a thousand miles back to where it normally sat, we could cut the corner early and gain on the boats ahead. When Raphaël crossed us, I'd worried that he'd wonder why we were headed further east and deduce our idea. Several days later, the high started to move. By the time we got there, it was back in its usual position, we cut the corner and picked up nearly a day on the group ahead. *Merci, Jean-Yves!*

Our MaxSea program, through a dizzying series of non-intuitive dialog boxes, could automatically download needed GRIB files via either of our 2.4k baud rate Iridium telephones, or our big 56k baud rate Fleet 77, the meter diameter white dome seen on cruise ships with a motorized, satellite-tracking dish antenna hidden inside.

Fearing a software glitch in this complexity needed for the GRIB files, I had programmed an HTML page with 87 weblinks to standard weather maps needed on our route. To save time and expense, given slow baud rates, these links bypassed homepages of NOAA, Météo France, Sydney or the Hong Kong Observatory, and linked directly to specific URLs that were continually updated map, photo, text or animated gif files. I was proud that Mark Wylie liked this idea enough to install it on other Open 60s that he worked with. Globally, we had: regional maps of wind strength, direction and isobars, for 00 hours, 24 hours, 48 hours, 96 hours; infrared or visible spectrum satellite photos; animated gifs showing progression of systems; 500 millibar maps showing higher altitude systems that affect the surface systems; strings of weather buoys with real-time data in the North Atlantic and South Atlantic; iceberg limit maps; sea surface temperature maps; wave height forecast maps; ocean current maps.

Racers spent hours and hours analyzing the weather and their intended routes. Gains made by brain analysis of your route were more valuable than those made by brawn on deck, for the latter entailed risk and fatigue to both skipper and boat.

§

At race's start, our sitesALIVE! program had 25 U.S. newspapers, some big, some small, scattered nationwide, under contract to market, publish, and distribute our Teacher's Guide and 15 part weekly series. In the race's first four weeks, I'd worked hard, a half dozen drafts each, on my four essays for the newspapers, plus calling in our daily audio report, writing a daily Ship's Log of data and comment, and taking and editing photos (the handheld video camera could take still photos, although with an odd time lag that often missed the target shot) and videos, then FTP'ing them into an online cache for Neal to post to our website and YouTube.

Yet my favorite task was answering Q&A: Matthias from Switzerland – are the prayer flags Buddhist?; Goncalo from Portugal – how long for boat preparation? (three years); Timmy from USA – do you fish? (no, the boat is going too fast to fish!). No matter my level of fatigue, these were our *raison d'être*, and I loved to write my answers.

Nepalese Prayer Flags Blessed by the Monks

On the prayer flags question:

They are prayer flags from Nepal. A friend of mine, Scott Hamilton, gave them to me before we left at the start. Scott has been to Mt. Everest four times, three of which were for research. It would be best, and very interesting, for Scott to answer your question, because he can explain the significance of each flag. Although I am not Buddhist, I flew the flags, and will fly them again, because when a good friend gives you something of great emotional significance to them, and spiritual significance for an expedition like this one, one pays attention and flies the flags. I am honored to do so.

Neal forwarded Mathias' question to Scott for amplification:

Yes, indeed, what you saw in the video are Buddhist prayer flags. I gave them to Rich in Les Sables d'Olonne just before he started the Vendée Globe Race. I got them in Kathmandu in the Himalayan country of Nepal. They were then transported by aircraft, by foot and on yaks to the Tengboche Monastery, where they were blessed by the High Lama in a special prayer ceremony to "activate" their powers. I then carried them to Mt. Everest.

The colors each symbolize elements; yellow = earth; green = water & growing things; red = fire; white = air & wind; blue = sky. In the center is Lung-Ta, the wind horse, who symbolizes speed, health, and good fortune. On his back he carries the "wish-fulfilling jewel". The prayers printed on the flags are carried away by the winds, to be shared with all creatures on Earth. The Vendée Globe race is considered the Mt. Everest of sailing, and shares many of the same risks and challenges. Rich is my friend and I thought these flags would be good on Great American III, from one Everest to another!

Could it get any better than that? Almost!

For the South Atlantic, bordered by 14 countries, we'd scheduled our classroom topic "Invisible Places", a class exercise that imagined places, peoples, and cultures invisible over the horizon as we sailed past. Capt. Wallischecke, Acting Superintendent of U.S. Merchant Marine Academy and one of our Experts, cleverly turned the topic around and wrote that the oceans are what is invisible, not the land, as the ocean is 70% of the planet's surface, but you can only see 2.4% of it from coastal lands! A provocative thought from an authoritative source!

I was so psyched. Amazing people had agreed and wished to participate in our Team of Experts, and I was as proud of that and sitesALIVE! as I was of racing the Vendée Globe. You had to have a really good reason for racing this race - and we had it.

§

After the Bay of Biscay carnage, the fleet had stayed nearly intact, losing only Jérémie Beyou aboard *Delta Dore* to a mast rigging problem that forced him to abandon from the lead pack to Brazil. Alas, the south would exact its toll.

In turning the corner around the oddly placed high, the lead pack had stayed close together. Heading east toward the Indian Ocean, only 100 miles still separated the first nine boats. The lead changed hands several times as the pack headed downwind before the westerlies. In each skipper's individual determination of route, often boats would be on different gybes, but in the vast expanse of the sea, a randomly adequate distance normally separated them. Not so one day, when Vincent Riou aboard *PRB* noticed Jean-Pierre Dick's *Paprec-Virbac* crossing his path on a collision course. Vincent called on satellite phone, then VHF radio, and got no answer as Jean-Pierre was sleeping with his boat on autopilot. So, 1000 miles from land in any direction, Vincent changed course at the last minute to clear his competitor's stern by a boatlength.

Michel Desjoyeaux, sailing *Foncia* as if possessed, had pressed, pressed, pressed through the Atlantic, and by Rio de Janeiro caught up to the tail of the lead pack. He uploaded a photo of himself with a placard proudly proclaiming "Top 10!" He reported in a blog that he had hand-steered 21 of the previous 24 hours, to get each last 1/10th of a knot out of his boat. *Le Professeur* was coming. And the leaders knew it.

Unlike Michel, I hand-steered infrequently, usually only after sail or course changes, to see how the boat liked the new setup, or when in a gale and big seas, to see what loads were imposed on the autopilot and the rudder system. For me hand-steering wouldn't make as much difference in the race as it might for him. Plus, steering in our cockpit exposed me to wind and cold and spray, whereas his new generation boat had a beautiful sliding cockpit cover with a Lexan bubble for his head that protected him from the relentless wind and spray yet allowed him to see everything going on as he steered. His new generation of boat had made purposeful strides toward protecting the skipper, as a protected skipper would be a faster skipper.

The disparate 2nd group of Brian Thompson on *Pindar*, Samantha Davies on *Roxy*, Dee Caffari on *Aviva*, Arnaud Boissières on *Akena Verandas*, and Steve White on *Toe in the Water*, was spread over an increasing range, and our third group spanned 500 miles. Jonny Malbon on his new *Artemis* was in front, then us, then Jean-Baptiste Dejeanty on *Maisonneuve*, then Unai on *Pakea Bizkaea*, then Derek Hatfield on *Spirit of Canada*. Hundred mile gaps separated us. Both Jean-Baptiste and Derek had returned for repairs after the Bay of Biscay gale, and had set out again. Jean-Baptiste, the youngest skipper in the fleet at 30 (about half my senior age!) had set a blistering pace after repairing the big crack in his deck, and pushed Derek down the Atlantic at high speed before finally overtaking him off Salvador.

Raphaël aboard *Fondation Océan Vital* and Norbert Sedlacek aboard *Nauticsport* trailed our group. Raphaël had taken a dramatic detour west toward Isla Trindade, a small group of islands 250 miles east of Rio de Janeiro. His mainsail halyard, a rope with an inner load-bearing core and an outer protective cover, had suffered a break in that cover which now bunched up and jammed when it went through a block, preventing the line from moving in either direction. With his mainsail double-reefed, Raphaël was unable to raise or lower it. It would be suicidal to go into the gales of the south with a stuck mainsail. He sought calmer seas in the lee of the islands, to anchor, go aloft, and make a repair, either by leading a new halyard, or stitching the cover back smoothly to the core, so that it would run through the blocks and stoppers. Reaching the island, he found no anchorage nor shelter, as the sea swell wrapped around even the biggest island. He sailed for the coast, a day's sail away. En route, a calm day allowed him to go aloft and stitch a repair. He turned south, racing again.

With the leader approaching the first ice gate, the Race Office emailed new coordinates for the second ice gate, located southeast of South Africa, and northwest of Kerguelen Islands, moving it 600 miles west and 130 miles north due to new satellite photos showing more icebergs that had broken off Antarctica. Coincidentally timed, Dr. Jan Witting of SEA, author of their curriculum on Oceans & Climate Change, wrote his NIE essay on "Antarctic Ice Shelves". An Expert writing on Antarctica, a race-altering order from the Race Office due to more icebergs breaking off Antarctica, what useful live input for our teachers on that week's Teacher's Guide activity "Climate Change"!

The Race Office also emailed the time penalty that six of us would have to pay for not properly respecting an unnoticed buoy controlling the spectator fleet at the tumultuous start. They'd informed us of our error that afternoon, but didn't define the 30 minute penalty until now. Each boat had to arrange an agreed waypoint with the Race Office, sail through that waypoint once, then sail through the same point again 30 minutes later. I decided to deal with it right now since I had manageable sails up, with two reefs and the staysail, it wasn't howling out, and if I waited, I knew that I'd just worry about it. I picked a latitude/longitude waypoint, emailed Julian Hocken in the Race Office my intention, received his approval, sailed through the point, turned around and sailed north for 15 minutes, then turned back south, and sailed through the same point again 36 minutes later. Julian recorded our times and positions by satellite. Penalty paid; that worry is off the plate.

I'd first met Julian when he worked on the Transat 2004. Among the interesting other jobs that he'd had in the past was to manage a 10,000 head dairy farm in Indonesia! Such interesting people on the short-handed ocean racing circuit!

December 1, three weeks since the start, I hadn't yet gotten into the bunk because of the pain in my ribs. Yet now I began to defer less to them. It had been a tough slog, day in, day out, sailing this huge boat for three weeks with that constant pain. Now, for the first time, I was able to climb in. Boy did that feel good! I had four 50 minute, blissful naps, cozy and warm, tucked into my forty degree sleeping bag. From the Rime of the Ancient Mariner, memorized long ago, my mind recalled the appropriate stanza:

Oh sleep it is a wondrous thing
Beloved from pole to pole
To Mary Queen the praise be given
She sent the gentle sleep from heaven
That slipped into my soul...

Awakening, I panicked, not seeing the array of backlit, flickering, chart table instrumentation LEDs in front of my face. Have we had a total power failure? Then I remembered that I was in the bunk and couldn't see the chart table directly.

Well after midnight, a real worry took over. A loud, high-pitched whine emanated from forward. Grab headlights and go, now, through the boat, isolate the noise – OH NO - to the keel compartment.

Open 60s are notorious for having keel problems that are race-ending if not life-threatening. I thought that we were immune because of our keel's five foot long lever arm versus the tripled loads of the 18" lever arms of the hydraulically controlled keels on the modern boats.

Crawling forward through two compartments into the sail locker amidships, I undid the 8 wing nuts holding the inspection port, put them in my mouth for safekeeping, then stuck my head through it. The bottom of the keel compartment was flooded with noisily churning water that rushes in and out around the hinge through the bottom of the boat - that was normal. The high-pitched whine was abnormal and was really loud in here.

No apparent problems with the huge bolts holding the keel onto the bulkheads. Stretching further, I stuck my hand deep into the cold rushing water to feel around the exit - nothing noticeable. I trusted that the block and tackle system wouldn't fail at that instant; if it did, the lever arm would swing back toward the high side of the boat, and crush me. The whine was steady - what could it be? Perhaps those two fairings on the outside, fore and aft of the keel hinge pin, were peeling off the boat and vibrating. Not structural, they smooth the water flow.

Back to the chart table, I zoomed on the group of islands called Tristan da Cunha (after which Tristan Jones, the great Welsh mariner and writer, was named when he was born on a cargo ship sailing past) to Inaccessible Island. It provided a lee from a northwest wind. Maybe I should sail there, stop the boat, swim underneath to take a look, before entering the Indian Ocean with a questionable keel. It's an option, but we won't decide yet.

Vendée Globe shore crews, friends, and helpers, all say - "Call anytime" - and they mean it. Yet even though the sailors were keeping 24 hour schedules, you try to respect the time zones, and sleep hours of those leading civilized routines ashore, and not call at night. But this was a keel problem. I called Brian at home, well past midnight for him, knowing that in just a few hours he had to be back at the shipyard, his wife Alison had to teach school, and 5 year old son Jackson would be at kindergarten.

He answered groggily "Hello?"

"Hi Brian, it's Rich."

"Hi Rich, how's it going?" He was instantly on high alert.

"Sorry to call so late."

"No problem, what's up?"

"We've got a loud, high-pitched whine coming from the keel compartment. It started suddenly. I've been into the keel compartment and can't see anything wrong, felt all around, looked with a good light. Any ideas?"

"Is anything caught in that gap between the keel and the hull?"

"I felt in the water all around there and didn't feel anything."

"Maybe something's caught on the keel, or maybe it's those two fairings on the bottom of the hull, fore and aft of the hinge pin. Those fairings are just shaped styrofoam fibreglassed over, with no structural strength. If you hit something, maybe it cracked one of those fairings, and its just whining in vibration with the water rushing past."

"I thought about that. Really no way to check."

"Are those huge stainless steel slabs OK that hold the keel on?"

"Gave them a good look, can't see anything wrong, no loose bolts. It really sounds bad. But the sailing characteristic of the boat hasn't changed any."

"Well that's good. I think it's going to be one of those fairings. After a few hours maybe it will just break off and the sound will go away."

"OK, I'll keep you apprised. Sorry again to wake you."

"No problem, call anytime. Let me know how it goes." Brian went back to sleep. I went back into the keel compartment to look, feel, and listen again. Eighteen hours later, as quickly as it started, the sound stopped. I didn't know why.

After crossing the shipping lanes from Buenos Aires to Cape Town, I tried to get more sleep. I was eating well, that being the 1st item on the daily job list: four full meals a day, snack in between, drink constantly, with bottles of water and Gatorade always topped off. The 40°F sleeping bag went to the chart table for naps, the 20°F bag was unpacked for the bunk.

We were into the cold that had arrived as Jean-Yves suggested – suddenly, and as John Kiley had worried – intensely.

After my search for a boat, I had visited John, a friend since the second grade, and an expert mariner and naval architect, having completed a correspondence course on his five year 'round the world small boat voyage. I'd shown him all the photos:

John, here's the keel, the cockpit, the cabin, the compartments, the steering system, the rigging, the sail plan, the electronics. What do you think?

He quietly reviewed it all and finally said:

For you, the problem is the cold. You'll be in the cold for seven weeks in the south. You've always been thin, no insulation. You need to solve the cold.

How insightful! Ask the smartest people you know a serious question and they will give you useful, often unexpected, answers. We installed a diesel heater in the cabin.

40° F air temperature in 25 knots of wind gives sub-freezing wind chill. And that would be a good day. Gone were the sun and the tropical warmth and the flying fish. Now we had summer in the south: cold, wet, gray skies, albatross, big swells, and a weightier wind from the west.

Through the Atlantic, despite the ribs, I'd maintained our routines. Keep tabs on the freshwater fed by the desalinator, and never let the 78 litre tank go below half full. This diligence was strengthened when I heard that Jonny Malbon had a desalinator problem and was down to 3 litres of water before happily being able to make a repair. Fire up the engine twice daily, charge batteries for an hour, or until the charging rate came down on the 165 amp alternator to 70 amps. No sense in charging at a lower rate than that and simply wasting fuel to produce few amps. We'd re-programmed the voltage regulator to lengthen to its maximum allowed hour the first bulk phase of the three phases of charging. Consultation by Brian with both an electronics expert and the battery manufacturer advised that we couldn't hurt the batteries with our alternator capacity if we wanted to jam amps into them in as short a period of time as possible. This would mean less wear and tear on all parts of the engine and alternator, including belts and bearings. I'd had a scare early on when starting the engine and noticing in my first check of the system that the water pump wasn't pumping cooling seawater through it. It alarmed me until I found its slipping belt, got out the big wrench, used the big screwdriver as a lever, and tightened it. The house bank voltmeter and ammeter were mounted at the chart table; I checked them constantly.

Our five solar panels had 7.5 amp capacity, yet realistically gave 5 amps in the tropics, with clear skies, no sail shadow, and the sun at a high angle overhead. The wind turbine at the stern didn't mind nighttime and was very effective when sailing upwind, when the boat's speed into the true wind speed amplified it to the apparent wind speed that the turbine saw. With 20+ knots through this elegant device, a sculpted body and three aerodynamic carbon blades, it could generate 10+ amps, which would almost power all the systems aboard, on average, including autopilot (the big user), computer, monitor, instruments, satphones, pumps, and running lights at night. For safety, we'd stuck a square centimeter of reflective tape on the tip of each blade, front and back. At night, the tape reflected your headlight to define a perfectly lit circle from the thousand rpm turbine blades. An intruding finger or ear would be sliced off if entering that circle.

Pushing Hard

I went through the boat daily looking for problems. The crashing wave that had thrown me across the cabin, hammering my ribs, had also knocked off half of the hooks that we had glued inside the boat, to hold spare lines, duffel bags of supplies, transparent backpacks showing spare parts for various maintenance needs, and tool bags. Yet my ribs had hurt so much that I hadn't been able to go back and re-glue them. For three weeks piles of this gear had been strewn randomly about. On a reasonable weather day I set about that task. I wanted every system to be as squared away as possible, and every pathway clear, before entering the Indian Ocean.

On day 25, we passed north of Tristan da Cunha Islands in the central South Atlantic without seeing them. Up ahead, Yann Eliès aboard *Generali* had taken the lead.

Approaching the first ice gate, southwest of South Africa, the position reports showed Unai making only 2.6 knots. I emailed Julian asking the situation and that I was closest if need be. Bad news, his starboard rudder system was broken. He sailed north for a day on the port rudder, for lighter wind and seas at the center of the high pressure system, to try to make a repair. After 36 hours of effort, he couldn't fix the broken carbon fibre support structure. Deeming it unseamanlike to attempt the south with only one rudder, he abandoned the Vendée Globe. Unai being Unai, instead of sailing 500 miles to Cape Town, he turned north for home, 4,000 miles away. Northbound through the southeast then northeast trades, his good port rudder would be in the water. A true mariner, a worthy competitor in the Vendée Globe, a great new friend, he sailed home to Spain on that one good rudder.

Our third group was now four. Though separated from the lead pack, at the longitude of Cape of Good Hope near the southern tip of Africa, we were 1300 miles behind the leader. Given Michel Desjoyeaux's comment about our having 30% less horsepower than he did, I thought we were hanging right in there! Yet that was about to change, as much of the race so far had been upwind, and in the strong downwind conditions of the south, their width and stability would broaden their advantage.

Those ahead, now deep in the south, were rocketing along, and being honest about it:

Mike Golding: I probably pushed it a little too hard and frightened myself stupid.

Loïck Peyron: The wind peaked at 35 knots and we recorded a surf of 28 knots whilst I was in my bunk – a bit full on. I broached on several occasions, one of which ripped off my Inmarsat C aerial which used to be at the rear of the cockpit.

Samantha Davies: I was awoken by the sound of a waterfall coming in the hatchway. Quite scary to wake up to that.

Bernard Stamm: If you wanted to be at the helm in these conditions, you'd need deep sea diver gear.

Dee Caffari: Seeing Bernard steam through makes me realize that his several laps [circumnavigations] in this direction counts for quite a lot. I feel as if I am in the deep end of the swimming pool for the first time and frantically paddling to stay afloat. It is intense and a little stressful and you feel that at any moment it might all be over.

At night, we hit 22 knots of boatspeed, exhilarating, yet risky. In 30 knots of breeze I decided to reef from the 2nd to the 3rd. Changing protocol, I brought all 20' of the reef down at once rather than my usual 5' at a time, then pull in the slack in the lines, then repeat. What a mess! The sail billowed out between the lazy jacks, the 3rd reef downhaul got hooked around the spreader, and the outhaul wrapped around the end of the boom. No solution except to crawl out there on the slippery, loose folds of wet sailcloth, boat still going 14 knots with the staysail, me hanging out over the water, flat on my stomach, hooking the lazy jacks with my feet and the tether, get the reefline untangled, hustle back, and take another 30 minutes of exertion to sort the mess made trying to save 10 minutes.

The next day, the autopilot alarm struck fear - BEEP BEEP BEEP - disengage the clutch, re-boot the electronic compass then processor then instruments, re-engage the clutch, it defaults to steering by compass, and won't steer by the wind direction. Watch the instruments, and - big problem - we're not getting wind angle on the primary instruments aloft. This defaulting to compass if it loses the input for wind angle is fortunate since the boat will then continue on its same course, but this is a problem for sure. If the pilot can only steer by the compass, and the wind changes direction, we could gybe accidentally when I'm napping, and there are only so many times you can expect the rig to withstand that shock load before something breaks. I recycled the instruments several times, and an hour later, aha, wind angle is back. I'll have to inspect the twelve reachable wire connections to see if corrosion is the culprit. Put it on the list.

GA3 passed the first ice gate, properly respecting it and reporting same to the Race Office.

An email arrived from Neal:

"It seems we have a lot of activity in Missouri. A bunch of newspapers are downloading the .pdfs of the 1/4 page weekly feature."

"Are they just downloading and posting the .pdfs on their websites? Or are they actually publishing the features in the full run of their papers?"

"I'll find out."

Later, fantastic news from Neal: "I spoke with Dawn (Kitchell, NIE coordinator for Missouri), and she checked, and we have 25 extra newspapers, all in Missouri, that are publishing our series. It must have been that full front page story on our program that she ran in The Missourian. She said it's amazing because nobody has ever published a 15 week NIE program before, 8 weeks has been the longest until now. And some of those papers are weeklies, so they're allocating a big percentage of their news hole to Ocean Challenge Live! Plus, it's going through the Christmas and New Year's holidays and they never do that!"

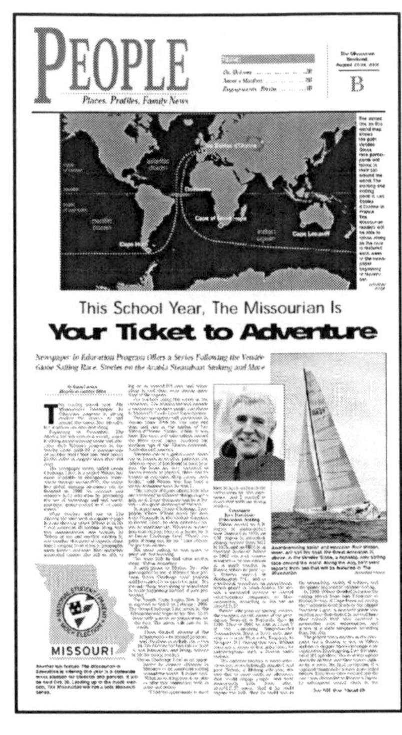
PEOPLE

Places, Profiles, Family News

B

This School Year, The Missourian Is

Your Ticket to Adventure

Newspaper In Education Program Offers a Series Following the Vendée Globe Sailing Race, Stories on the Arabia Steamboat Sinking and More

MISSOURI

Fantastic! Missouri! About as far from salt water in any direction as you can get in the USA! If loads of middle school classes in the state of Missouri were following the lone American entry in a French yacht race around the world that wouldn't come anywhere near America, then obviously the American public was ready to receive the Vendée Globe. And just as obviously, the general media and potential American corporate sponsors, who were uniformly ignoring our participation, were missing the boat. The New York Times had published an article about the start of the race, and was clueless to the fact that there was an American entrant!

But forget The New York Times, we had the Joplin Globe and The Kearney Courier, the Boone County Journal and the Webb City Sentinel, the Steelville Star and twenty more. Missouri was following the Vendée Globe! This was the whole point of our effort. Excite and engage the kids! Onward *Great American III*! Sail well, write well, and make them proud!

§

As the Vendée Globe was a journey, so sitesALIVE! had been one too. What a challenge our new idea for K12 had been. Bumps and bruises along the way might not have been physical, but they'd been just as difficult. My elation at Missouri drifted backward into memories...

To promote our NIE programs, we'd exhibited yearly at the annual Newspaper Association of America Foundation NIE conference. For our online programs, we'd exhibited at the national K12 conferences of National Science Teachers Association, Florida Educational Technology Conference, National Education Computing Conference, and many more. Our sitesALIVE! booth and staff showcased our live programs to teachers.

Sometimes we could sell our programs as content to NIE, yet often not. The papers had to be paid for to count as circulation, yet often the schools had no money, so sometimes we would have to subsidize interested schools' participation and buy the papers on their behalf. This seemed crazy, but we were trying to build our audience, so we did it.

Online, we offered single programs, groups of programs, by semester or full-year, all manner of combinations, for sale. Yet it was all so new: online payments were new, online audio was new; online photos were new; online videos didn't exist. Within the schools, at first there were not enough computers (a wealthy town's computer lab had only six laptops), then not enough Internet connectivity (a school with fifty new Macs in its lab couldn't access our website because they all went through a single 28.8K baud dial-up modem), then teachers could not, or would not, use the Internet in their classrooms (i.e., the teacher who asked if www.sitesalive.com needed a computer). The kids loved computer technology and were facile with it, which told us that tools using this technology would excite and engage them, thus helping teachers. Our NIE programs, often oversubscribed, proved that the concept of bringing the real world to classrooms was correct, as had Prodigy proven it online reaching 100,000 children at home. It seemed that I had misunderstood how unusual our Prodigy early adopters were.

An unspoken worry had begun to lurk – were we too early?

Yet we did have successes. The Los Angeles Times signed up its quota of 750 teachers in just 48 hours for our 2003 Hong Kong-New York voyage program that wouldn't physically come within 9,000 miles of L.A.! With the Wichita Eagle, we won the 2001 Newspaper Innovators in Education Award, when they published five different programs of ours over five consecutive semesters, totaling 65 weeks of live NIE content. Online, we were Finalists in both Education and Children's categories for the Ziff-Davis Global Information Infrastructure Awards, an early website accolade.

We'd pressed on. And regardless of the circuitous and often tortured path to get here with this new idea – to make sitesALIVE! global - here we were, tearing through the South Atlantic Ocean, en route for the south, with a big chunk of the Show-Me state's students along with us, not to mention their colleagues in Colombia, Argentina, the Azores, Italy, Latvia, Taiwan, the Philippines, and elsewhere around the world. Even if we weren't getting the multitudes that we'd wanted via NIE globally, we were getting a diverse group of international students. And that felt good.

§

Thus energized, time to tackle more maintenance before the Indian Ocean. I re-sealed a stanchion that was leaking onto the port bunk, lubricated the sets of 10 pulleys that guide the keel control lines on each side, and bailed more water from the forepeak. I put a big charge into the batteries and desalinated a full tank of 78 litres of freshwater. The battery monitor had mysteriously shown that the capacity of the house bank was declining, a serious worry since the batteries were new, and if they were faulty and died, we'd be finished too. I consulted Brian about it, he thought that the monitor needed to be reset. Before straining my eyes on the 6 point type of the manual, I decided to charge the batteries down to almost no amps charging.

Bingo! All of a sudden, the 50% readout clicked over to show 100% capacity. OK, we understand better now...or... maybe not...

The wind system in front of us was receding, we encountered a light area and did two gybes, before the wind strengthened from behind again, and off we shot at 18 knots of boatspeed. But the autopilot was wild, all over the place, and we broached several times. I couldn't figure it out. The wind instruments were providing data continually, both wind angle and wind speed, so it couldn't be that. We'd take off, the pilot would go ERRRR...ERRRR hard, and the boat's heading would be veering hard to port then hard to starboard. What could it be? Can't go into the south with this. Then I remembered. In the light wind spot, I switched the Autopilot setting to Fixed Boatspeed. The pilot takes wind speed and direction, and boatspeed into calculating the True Wind Angle, then can steer by that downwind. But if the boat is going less than 4 knots, the Manual's recommendation is to switch the setting to NOT accept the speedometer input, but to just tell the pilot we're doing a steady 4 knots. This smooths the variations in the calculations at low speed. But if the pilot tries to steer as if we're going 4 knots by pushing and pulling the rudder with the big angles needed at low speed, yet we're really making 18 knots, well, the wild zigzagging is impressive, scary and dangerous. That's an oops on me. OK, re-program the pilot to use boatspeed input. The pilot settled down immediately.

Whew, these boats are complex. There's so much to remember. And especially when you're tired.

Yet I reveled in this successful maintenance, and the battery and pilot solutions, I was taking care of the boat, doing what I was supposed to be doing as we headed past Cape of Good Hope then Cape Agulhas, the actual southern tip of Africa.

I'd been around these Capes twice before, most recently on our 2003 Hong Kong to New York westbound passage. We'd come in close to the south coast, even seeing car headlights and lit houses at night, to get a boost from the strong and favorable Agulhas Current that sweeps south down the east coast of South Africa, then wraps around to the west across the shallow Agulhas Bank and past Cape Agulhas.

Why so many phenomena named Agulhas? Portuguese ship captains discovered that at that location a magnetic compass needle which naturally points at the magnetic North Pole was also pointing at the geographic North Pole, a rarity globally. Usually there is a Variation between the two directions that can be as great as 40 degrees. “Agulhas” in Portuguese means “Needles”, thus Cape Agulhas.

On that voyage, becalmed and drifting in a circle without steerage way, I’d noticed by the GPS that we were making 5 knots backwards toward New York in the Agulhas Current! Progress! Yet it’s a scary place, because if that strong west-flowing current encountered a strong gale from the west, current into wind on the shallow Bank, the combination could produce monstrously steep seas that have broken ships in half, when bow and stern are suspended on two waves with no support amidships, or when perched amidships on one single wave with no support at bow or stern. Later passing Robben Island off Cape Town, we’d soberly admired the nobility and actions of Nelson Mandela.

On our other rounding, eastbound from New York to Melbourne, we’d passed five hundred miles south of the Cape. Now we were even further off, 700 miles south, and heading eastbound for Cape Horn 10,000 miles away. Now we were entering the dreaded Indian Ocean.

"I hate the Indian Ocean."
...Captain Murray Lister

Chapter 8: Gales of the Indian Ocean

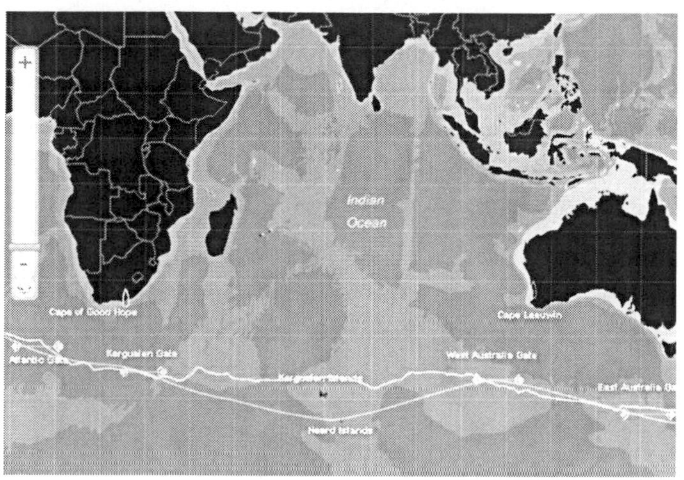

On our 2001 New York to Melbourne voyage I had plotted the clippership record-holder *Mandarin*'s elegant route in 1855. Captain John Parritt had taken her south of the Kerguelen Islands, a desolate outpost of barren rocks nearly equidistant from Africa, Australia, and the South Pole, and inhabited now only by a lonely French research station. I'd emailed Murray Lister, whom I knew as Chief Mate aboard *New Zealand Pacific* during our rescue, and currently serving as Master aboard the containership *Cape York*, exiting the Persian Gulf and bound for the Straits of Malacca (Murray's routes always conjured Joseph Conrad). I described *Mandarin*'s route in the south. Murray replied by Inmarsat C:

> *The Indian Ocean is an awful place. We would have never considered taking New Zealand Pacific, at 815' long, south of the Kerguelen Islands. It's just too dangerous.*

For *GA3*, the great circle route between our first Indian Ocean ice gate and the next West Australian ice gate lay south of these islands. I pondered the choice. South would be shorter, but with more chance of ice, and you could get trapped there unable to escape north in a storm. The route had macho in it, which was not me, and I was pretty sure I wouldn't go there. It was fun to imagine, though, a good story for drinks at the bar.

Just as the hot interior of northern Africa generates the low-pressure systems which migrate westbound across the Atlantic and may become hurricanes for North America, so the hot interiors of South Africa and Madagascar generate lows that develop into storms that then spin southeast into the Indian Ocean and continue across the Pacific. From Australia, heat generated lows, per Jean-Yves Bernot's description of a "bomb", can pummel the Pacific. And more can join the procession from South America, as we would later learn.

My fun imagining lasted until I saw the next weather map. A huge and growing gale was racing across the South Atlantic and lining us up in its worst, northeast quadrant, where its eastbound system speed adds to its rotational speed to give the strongest winds and the biggest waves.

That afternoon's boat inspection was thorough. I planned the sail change sequence: 2nd reef to 3rd reef in the mainsail, then staysail to storm jib, then 3rd reef lowered to the boom if need be. I brought spare lines from the forepeak to the cockpit. This weight transfer lightened the bow, thus reducing the risk of it burying itself in a trough, and added weight to the stern to help keep the rudders in the water. Plus, if we needed to drag the lines overboard to add friction to slow the boat and prevent it nose-diving into a wave, they would be at hand. In our cataclysmic storm off Cape Horn, before our capsize and rescue, we had dragged such "warps" for three days and they had reduced our speed from an out-of-control nineteen knots in forty knots of wind with no sails up, to ten knots even when we got 85 knots of wind and mountainous seas.

I studied extra weathermaps searching for hints of moderation. There were none. Sobering news from ahead interrupted my study.

A month into the race, after leading the fleet through the Atlantic, *Gitana 80*'s mast had exploded a day after Loïck Peyron had climbed it to retrieve an errant halyard. Everybody thought, but nobody pondered publicly, what would have happened if Loïck had been aloft at that moment. He abandoned the race, put up a pre-planned jury rig (the French are exceedingly well-prepared), and headed for Perth. Good-naturedly, via his high speed 56k baud rate satcom, Loïck joined the 300,000 players onshore who were racing the Vendée Globe vicariously in the online Virtual Regatta! One report's hint that a running backstay had contributed to the *"dematage"* cued me to spend the afternoon adding backup lashings to our running backstay blocks.

In studying with Jean-Yves Bernot, we'd lunched one day in La Rochelle, where several Open 60s were based. Dominique Wavre's new *Temenos II* was out of the water, on her stands. I'd met him just once, when he'd showed us his previous boat, and didn't expect him to remember me, but when we circled to the stern, *"Bonjour Jean-Yves, ça va bien?* Hi Rich, how is your boat?" The Vendée Globe is the hardest sailboat race in the world, and also the friendliest. Sadly now, that senior Swiss statesman, the President of IMOCA (the Open 60 Class Association), in his 8th race around the world, suffered a disastrous breakage.

The short lever arm of his canting keel, controlled by hydraulic ram, had broken off, leaving the 14' carbon fin, with 3-ton lead bulb, swinging freely. He tried to stabilize it with ropes, a challenging if not impossible task, and turned to head for the one semi-sheltered bay of the Kerguelen Islands. With no hope of solo repair, he abandoned the race. Arriving safely, he awaited a piece of stainless steel fabricated to lock the keel on centerline for his sail to Perth. From there, the boat would be shipped home to Europe. I emailed him, saying that the position reports would just not be the same without his name up there among the leaders. He replied thanking me for my kind words, that he'd see me at the finish.

Jonny Malbon & Dame Ellen MacArthur

The Iridium phone rang:

"Hi Rich, it's Jonny aboard *Artemis*. I just saw an iceberg, and you're following on about my same track about a half day back, so thought I'd let you know."

"Hi Jonny, thanks hugely for that, I'll be on high alert when I get to your area. Did you catch it on radar, or visually, or both?"

"Both."

"OK, good, other than that, how's it going up there?"

"OK, boat's a bit of a handful, we damaged the starboard daggerboard in a collision with a small marine mammal in the South Atlantic, sad for us, sadder for the creature, but we're coming along OK, learning a lot. How about you?"

"Same thing here, making progress. Broke a rib or two early on, but they're feeling better now. Thanks a lot for the call, I really appreciate it."

I'd sat with Jonny Malbon at a skipper's luncheon before the start, but didn't know him well. His *Artemis* was a powerful new Open 60, a hundred fifty miles ahead of us, and his path was 80 miles further south. We weren't directly behind him, but where there was one iceberg...

Bernard Stamm, Dominique's countryman, reported a broken rudder structure. He turned for the same bay in Kerguelen, planning to anchor, try to repair it alone, then rejoin the race. After breaking his bowsprit in the Bay of Biscay gale in a collision with an unseen fishing boat, he'd returned to Les Sables d'Olonne for repairs, re-started and streaked through the Atlantic, climbing the standings all the way south. Arriving at Kerguelen, he anchored in 45 knots of wind, the anchor didn't hold, and the boat dragged toward the rocks. He hadn't requested assistance, because he would be disqualified if he'd accepted it. Ashore, Dominique saw what was happening and rushed out in a Zodiac to try to help, but he was too late. *Cheminées Poujalat* struck the rocks and there was no way to pull her off. Bernard, a fierce and friendly competitor, lost his boat. He was shattered.

The gale approached relentlessly. A building swell confirmed the weathermaps. Aboard *New Zealand Pacific*, Captain Watt had recorded sea height as two different wave trains, like sine curves. The first was the underlying swell, high in amplitude and slow in frequency. The second was the cresting sea on top, lower in amplitude yet faster in frequency. In that storm he had recorded 15 meter swells, and 5 meter cresting seas. Given the different speeds, these would either combine to 20 meters (65') or subtract to 10 meters (33') or any combination between. A big one had "pooped" his ship, breaking over the stern, and crushing the tops of the stern-most row of containers, 37' above the waterline. The Southern Ocean could clearly overwhelm you.

Sea Getting Up

The wind strengthened, the barograph trace headed down. Soon we had the 3rd reef, the smallest mainsail configuration before it comes down to the boom. At 40 knots windspeed, we surged past 15 knots in 15-20' seas. I rolled up the staysail to set the storm jib, according to plan. But despite the sunny day, I hesitated to go on the foredeck. We were making 15 knots comfortably with only the 3rd reef, this is good, no need for more sail, I'll go with that.

Big mistake not to follow the plan.

As the sun set, and darkness enveloped us, the glass continued to fall; the wind, seas, boatspeed and noise continued to increase. At midnight, with the wind at 50 knots, I eased the mainsail to slow the boat, hitting 20 knots now thunderously and regularly.

§

Many think sailing is a peaceful, quiet sport. Maybe on a lake or a coastal summer's day on the ocean, but not in a gale in the south. Twenty, thirty, or forty foot seas or the sixty foot monsters we'd had at Cape Horn are like city blocks racing and cresting at 30 miles per hour, each one of a thousand threatening to obliterate you. Inside the boat in a storm is like being inside a drum that's being beat on and thrown violently about. The wind is howling, the waves are crashing, the wind turbine is screaming at a million rpm. The noise level indicates the threat level. After college, I worked part-time doing security at rock concerts. We'd stand in front of banks of speakers at a Rolling Stones or a Beach Boys concert with 20,000 screaming fans. It was deafening, but it didn't signify danger. The noise at sea does. And in a storm, it never stops. The stress on your mind, imagining what you can't see in the dark, of the huge cresting seas, of what's happening unseen up the mast, or underneath the hull with the keel, daggerboard and rudders knifing through the ocean at waterskiing speed, is enormous, and it never stops. You're wet, you're cold, you're tired, you're hanging on physically and apprehensive, on highest alert, if not actively fearful, you've been at it for months already, and it never stops.

Solo at sea, nobody is there to share the physical load, and nobody is there to share the mental and emotional loads. There is no sport like this one.

§

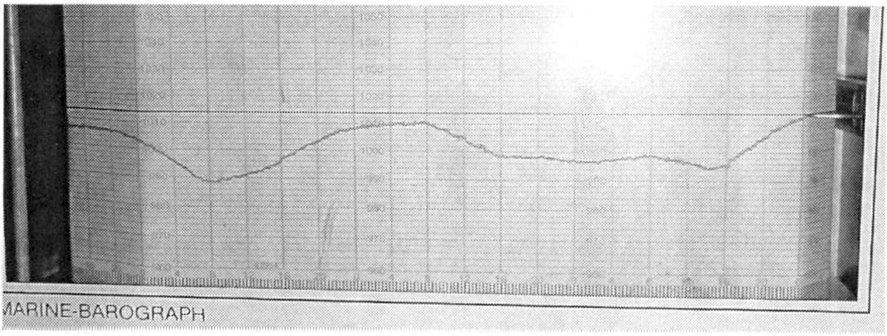

Two Depressions on the Barograph

The glass fell further, the wind gusted past 60 knots, hurricane force, the boatspeed sprinted to 20+ knots, giving no advantage of sustainable speed, only the disadvantage of risk. The 3rd reef was too much sail, but now there was no way to get it down. If I let off the halyard, the sail would blow against the rigging, chafing both, and staying up. The only solution was to sail the boat upwind into this 60 knot gale, into these 25' breaking seas, then the mainsail would flag back from the mast and rigging, and could be winched down, sail slide by sail slide.

But I couldn't sail upwind to lower the mainsail, because, upwind, I needed the storm jib to keep the boat moving once the mainsail was allowed to luff. I hadn't set it when I had the chance at 40 knots in daylight; now I had to set it with 60 knots in the dark.

Have two glasses of milk, a couple of Baby Bels, a handful of Fig Newtons, think it through step by step. Check the barograph, might it be leveling? Wishful thinking, no, it's still going down. OK, here we go, full on safety awareness, talking myself out loud through every step.

Go on deck with stocking cap, gloves, foul weather gear, seaboots, harness and tether. Acclimate my night vision with my headlight. Hook the tether on the jackline. Work my way forward past the mast to the foredeck and the babystay. Down on hands and knees. Sense the seas and boat's motion always, ready to leap to bearhug the mast if a sea threatened to come aboard. Unlash the halyard and sailbag holding the storm jib, pull out the sheets, lead them back to the cockpit on each side, holding on, calibrating every move by my sense of the sea, the motion of the boat, the sound of what was coming. A sea crested aboard amidships - I leapt onto the boom to let the solid water pass underneath. Back and forth, mast to cockpit, for the sheets and to hoist. En route, look at everything - do I see any other problems - since I'm here?

OK, time to hoist, hand over hand until the heavy duty, 250 square foot storm jib was up hand tight. Wrap the halyard around the winch, put the winch handle in and began to grind for proper tension. The sail was luffing madly in the 60 knots of wind, and the sheet was flailing like a whip, and invisibly. WHACK! It hit me hard on my ear, knocked me to my knees. Dazed, I hugged the mast for support, not wanting to slide down the deck into, or maybe through, the lifelines, felt around my ear, nothing to learn there, can't tell if the wetness is the blowing spray or blood, OK, jam off the halyard where it is, crawl to the cockpit, trim the sail so it and it's sheet are not thrashing, into the cabin to get my helmet with full Lexan visor that we have for going aloft, put it on, then back to the mast to grind the halyard taut, then to the cockpit again.

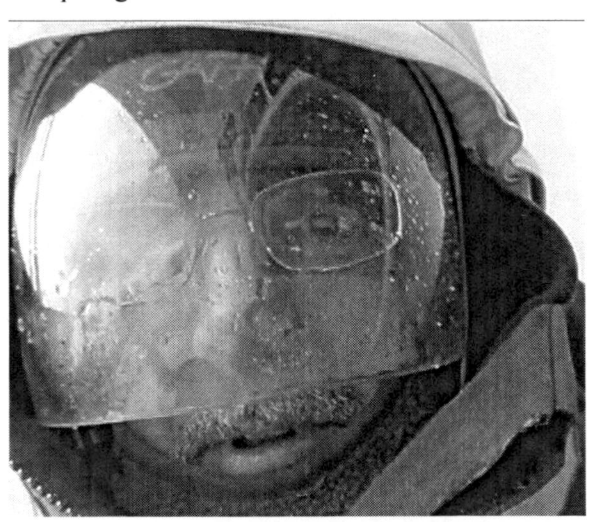

Helmet with Full Lexan Visor

I was beat, but so what? This sail maneuver is far from over. Now for the hard part. Even though I just hoisted a sail in 60 knots of wind downwind, now I have to sail upwind into 60 knots to get the mainsail down. Stuff my hands, numb from the frigid cold, into my ski gloves for a few minutes to warm them up. Then a swig of Gatorade, here we go.

Disengage the autopilot clutch, stare into the wind and the dark trying to sense or discern approaching seas to time our turn. Was there a really bad one coming? Not sure, can't tell, don't think so. OK, turn the boat rapidly toward the wind with the tiller, to a close-hauled angle to the wind, now engage the autopilot. How's she doing? Is the storm jib, with the mainsail eased and doing nothing but luffing, enough by itself to keep our direction into these seas? Seems so. OK, let's lower the mainsail.

Off came the halyard. With no load on the mainsail it came down 5' and stopped. Is it stuck? No, the wind is just blowing so hard it won't come down. OK, back to the mast, holding on for dear life as we crash up and over the seas now instead of riding them downwind. I'd brought two pieces of line, 15' each. Tie both at the bottom of the sail, lead one up and over the next slide on the track, lead it to the winch, grind the sail down five feet, tie it off. Take the other line, climb up onto the winch to reach the next slide and feed the line over it, lead down to the winch, grind that slide down. Untie the first, lead it over the next slide, grind that one down, and so on, until the mainsail was down on the boom. Climb up to the sail on the boom, crawl halfway out to the end, and tie the two sides of the containing lazyjacks together, like cinching a purse. "OK, that mainsail is not going anywhere." Down to the deck, then to the cockpit. Time the seas again, and turn the boat downwind to course, storm jib only now, 12 knots of boat speed. That's better. Into the cabin to warm up, closing and dogging the door behind me, to keep out the cold wind and spray, and the never-ending noise. The helmet had proven a lot warmer for my head than those porous stocking caps that the wind and spray go through freely. Take off the helmet and foul weather gear jacket. Spent. Milk and Ensure, hot oatmeal and raisins, Ramen noodles, a few Baby Bels and dried apricots to recover.

The pilot seemed to be holding her, so I rested at the chart table bench, ready to go on deck quickly if need be. A few worried hours later, with daylight brightening the east on our bow, the wind eased to 50 knots, then 40 knots, and the glass began to rise. With the wind down, we turned back into the leftover sea to hoist the mainsail to the third reef, then turned downwind, doused the storm jib, rolled out the staysail, and were on our way.

In the afternoon, I made a thorough check of the boat, above and below decks. Finding water sloshing in the forepeak I bailed it out, lifting bucket after bucket over my head, through the foredeck hatch, then dumping the frigid water, mostly on the deck to drain overboard, yet some on my head and down my neck.

One Indian Ocean gale down.

§

More bad news from the lead pack pressing hard. Jean-Pierre Dick, aboard his blue *Paprec-Virbac*, hit something in the water and broke the connecting rod to his port rudder. Like Unai in the South Atlantic, Jean-Pierre turned north for calmer winds and seas, to make a repair. After a day-long carbon repair job, he rejoined the race.

Were the leaders pressing too hard? Only they knew, and you wouldn't catch me second-guessing the legends in that group:

> *Jean Le Cam (2nd place Vendée Globe 2004-5): In a gang of ten who are crazy, who are fairly often taking things to or beyond reasonable limits, I think I am being reasonable, but difficult to know where to set the cursor. You get used to the excesses.*

> *Brian Thompson: The real top speeds are always under pilot, as the pilot has no fear.*

> *Michel Desjoyeaux: Hit 30.44 knots under pilot.*

> *Dee Caffari: I had a couple of days when I freaked out a bit and was super sensitive about everything. I phoned my boyfriend in a flurry of tears. It was a combination of everything – I was in the south, it was full on and would be for a while, I had never done*

this before and I was on my own. Its fine now but I just had a small panic, which is a bit weird because I'm enjoying it.

"Weird" is the right word, because I felt the same way. In the big seas and gales I was frightened, tired, cold, a long way from land or help, my muscles hurt, my joints hurt, I was unsure of my decisions, yet I felt myself utterly alive, using every faculty that I had in this world to its utmost.

§

My preoccupation with our gale's approach had limited my weathermap analysis to our immediate area. When I looked for a broader perspective with our next map, looking behind us again across the South Atlantic, my heart skipped a horrified beat. A second huge storm was coiling behind us.

The track of its center lay north of us, so when it hit, the clockwise rotation would give us headwinds. Oh brother. Sure we had weathered the first gale, but that didn't mean anything for this next gale. Well, this is going to look odd to the folks following at home, but we're going to turn northeast, from our east-southeast path, and try to get far enough north so that we'll be on the downwind side of this next system when it gets here. That's the prudent thing to do, the seamanlike thing to do I told myself, not wanting to think I was chickening out.

Our second gale arrived in the night, glass falling, wind and sea rising. That first gale had been cold, cold, cold. This second one was frigid. The storm was so big across that it was sucking Antarctic continent air into its vortex. I went forward with ski gloves on to set the storm jib, found I couldn't do anything with them, took them off, and held them in my teeth. When I got back to the cockpit, I couldn't feel my fingers OR my toes. Three reefs and the storm jib, winch the mainsail down again as the wind passed 50 knots en route to 60 knots. Hail chattering on the deck, windchill at 10 degrees, freezing out.

Welcome to summer in the Southern Ocean.

A situation. How could this happen? How did I let this happen?

Our path to the northeast to get on the downwind side of this next swirling storm had placed us close to the south coasts of Isles Crozet. You have to be kidding - we're in the middle of the Indian Ocean, and we have a lee shore? A sailor's worst nightmare is being blown downwind onto a lee shore, and ours was a rocky coast, in 60 knots of wind. Two islands, Île de la Possession and Île de l'Est, each 10 miles long, 10 miles between them. We're 9 miles off, it's a 30 mile overall length, we're making 9 knots, we have to sail at 90 degrees to the wind to parallel the coasts so we're going to get hammered not being able to run off downwind. This is unbelievable. How did I let this happen? Two lee shores nearly two thousand miles out from Africa in the Indian Ocean.

I turned on the radar to search for the coast. Nothing showed. I can understand if the radar's reflected signals are smothered by the hail squalls outside, but in between them it should see the coast. I tried the longer range settings on the radar, nothing. This is odd, the chart shows that those islands have some height to them, good for reflecting radar. Into the cockpit to shine our million candlepower spotlight on the radar antenna mounted 20' up the forward side of the mast. Ah, there's the problem. The antenna is on a hinged bracket. As the boat heels, the bracket hangs vertically to keep the antenna level with the horizon. Problem here is that the 60 knots of wind are blowing the bracket and antenna out at 90 degrees, like a flag, so the antenna is calmly scanning a vertical slice of the sky ahead, above, and astern, not a horizontal slice across the sea. Well, that's a new one! Nothing to do about it, back to the chart table to check our three GPS units - do they agree? Are we actually where we think we are? Yes, they agree, nine miles off the lee shore. OK, we're just going to stay up and watch this until we're past. I winched two feet of daggerboard down to reduce our sideways slip toward the lee shore.

Three hours later, we cleared the end of the second island and I went below. The noise and fear was worse in the cabin because you couldn't see what was generating the noise: the howling wind, the seas crashing, the hull streaking through the water. After the solo Transat 2008, from England to Boston, Samantha Davies had sailed back to France with full crew aboard her *Roxy*. Why not practice solo on the way back, as that race's winner Loïck Peyron had done?

Because she wanted crew to push the boat hard, so that she could practice sleeping with the noise and vibration of the boat at high speed. A great idea from a great sailor.

In trying to manage your mental state, to either calm or invigorate, one tool is music. If you're going to make a big sail change, listen to Bruce Springsteen's "Thunder Road" on the iPod to get yourself pumped. If chaos reigns outside, and your mind is creating visions of a watery Dante's Inferno, try to calm down with some classical music, or, better yet, the soothing human voices of the St. Benedictine Monk Choir that Ellen had given me on a CD. There were 18 chants. I listened to the entire CD four times that night, 72 chants in a row into my earbuds. A hurricane blowing outside, 25' frigid seas breaking thunderously around us, hail chattering on deck, wind screaming in the rigging. The 72 chants helped.

Another six hours and the breeze and seas began to drop, the glass to rise. After mopping condensation in the cabin dripping across the instruments, I went into the bunk for a series of naps. The storm wasn't quite done, and a last gasp puff knocked the boat over. Launched from the bunk, I fetched up 12" away on the bulkhead, hard, with my left ear cushioning my skull. It hurt, a lot.

On we raced in the Vendée Globe.

Later, checking forward, I found the bracing pulpit on the leeward side of the mast broken. It's there to lean against when working at the mast. The free ends of the spinnaker and reacher halyards were tied to it. The 60 knots of wind had set the two halyards swinging back and forth rhythmically and so violently that the load of the swinging halyards broke a weld in the 1" diameter titanium tubing. Amazing! The exposed edges were razor sharp and would slice any sail or line or finger that came near. I lashed the two pulpit legs tightly together so that the break would not open, then wound a long strip of adhesive dacron tape, for sail repairs, around the break to cover the edges. Good for now.

All was not sanguine for everybody however. When I'd turned northeast between the gales, I'd watched on the daily position charts Jean-Baptiste, a bit south and behind us aboard *Maisonneuve,* continue on. I'd worried that he was going to get hammered sailing upwind into that second storm, whereas we would get hammered, but be sailing downwind, easier on everything including skipper. He did. He suffered autopilot failures as well as rigging failures. Unable to fix them, he had to abandon, turning northwest for Port Elizabeth on the southeast corner of South Africa. En route he endured seventy knots of wind.

Our group was now three: Jonny, us, and Derek.

An email arrived from a friend ashore:

Rich,
I can't imagine how emotional and lonely this must be for you. Such a grueling race. I was trying to think of what, on a much smaller scale, of course, I could equate this to in my life. Started thinking about two years ago when I was going through my horrible series of surgeries for breast cancer. I had one friend who, desperate to figure out some way to help, brought me a warm muffin every few days. Of course food wasn't exactly what I needed as I was getting absolutely no exercise but her kindness made me weep every time. I don't know whether emails from friends are like muffins but please know that you are not alone out there. We are all sailing along with you and will keep sending email muffins. Be safe.
Fondly,
K

Day 37. Our sail number. Decades ago I'd asked my mentor Walter Greene why he had 35 as his sail number. He said it was his age when he started solo sailing. Good enough for Walter was good enough for me, so I picked 38 for *Curtana*, my age for my C-STAR. Then both *GA* and *GA2* became USA 38. With *GA3*, I'd asked IMOCA for USA 38 only to find it was still reserved by an old Open 60 in the U.S. that wasn't racing. So, either go with 37, which was my age for qualifying for the C-STAR in a solo race Bermuda – Newport, or 58, my age now in the Vendée Globe. I liked 37, a prime number, and besides, Ellen had said, "When you look aloft in a big storm, do you want to be reminded that you're 58?!" I picked USA 37.

Ahead, Mike Golding, like Dominique in his 8th race around the world, was leading aboard *Ecover*. When I met him in Le Havre before the start of the race to Brazil, he had said kindly, "Hi Rich, glad to have you in the fleet." An ironman competitor, he'd taken a gybe deep south for more wind before coming back toward the next ice gate. Watching the instruments below, a 55 knot squall had overtaken him, pushing his boatspeed to 32.5 knots. Zipping up his foul weather jacket to go on deck to ease everything to slow down, his overloaded mast exploded and crashed into the sea. He cut it away, put up his boom and storm jib as a jury rig, and disappointedly headed for Perth behind Loïck.

By mid-day, the amazing Michel Desjoyeaux, *Le Professeur, Mon Professeur*, pushing *Foncia* brilliantly and relentlessly, took the lead 750 miles south of Cape Leeuwin at the southwest corner of Australia.

The fleet was being decimated. Kito, Alex, Marc, Yannick in the Bay of Biscay, Jérémie and Unai in the South Atlantic, Loïck, Dominique, Bernard, Jean-Baptiste and Mike in the Indian Ocean. A million sea-miles between them, all abandoned. Nineteen left racing.

Worse was to come.

The yellow LED on the Inmarsat-C glowed - mail was waiting. I read it, and caught my breath. Yann Eliès was in trouble, 800 miles south of Australia.

I'd seen Yann the day before the start, riding his bicycle slowly through the marina, standing up on his pedals with his young daughter seated behind him, her arms around Daddy. He saw me, and rode over to introduce her to *"l'Americain"*. He was 34, a soft-spoken, friendly, expert ocean sailor who had crewed with Loïck's brother Bruno aboard the giant catamaran *Orange* when they set the around-the-world record for the Jules Verne Trophy.

Re-leading a line on his bowsprit, with *Generali Concorde* at 12-14 knots, the boat surfed down a sea to 22 knots, buried the bow and Yann deep into the next trough, nine tons of boat at speed piercing the sea, crushing him against the stainless steel bow pulpit. His 2,000 pound test tether broke, and when the bow rose and the sea released him, he found himself overboard, holding onto the pulpit overhead with his left hand. Somehow he got himself back on deck, a superhuman effort.

In excruciating pain, he dragged himself backward along the deck, into the cockpit, into the cabin, and got himself into a position of less pain than all the others. Calling the Race Office by satphone, he reported that he thought he'd broken his femur (thighbone), the strongest bone in the body. Race Director Denis Horeau immediately contacted the two closest boats, Marc Guillemot aboard *Safran* 100 miles ahead in 8th place, and Samantha Davies aboard *Roxy* 450 miles southwest in 11th place, and requested that they head to his position. Both immediately stopped racing and headed for Yann, with their specific brief from Race Doctor Jean-Yves Chauve to "lend emotional support". Horeau then contacted the Australian Navy to request assistance. They immediately initiated deployment of the 385' frigate *Arunta* from Perth, with ETA at Yann's position in 48 hours.

The tradition of the sea is to go the aid of a mariner in distress, no questions, no debate. If asked, you go. Marc, Samantha, and the Australian Navy went.

Likewise, in the 1996 Vendée Globe that lost five boats, when Pete Goss had been asked by Race Director Philippe Jeantot whether he could lend assistance to Raphaël Dinelli, 160 miles behind and upwind in the 60 knot gale, he went. Asked later about the decision to go or not go, knowing that he was putting his own life at risk, he replied simply that the decision was easy: you either live by your morals and principles, or you don't. He did, so he went.

In agony, Yann was unable to reach his severe pain medication, stowed only six feet away. Hearing this by radio, Marc mixed up his own pain medication in plastic bottles, and when he arrived 10 hours later, sailed close aboard and tried, unsuccessfully, to lob these down the companionway hatch to Yann. Yet his presence was reassuring and Yann's spirits were lifted. Besides being close friends, Marc had broken both his legs in the somersaulting capsize of the 75' catamaran *Jet Services* in 1985, so brought personal understanding to the situation. Marc suggested to the Race Office that he could try to get off onto *Generali* to help, but was dissuaded from this, since he might be injured in the surging together of two nine ton boats in a seaway.

Samantha had closed to within 70 miles when the Australian Navy arrived. In acceptable seas, they deployed a rescue Zodiac, boarded *Generali*, strapped Yann to a stretcher, and transported him to the frigate. Halfway between Australia and Antarctica, on a little used trade route, *Generali* was deemed a minimal hazard to navigation, and was left to drift.

Australian Navy Rescues Yann Eliès

Two days later, Yann was operated on in Perth. In addition to his thighbone, he had broken his pelvis and back. Dr. Barnewolt told me later that a broken femur is the most painful injury a body can sustain. Furthermore, the broken end of the bone could lacerate the major artery running up the leg. If so, the victim would bleed to death in two minutes.

The Race Doctor communicated fleetwide, directing all skippers to move their medical kits to their chart table, the most central location on their boats. IMOCA 60 Class Rules were later revised to specify this central stowage of the medical kit.

Marc and Samantha turned east, and resumed racing. Météo France would estimate where they would have been had they not diverted, and calculate a time compensation which would be applied to their finishes in Les Sables d'Olonne.

The fleet collectively exhaled. One could sense that new precautions were being taken - if that injury could happen to Yann – young, fit, experienced - it could happen to anybody.

This episode prompted a sitesALIVE! student's question about the tradition of going to the aid of a mariner in distress. Who better to answer than our Expert Sean Connaughton, Maritime Administrator for the U. S. Government? He began by an inspiring quote from the 1885 Annual Report of the Operations of the U.S. Life Saving Service, precursor to today's Coast Guard:

> *These poor, plain men [U.S. Life Saving Servicemen], dwellers upon the lonely sands ...took their lives in their hands, and, at the most imminent risk crossed the most tumultuous sea..., and all for what? That others might live to see home and friends.*

Approaching the Kerguelen Islands, we passed north as expected, heeding Murray's warning. Brian and Dee had sailed north too, and they were as brave as they come!

§

Crossing this longitude line, not only of the Kerguelens fifty miles south, but also of Diego Garcia, an atoll 2400 miles north, triggered a cascade of memories. Westbound, en route Hong Kong to New York, passing south of that huge British and American military base, had led me to email my concern for his safety to Bill Griffen in Kuwait. Though preparing to go into Iraq, ever the modest Marine, Bill emailed me back saying he thought it was safer where he was than where I was.

At that voyage's start, our pre-departure party at the Royal Hong Kong Yacht Club was delayed awaiting the Commodore, a doctor in his working life, who had been at the hospital since dawn, as they attempted to understand a new pneumonia-like affliction, to be named SARS later that weekend.

A week into that voyage, transiting the South China Sea, we'd entered the territorial waters of Indonesia, the largest Muslim country in the world, with a boat named *Great American II*, only three days after that Iraq invasion had begun. On top of piracy considerations (for which Murray was our expert advisor, having been boarded twice by pirates in his career), we couldn't be sure how we would be regarded if we were noticed sailing through those waters, so per our advisor, we ran without running lights at night.

Earlier still in our sitesALIVE! history, we'd arrived in New York for our departure to Melbourne late in the evening of September 10, 2001. Docking at Chelsea Piers, two miles north of the World Trade Center, we were there the next morning when the towers were attacked. Both my shipmate Bill Biewenga and I had friends aboard those flights.

By 11 am that morning, a hundred bed operating room was set up and staffed in the cavernous spaces of Chelsea Piers, the former Cunard Lines terminal where *Titanic* was supposed to have docked. We volunteered, I in the respiratory section, and Bill in the triage unit as he had experience from the Vietnam War. Yet there were no patients, at least until midnight when exhausted Policemen and Firefighters came in, with breathing problems, or just needing to talk.

Polling teachers whether we should sail or not, they responded: "Yes, there will be a lot of bad news coming, give us something good for the students." We sailed. Arriving Melbourne 68 days later, I was invited to be a guest speaker for the local high school graduation. With 900 students in the auditorium, you could have heard a pin drop in their hanging on my words describing New York after the attack.

Besides the disconcerting notion that we seemed to be at sea during times of national emergency, the obvious interconnectedness of the world by the sea gave new ideas. Perhaps these international episodes had planted a glimmer of globalism in my thinking about sitesALIVE! that had opened a door to the Vendée Globe. And so far the racing was confirming that notion: look, we're sailing around the darn world in one fell swoop – it's big, but it isn't THAT big, and it clearly demonstrates that we're all on this planet ride together.

§

Once past the confused seas of the shallow Kerguelen plateau, we steered for the West Australian ice gate. Fatigue, from both physical exertion and sleep-deprivation, was serious. Sailing in a daze, I fell asleep at the chart table, face down on the keyboard. Waking 4 hours later, my longest sleep for the 40 days of the race, I found the boat doing 7 knots with the wrong sails up, and those badly trimmed. The GPS log tripped over: 10,000 nautical miles for a 10.5 knot average

Finally, a stretch of 20-30 knot winds, moderate for the south, allowing high mileages. I always wore the helmet on deck now, and began to wear it in the cabin at these high speeds. Knowing Mom would enjoy that we were near the exotic Kerguelen Islands, I called via Iridium. Our conversation was wonderful, yet emotionally trying because it focused again the stark question of whether I should be out here or not, as she was 92.

Our 3rd gale overtook us with 35-45 knots. It wasn't the 60 knots of the first two gales, but it still hammered us with big breaking seas. *GA3* hit 23 knots down a wave with three reefs and the storm jib. I was getting good at setting the storm jib and felt confident in the procedures on the foredeck. An AIS target appeared on screen, and after 2 hours of looking over and around the waves, a big fishing vessel appeared, paralleling us a few miles south. I called Jonny to alert him that there might be ships in his area ahead. He had 50 knots in our gale.

When the barograph rose after the gale receded east, with clear skies and sunshine, and Christmas approaching, I declared another maintenance day. Snugged the dozen clamps on the desalinator's hoses and valves improved the suctions as discerned from an immediate audible difference. After 100,000 sea-miles listening to desalinators through the years, I could tell from subtle sounds its functionality. I transferred five gallons of diesel from a jerry-can into the main tanks, checked the engine's oil and coolant levels, then bailed the forepeak, and washed clothes in the bucket. Finally, with the sun still out, I decided on a shower. The newly desalinated water retained the ocean's 45 Fahrenheit degrees. As the black solar shower bag didn't have enough late afternoon sun to warm the water, the shower in the cockpit was frigid and consequently brief. Yet it felt good. I changed clothes for the first time since the South Atlantic.

Despite the hardships at sea, sitesALIVE! was always on my mind. I delivered on deadline my daily audio, ship's log and journal, and weekly tasks of the formal NIE essay plus Q&A, photos and videos. Our primary objective, I worked at it intently two hours daily.

My weekly essays for the newspapers were the biggest effort. On our doublehanded voyages, I'd hammered on them for 9 or 15 drafts sometimes. If you have the chance to write for 7 million readers, and 200,000 students, you NEVER send your first draft, or your third. You have an extraordinary chance to have an impact, and you must edit and polish, per Dr. Pariser, and particularly in the confines of our NIE essay's limit of 225 words. But the fatigue of sailing this big boat, alone, in the south, shrank my editing to 4 or 5 drafts. I had to keep pushing the boat, I couldn't be last; if we were last, I feared that the kids would stop paying attention.

I loved to read the essays that our Team of Experts wrote. Here in the south, Sam Scott of Peabody Essex Museum wrote on "The Southern Ocean." With exquisite timing, PEM had opened a Polar Marine Art exhibit a week before the Vendée Globe start and scheduled to close near its estimated finish!

Whenever I got down in spirit, whenever I was exhausted on deck or below, when I got to 400 grinds on the pedestal, and didn't think I could do another single one, but knew I had 100 to go, I thought of our school program. This is why I was out here. And beyond the subjects of geography, math, science and history that we were expounding upon from sea, we also had to show them perseverance, tenacity, and that we would never, ever quit. My challenge was at sea, with the boat, oceans, and me; but our bigger challenges were onshore, to show as much of the world as we could to the young students.

I remembered our sitesALIVE! feature, dubbed "Win-A-Call", that we'd had on our Hong Kong – New York passage. Website participants would enter their email address for a weekly drawing; the winner would get a call from us aboard *GA2*. Approaching

Madagascar from the Sunda Strait, I'd called a ten year old boy in Alberta, Canada. Diabetic, homeschooled, with a single mother, we spoke intensely for 50 minutes via Iridium. We talked about our chronic afflictions, his diabetes and my asthma, then about the oceans, stars, school, birds and boat. After finishing in New York, a letter arrived from his mother: "We loved following Ocean Challenge, so we've changed our summer vacation plans. We're going to Vancouver so that my son can see the ocean. He's never seen the ocean before." Recalling that episode, I just about cried.

On the plus side of the Southern Ocean ledger are the albatross that continually surround the boat. Huge, powerful birds, with a wing span of 9'-10', they glide and soar, almost never flapping those wings. Grabbing deflections of wind over swells for a lift, they swoop down into the troughs, close to the water, at high speed, banking, feeling for the water with a wingtip, looking for food churned up by the boat's wake. If it's blowing hard, they may hover near the cockpit, watching the wake, and you can inspect and admire these creatures who are completely at home where we humans are not.

On our 1993 San Francisco to Boston passage aboard *GA2*, we saw albatross near Cape Horn. Online with Prodigy, a student had sent a question, signing his handle as "Fish". I answered his question, and sent back my own: "Since you're name is Fish, can you find out from the library - what do albatross eat?" A few days later came his answer: "Albatross eat squid. And don't throw overboard any plastic six-pack holders - they can choke on them." A budding ocean environmentalist!

Watching from the cockpit one day, starboard gybe, an albatross banked in toward *GA3* from leeward. Coming fast, he suddenly nose-dived into the water just short of the hull. I guessed that he had thought that he could bank easily to clear the bow, but the invisible air turbulence behind the sails had confused his plan, so he crashed into the water instead. Had this albatross made an aerodynamic miscalculation?! The question sounded absurd.

The next day, watching instruments in the cabin, there was a huge crash on deck. I ducked and recoiled instinctively, then looked forward through the cabin windows for breakage. A huge albatross had crashed on the mid-deck and was in an awkward, flailing kerfuffle! He clawed at the heeled deck with his webbed feet, flapped his wings, somehow got off the deck between two lifeline wires and tumbled into the sea. Bobbing to the surface, he ran across the water, flapping wings determinedly, and got airborne. Was it the same bird as yesterday?! Another aerodynamic miscalculation?! I wondered who was more surprised, he or I.

Albatross

Rocketing downwind, I spent considerable time stretched flat on my stomach at the end of the boom tying in a backup lashing for the mainsheet block. The massive 1" diameter spectra line, 100,000 pounds test strength, was slowly chafing on the boomvang. Preventive maintenance is key, keep at it. Find and solve potential problems before they become real problems. But don't email my mother any photos from that precarious perch!

Christmas Eve, 45 days in, 11,700 miles on the GPS, we passed the West Australia ice gate. Our 4th Indian Ocean gale hit, 45-50 knots of wind, 20 foot breaking seas. I tried to slow the boat to save it, 3rd reef in main only, yet *GA3* hit 23 knots anyway. Despite the growing familiarity, an Indian Ocean gale is never routine. Storm jib work on the foredeck, with the frigid windchill a constant, was now informed by elevated caution due to Yann's close call.

I emailed the Race Office staff:

Dear Denis, Julian, Mathias, Marko,
Thanks for your concern and good wishes on this Christmas Eve. In any race, it's nice when the organizers truly care about the competitors, each and every one of them. And for this most challenging race the Vendée Globe, I, out here alone, feel truly that you all are back there pulling for me, taking every wave hit as I am, and that gives me a good feeling. Weather files suggest 4 more days of this hard weather. Have developed a nice Iridium chat bond with Jonny Malbon; he's getting hammered too, and that's nice because I've a brother-in-arms out here.
Merry Christmas to all - Joyeux Noël a tous....
Rich

A 5th gale of 40 knots struck on Christmas Day. I tried to be Merry, opening some presents sealed in Ziplocs, and wished for moderating conditions. Then Iridium calls to Jonny ahead and Derek behind, to wish both a Merry Christmas. Recording two holiday greetings, in English and French, I uploaded them via satcom to our, and the race's, websites, the file transfer slowed by the clogged Inmarsat bandwith as every Indian Ocean ship's crewmembers must be calling home.

On a long call with Mom, we were both upbeat - and hiding our true feelings. From her work in Alaska, she knew far better than most how debilitating and dangerous continuous wind and cold could be. Well aware that we'd sustained 5 gales in this awful ocean, never once did she express her worries to me, knowing that her concerns would compound my own. From the other side of the world, she did what she could to help her son.

With Ellen, not needing to keep up my public face, I could vent or muse or agonize, on seagoing fears or those about Mom. On Mom, she could give a true status report, having kindly visited her regularly. She was a pressure release valve – always there when needed. Yet that kindly offered role bore a toll. For me, after a good venting of fear or frustration or fatigue, something would happen aboard which would move me off that episode forward to the next, whereas she was left bearing my unloaded anxiety, yet without knowing until our next exchange how it was playing out at sea.

If the solo sailor admits needing help from shore, you're tacitly admitting you can't do this alone. Yet the solo sailor in the gales of the south thousands of miles from safety must absolutely believe that he or she can do exactly that. Thus one is reflexively slow with immediate public gratitude for those that you know you really couldn't have done without, so as to not dampen your own confidence.

A wondrous and unexpected present – Merry Christmas wishes arrived via Lorraine from schools in Poland, China, and Australia. sitesALIVE! was reaching globally, as was our goal. Fantastic.

The day after Christmas – might we get a reprieve from King Neptune who had long since made his point? Not a chance. Our 6th gale with 35-45 knots. Our poor 3rd group, hammered to three boats by the Indian Ocean. I couldn't differentiate between these last four gales in my mind anymore. It all blended together as one massive beating.

The cold was wearing. Expedition-weight long underwear, thick wool sweater, down vest, two pairs of wool socks, fleece neckwarmer, wool stocking cap or fleece balaclava, sometimes wool stocking cap on top of fleece balaclava. If staying below, a huge purple parka with hood, plus wool gloves knit without fingertips, plus down moonboots; if on deck, foul weather gear top and bottom, seaboots, leather sailing gloves to protect my hands, and helmet, with the visor down.

In the south, I'd fired up our diesel heater several times to try to take the edge off the cabin frigidity, maybe get the temperature from 40 degrees to 50. Yet an exhaust problem limited its use.

The unit was installed in the engine area to be near its fuel source, our diesel day tank. Its heated air blew into the cabin under the chart table bench. We exhausted the heater into the keel compartment, which had two vents onto the deck. Since water could surge in and out around the keel hinge pin, the deck vents allowed the air pressure in the compartment to equalize. We thought that the vents would therefore vent the diesel heater exhaust. They didn't. Instead, the exhaust fumes came into the cabin through the holes in the bulkhead through which the keel control lines were led. The gap was tiny, ¼ inch at most around each line, yet after fifteen minutes of the heater, I could smell the diesel fumes, and had to turn it off, or risk carbon monoxide poisoning.

Ironically, a heater was a double-edged sword. If you get nice and toasty in the cabin, will you resist going on deck into the cold, wet and storm when you know you must? If cold in the cabin, the transition to the deck doesn't seem as bad. Always try to find a bright side!

Two autopilot alarms froze me with fear - if the pilots go, we're done. I re-booted the three separate systems sequentially each time: hand-steer, then dash below to re-boot the electronic compass; hand-steer, then dash below to re-boot the processor; hand-steer, then dash below to re-boot the wind and boatspeed instruments. The autopilots revived.

I crawled back through the cramped passageway to check for water in the stern compartment. We'd been hit so many thousand times in the transom by waves, that water must have gotten through the dogged escape hatch. Happily, only a bucket of water in the steering mechanism area. A lot of machined metallic corners though, glad I wore the helmet, you could get killed back there in a seaway.

Sebastien Josse had sailed his *BT* 20,000 miles in practice the summer before the start. In 4th position, he reported sailing "comfortably" in 65 knot winds with staysail and 3rd reef, when the boat was knocked over by a wave, mast under water. When it came up, there was water sloshing in the cabin, and he noticed with horror that the cabin top had broken off its epoxied foothold on the deck, exposing an open crack to every wave that came aboard. Discussions with his designers, engineers, builders and shore crew offered no reasonable plan for repair, so he had to abandon, and turned for New Zealand. Better not to face Cape Horn with that damage.

The Vendée Globe is hard enough if everything goes perfectly, but it doesn't, and not for any skipper.

Dee Caffari, aboard her new *Aviva*, reported that her brand-new laminated mainsail of Vectran fibres on a Mylar sheet, covered with Dacron for chafe, was falling apart. Vast swaths of the protective dacron taffeta had peeled off, exposing the interior load-bearing fibres, and now that interior was disintegrating. There were holes in the sail big enough to climb through. She had used up her sail repair materials, then her sealants and adhesives, and then her epoxy supply, to try to keep the laminate together.

As a teenager, I and a neighbor had fibreglassed the bottom of a 110 Class one-design boat, to keep it sealed. Our mixture of resin and hardener was slightly off, so that the applied layer stayed tacky. That mistake offered an idea now that I emailed to Dee: purposefully mis-mix the resin and hardener, so that the result would tackily hold the layers, but stay flexible and not crack. I added: "You won't want to bump up against this in your finest evening gown, but then again, that won't be a problem in the Indian Ocean."

Repairing a badly damaged mainsail like hers would be a monster effort. Ashore the sail would likely be thrown away. Perhaps the delamination could be addressed if spread out on a flat, dry floor, yet drop an Open 60 mainsail at sea, and it drops like a towel, in a heap and wet, all folded back on itself randomly. How do you even begin to make such a repair at sea? Not to mention the extra work re-hoisting the sail. Before the equator, I'd noticed that our mainsail halyard block had a quarter twist in its lashing. I lowered the mainsail to the deck, re-lashed the block straight, then re-hoisted, a thousand plus revolutions on the pedestal. Any extra work beyond the normal appalling workload of sailing an Open 60 alone was unimaginable.

Dee was in-DEE-fatiguable! Strong and beautiful, with a huge smile, in 2006, she had sailed a 70' steel cutter solo and non-stop around the world, in 164 days, westbound and upwind, becoming the first woman to do so. An important goal for her in the Vendée Globe was to become the first woman to have sailed solo non-stop around the world in both directions.

Conditions permitting, I napped more in the starboard bunk. In expedition weight long underwear (top and bottom), thick wool sweater, down vest, wool socks, stocking cap, in the 20 degree sleeping bag, after 15 minutes I would finally be warm and would fall asleep as the boat screamed along, pilot in command. I slept feet first, so that if we hit something, my feet would hit the bulkhead, not my head.

900 miles south of Australia, a breaking sea knocked the boat over, hard. Asleep, I came out of the bunk, was funneled head first through the access opening in the bulkhead, (the same opening through which I jack-knifed when I hammered my ribs, but in the opposite direction), flew six or seven feet across the cabin, and landed a one-point landing on my left eyebrow on the sandpaper-like non-skid floor. A full body weight hit, skull to solid floor. Now conscious, I picked myself up and leaned against the bench. It was 2 am and dark. *GA3* kept tearing along.

I felt the top of my head with both hands, seems OK; then both sides of my head, seems OK; then patted both sides of my face. My left hand felt damp. I turned on the cabin light - it was covered in blood. Two steps to the galley sink mirror, braced with a broad stance, I couldn't see the left side of my face for all the blood. I thought momentarily of taking a photo to send to the American media who think that sailing is such a sissy sport, but then thought that since I couldn't see out of that eye, it would be more prudent to get it cleaned up and find out what was underneath.

Blood was splattered on the floor, on my seaboots, on my blue down booties for long cold hours sitting at the chart table, on the vinyl pockets hanging on the cabin wall.

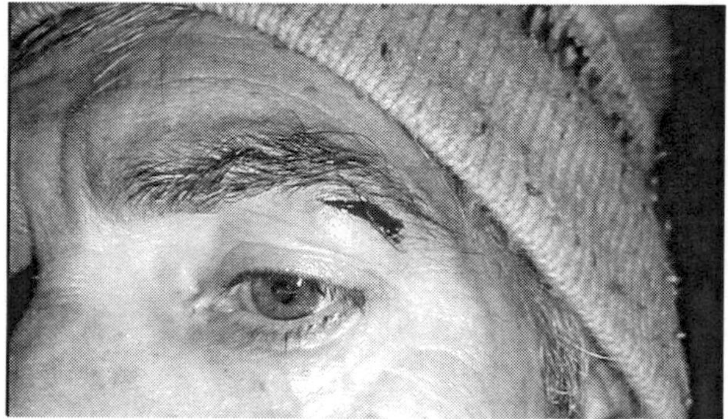

Bloody Gash

I got a new roll of paper towels, pumped a cup of fresh water, and dabbed gingerly at the blood. My head hurt. Slowly I got the excess cleaned up, but there was a gash in there somewhere that kept bleeding. I put a cold water/paper towel compress on it, and lay down on the bench, head up, to reduce the blood pressure on the wound. Unhelpfully, the gale continued, and the boat kept streaking along, crashing down the big seas at high and noisy speeds.

Over time, the compression slowed the blood flow. I called Brien, got through, and explained. I worried about infection. He said: “Facial cuts bleed like crazy, but that helps us, because it keeps the flow outbound, so it’s harder for an infection to get established. You took a real shot landing on your head. Do you have double vision? Look up, down, left, right.”

I followed his instructions, “No, seems OK. I can take a picture of this and send it in if you want.”

“Do that. You’ll have to get some tape across it eventually. That’s probably easier than staples. Since it’s under your eyebrow, it’s going to be difficult.”

“OK, I’ll keep the compress on a bit longer, then get a picture to you.”

I cut a piece of elasticized heavy-duty adhesive cloth band-aid, meticulously trimmed to fit and not overlap the hairs of my eyebrow. I lined it up, and lined it up, and lined it up in the mirror, trying to catch a steadier moment, then finally went for it and pushed it on, hoping I’d gotten enough on either side of the gash to hold it. I didn’t want to have to peel it off to try again - that would re-open the wound. Good shot, right down the middle. That's not bad, I thought. I took another photo, and emailed it both to Brien, and cc to Dr. Jean-Yves Chauve in France.

Brien called an hour later. "That looks really good! If you're looking for work after the Vendée Globe, we can always use a good pair of hands that can be meticulous under stress here in the Emergency Room!"

The next day, the next gale, our 7th in the Indian Ocean in a span of 17 days. A series of 55 knot nighttime squalls within the 18 hour long 35-45 knot gale. Will these ever end? I read in disbelief that Michel had reported 42 knots, "the most I've seen so far in the Indian Ocean", when on the longitude of New Zealand. What had our group done to King Neptune to deserve this treatment? Seven gales in the Indian Ocean. I agreed with Murray's opinion of the Indian Ocean.

These gales for our group had slowed us in the fleet. Entering the Indian Ocean 1300 miles behind the leader, we were now 2900 miles behind. Oh for the broader beam and stability of the new generation boats. And this hammering of the older boats didn't seem fair. Yet fairness has nothing to do with it. The ocean will challenge each and every one of us however it chooses. There is no complaint box. Do what the French asked – sail your best always, tell them about it, and come home – and we will all be winners.

Dusk, dark, dawn, day, dusk, dark, dawn, day, dusk, dark, dawn, day - we sailed around the clock, complete 24 hour cycles, one after another after another after another. Our original goal of 90 minute naps, to encompass a single complete sleep cycle, had fallen by the wayside in the Bay of Biscay with the rib injury pain and consequent inability to sleep. Mostly I'd gotten 30-45 minutes at a time of dozing or napping, then get up, go into the cockpit, take a good look around the horizon for ships, check the sail trim, loads, heel and keel cant, then back inside.

If the situation seemed stable, I'd try to "clusternap", a technique learned from Dr. Stampi where, if you wake from a nap, you can check things, and if you don't grind a winch or take a wave in the face to really wake you up, then you can go back to sleep, and re-gain more rapidly your previous sleep level. If you do a serious activity, if only for a minute, it will wake you further, making it harder to rejoin your sleep level as quickly.

Dozing at the chart table, the boat got hammered by a wave and knocked over. Waking, disoriented, in an awkward heap somewhere in the cabin, I thought the boat was upside down. Flashing back to our Cape Horn capsize, anxiety triggered an asthma attack, my first of the race. Chest severely tightened, I couldn't breathe. Try to calm down, breathe in, breathe out, breathe in, breathe out, my chest and lungs were seriously seized up. Where's my albuterol rescue inhaler? I found it and took two deep yet controlled puffs. Then a thought, hmmm, the inhaler was still in the vinyl pocket hanging on the wall, where it was stored, so the boat must not be upside down, or it would have fallen out of the open top. OK, that's good logic, we're still right side up. What a relief...

GA3 rushed through the dark, my asthma constriction loosening over the next few hours. I crawled forward to the bow and struggled to tie off the two roller furler drums. If a furling line broke and the sail unrolled, it would be trashed within minutes, and I wouldn't be able to get it down since the staysail and jib are lashed aloft without halyards. So to get one down, I'd have to climb the mast and cut it down. Precautions taken now could save potential disasters later. Beware A breaking leading to B breaking leading to C breaking and you then having to go aloft. Be proactive to save having to be reactive.

Just as Dr. Barnewolt had written his earlier mantra on shipboard precautions for my general health – wearing gloves and helmet - so too did Dr. Fanta in his NIE essay on asthma, describing its causes and treatments. I'd been rigorous on land about my asthma routine, and was doubly so at sea. Perhaps that rigor had saved worse trouble now.

Brian Thompson aboard *Pindar* had reported early on that he had rebuilt his alternator. Not having the tools or skill to do that, I opened the engine compartment every time I charged batteries to give the engine and alternator maximum cooling air circulation. This made an enormous racket in the cabin. That night, I charged past my usual stopping point at 70 amps, down to 50 amps, then to 25 amps, continuing charging at 10 amps, just wasting fuel. Then I kept it going for another 45 minutes. Why? It was preferable to listen to the steady, if deafening, uncovered diesel engine running five feet away, than to listen to the chaotic terrifying tumult outside.

The next day, a ship icon from the AIS blipped and disappeared on the computer screen at our position. I zoomed in on the screen, and the trail of its path was uncomfortably close to our path. I leapt into the cockpit and spent 15 minutes looking around. In a seaway, one circular scan is inadequate, as even a big ship could be lurking close behind a swell. You keep looking in each angular sector until you've seen to the horizon and can eliminate that sector. I didn't see anything.

Nevertheless, I was unnerved, because it looked as though we would have passed within a few hundred yards of the vessel, if there was one. Sometimes the receiver of the AIS will put our own transmitted AIS ID onto our own screen, a self-fake. Nonetheless, with Derek about a hundred miles back, I called to alert him. When he answered, I said "Hi Derek, it's Rich, I just had an anomalous reading on the AIS, wanted to alert you that there might be a ship in the area when you come through here."

"Have you heard?" he replied.

"No. Heard what?"

"Last night, in that last gale, we were under bare poles and got rolled upside down, the mast underwater. When we rolled back up, the two top spreaders on the port side of the mast were broken."

"Is the mast still standing?"

"Yes. I've put the extra halyards over to that side and so far the mast is stabilized. But we're done. We're heading for Tasmania."

Derek was disconsolate. He'd raised the money for his boat in many, small donations in Canada, and built the boat himself, a prodigious feat. The Vendée Globe was his Holy Grail. Years of work were finished in an instant.

A friend had sent me a packet of inspirational quotes to open when I needed them. So the next day I called Derek on the Iridium and read to him the famous "Man in the Arena" quotation from President Theodore Roosevelt, delivered appropriately at The Sorbonne in Paris in 1910:

> *It is not the critic who counts; not the man who points out how the strong man stumbles, or where the doer of deeds could have done them better.*
>
> *The credit belongs to the man who is actually in the arena, whose face is marred by dust and sweat and blood; who strives valiantly; who errs, who comes short again and again, because there is no effort without error and shortcoming; but who does actually strive to do the deeds; who knows great enthusiasms, the great devotions; who spends himself in a worthy cause;*
>
> *Who at the best knows in the end the triumph of high achievement, and who at the worst, if he fails, at least fails while daring greatly, so that his place shall never be with those cold and timid souls who neither know victory nor defeat.*

At the end I said, "Derek, you're the man in the arena. You built the boat yourself, you raised the money, you sailed well, you represented yourself, the Vendée Globe, and Canada well, you've nothing to be ashamed of, and you'll be back. I'll check in with you until you get to Hobart. Call anytime." I called him every day until he nursed the boat to Hobart. His spirits gradually rose as he began to plan for the future.

Our third group had entered the Indian Ocean as five. We left it as two, Jonny and I.

"A ship in a harbor is safe, but that is not what ships are built for."

...Unknown

Chapter 9: Halfway Home aboard *Great American III*

Halfway around the world, and half the fleet of thirty starters had been knocked out of the race, including eleven of the twenty brand-new, fully sponsored boats. Of these eleven, there were six broken masts, two broken hulls, two broken rudders and one broken keel.

GA3 and I weren't going as fast as they had been (both of us were older!), but we were still going, and whereas none of those new boats had circumnavigated even once, *GA3* was on her fourth.

It's said that in solo ocean racing, getting to the starting line is as hard as getting to the finish line. For the Vendée Globe, the concept graphs exponentially.

§

We had needed to acquire a reliable Open 60, at a fraction of the top sponsored boats' budgets, that gave a high probability of finishing, given our legally binding contracts to deliver content. Then we had to prepare and qualify her and her skipper for the race.

In fall 2005, I flew to Europe to look at four boats, mostly older generation. With the race unknown in the U.S., sponsorship was unlikely – we'd have to fund the effort privately. Sale of *GA2*, external investments, and my house, plus invested inheritance from Dad and two private donor sponsorships, together looked adequate to complete a low-budget project. We could afford a 2004 boat only with a solid sponsor, and a new boat would be out of reach cost-wise, not to mention the teething curves of a new design being too risky for our goals. A 2000 boat would not be competitive, but I'd accepted that - our goal was onshore as much as offshore.

In England, I saw a boat that had sailed the Vendée Globe and Around Alone, took a multitude of photos, then boarded the overnight ferry from Southampton to St. Malo, France. There, Myles Jessel picked me up. He had sailed as cook with my Dad on two transatlantic passages, and with us when we won the Bermuda Race. Though American, he had lived in France for thirty years as a translator, which eased the challenges of my 1960s high school French.

We drove to La Trinité Sur Mer to see Thierry Dubois' boat *Solidaire*, picking up Hugues, Flo and their son Benjamin en route. With Myles, Hugues, and me, it was a Wilson family reunion.

Solidaire was interesting. Saved by a second raft dropped by the Australian Navy plane in that 1996 Indian Ocean gale, Thierry built everything he had learned from that capsizing, re-righting, and re-capsizing episode into this boat. She was fibreglass, less stiff than carbon, thus necessitating two bulkheads running from bow to stern a meter in from each edge to give longitudinal stiffness, like an I-beam, so that the hull would not bend like a banana when the backstays were loaded. The resulting segmentation made the interior maze-like, yet gave ten watertight compartments, safer than the required five.

Her flat transom was recessed two feet into the hull, so that if the boat was right-side up, upside down, or laying on either side, that recess left a sea-level shelf that gave an overboard sailor a chance to re-board. The rope control system for her canting keel, though more arduous to do, also seemed more reliable in being less loaded than the shorter lever-armed hydraulic systems.

We sailed and got a sense of an Open 60 - big, powerful, and very physical.

We drove south to La Rochelle, to see a 1996 boat, available at a competitive price. With no canting keel, she had less righting moment and therefore less power than Thierry's boat. For comparison to modernity, we saw the 2004 boat of Swiss sailor Dominique Wavre. An inspiration at only five years younger than me, Vendée Globe 2008 would be his eighth race around the world. *Temenos* was more sophisticated in its carbon build, wider beam, internal tank ballasting systems, and electronics than the other boats, and too expensive for us without a sponsor.

In Le Havre, on the English Channel coast northwest of Paris, for the start of the Transat Jacques Vabre doublehanded race to Brazil, we met Denis Horeau, Race Director for two Vendée Globes, and likely for 2008 too. A scheduled twenty minute meeting of introduction lasted two hours as I explained our Newspaper in Education program. Denis felt that the great French races deserved more international exposure, and our sitesALIVE! NIE program intrigued him. Plus, he was pointed that the Vendée Globe is a human race, and although not decrying its growing professionalism, the story of a sole and senior American would be additive.

Returning home, I studied my photos, and began to settle on *Solidaire* as the best candidate. I talked with mentors Walter Greene and Phil Steggall about it, asking the same question as in Europe – do you think I can do this? - and getting the same soberly delivered reply: it's a big project, but you've put in the miles, and, yes, you can do it.

During the winter months I negotiated a purchase of *Solidaire* from Thierry, and went to France at the end of March 2006 to see the boat re-assembled, then to sail her home solo, so that I might imagine any changes to make for the Vendée Globe.

§

A week before arriving to stay with Hugues and Flo who lived a thirty minute commute from the boat, I'd received the terrible news that son Benjamin, at 27, had been diagnosed with leukemia. I offered to stay in a hotel. They said no, it will be good to have you and your project as a distraction. A brave young man, Benjamin began his treatments without once complaining. As Hugues maintained a fleet of charter sailboats, and Flo was a social worker for troubled youth, they were not wealthy, thus the free national health care system was essential for the expensive treatments, and would serve Benjamin well.

For the next month I watched the re-assembly of *Solidaire*. Friction surfaced on occasion. It was difficult for Thierry to have an older American come to take his baby, all the while having the audacity to think that he was going to race the Vendée Globe. Thierry had raced the 2000 race, completing the course, but not finishing officially after stopping for an alternator repair in New Zealand. In 2002, he'd finished second in the Around Alone race to Bernard Stamm. For Vendée Globe 2004, he chartered his boat to a French sailing journalist, who completed the course after repairing a broken boom in New Zealand, thus again not finishing officially. Nonetheless, three completed circumnavigations - did she have another one in her?

I saw how to bolt on the four ton keel that stood eighteen feet tall on the dock, and how the PBO rigging was lashed. Where most boats have turnbuckles to tension the standing rigging that holds the mast up, this boat had the rigging tied on to the mast and boat with 6 millimeter (1/4") diameter Vectran cord. The mast was pumped hydraulically against the rigging to 14 tons of pressure, then shims placed under the mast to keep it tight. PBO was a new synthetic fiber from Japan. Cedric Chauvaud, an oyster fisherman from Île de Groix, off Lorient, had been the first to rig sailboats with this remarkable fiber, light, strong, low stretch, yet which needed to be well sealed because it didn't like water or sunlight. While he was meticulously tying the 10 cables onto the mast, I asked him how many loops he did in each lashing. In his best broken English, he happily replied "Thirteen, for good luck!" When later rigging the cables ourselves, we always tied thirteen loops, to gain Cedric's good luck.

When a huge regatta filled La Trinité Sur Mer, we sailed the boat 30 miles north to Lorient, and tied up to the Base de Sous-Marins (submarine base) built by the German Navy and like the one in La Rochelle featured in the movie "Das Boot". Despite repeated bombings by the Allies during World War II, its massively thick concrete roof and walls had not budged. Now the long interior spaces housed mast-builders and riggers, not German submarines.

A big jolt came before departure.

The Vendée Globe is controlled by four sets of rules that fill a thick binder. The qualification rule, that a skipper must finish officially a solo transatlantic race in his or her boat, recognized that only three such races existed in the four year cycle and provided an exemption to sail a 4000 mile solo voyage instead. Two skippers from 2004, Roland Jourdain and Jean Le Cam, had done this when their new boats encountered keel problems before the last available qualifier race. They had sailed 2,000 miles upwind to Cape Race at the southeastern tip of Newfoundland and returned downwind to France. I had asked Denis Horeau if my voyage La Trinité Sur Mer to Boston, 3,000 miles upwind, could serve as my qualifier. He had said yes. A signed letter from the Harbormaster's office in La Trinité officially logged my departure for the committee.

With this qualifier completed, we could re-fit the boat in the U.S., and sail back to France in two years for the November 2008 start. The intervening time could be spent developing our sitesALIVE! program and practicing. I called Denis to confirm that the committee was receiving our tracking signal to monitor our progress. "Rich, the committee has determined that this will not count as your qualifier." No reason was given. Fatigued by the preparation, and stressed by the imminent solo voyage home, I was stunned. That one sentence rejection would force us to sail two more transatlantic passages to become an entrant in the Vendée Globe.

§

The next day I cautiously departed the dock, steered *Solidaire* through the tightly packed boats to the harbor entrance, then hoisted the mainsail to the second reef. Thierry motored alongside in an inflatable for our first mile before he gave me a big wave and turned back. I puttered along without hoisting appropriate sail, obscuring the real reason - my anxiety - with the disguising one of having to clear a rocky promontory.

Once past, I hoisted the staysail. Although the bigger jib at the bow was on a rollerfurler, this smaller jib was hooked to a stay and had to be hoisted at the mast. The autopilot steered while I worked on the foredeck. We headed west toward Belle Île, and then tacked north to sail the coast. I wondered if the small sailboat that watched us pass could sense the tension of the hopefully future Vendée Globe skipper alone aboard this big white boat.

Through the night we sailed northwest, past Lorient, past L'Ouessant at the northwest corner of France, across the east- then west-bound ship traffic in the English Channel at dawn, and continued north along the west coast of Ireland. The weather maps for this early May crossing of the North Atlantic showed a low pressure system stalled in the middle, so big that its edges touched Ireland on one side and Newfoundland on the other.

Willing to do anything to make this first passage easier, I sailed north until we could turn west and go over the top of this counterclockwise rotating storm. At 55° North, we turned to sail oddly downwind for North America. What makes the solo Transat Race so hard is that the direct race route is upwind in gales, fog and cold. Yet in this far north lane, we sailed downwind.

Five days out from La Trinité, broad-reaching at midnight with staysail and a reef in the mainsail, I studied by headlight the autopilot manual in the cockpit and adjusted settings to experiment. After an hour, I closed the book, took a good look around, no lights on the horizon, and went below to check the keel controls.

BAM...BAM...BAM..., three huge solid collisions stopped the 9-ton boat dead in the water from 12 knots. I rushed to the cockpit and could see nothing in our wake. What had we hit? What did it matter... With my headlight, I could see that one rudder was kicked up out of the water. I let out the mainsail to unload sail pressure on the boat, then sprinted forward to drop it fast into its lazyjacks. Back to the cockpit to trim the staysail flat to make it inefficient, to slow us, but also to help keep the bow blowing downwind.

The hinged, kick-up rudders were each fused by one centimeter diameter fibreglass rods, so that if they hit something sharply, the rod would break and release the rudder to spring up by pre-tensioned bungee cord, hopefully saving the rudder's blade and post. With the boat's heel, the windward rudder wasn't fully in the water, so that when we started moving again, we wouldn't have steerage and might crash-gybe, which would add to our woes.

I leapt below to cant the keel all the way to our starboard windward side, to heel the boat to windward, hopefully enough to put that windward rudder fully in the water. Heeling to windward would look odd, but here, 500 miles south of Iceland, in the dark, I was the only spectator, and I didn't care how it looked. Back to the cockpit – do we have steerage again? Yes.

Rushing back below, I grabbed a second headlight for backup, and climbed and crawled full-speed through the boat's interior, through all the compartments, looking for water coming in. We had hit hard, hard enough to be holed. All the way to the bow, listening, then gingerly opening the two sequential watertight doors forward to see if we'd broken the bow or punctured the hull. No, those two compartments were dry. Re-close and dog each door, turn around to come back and – OH NO... The forward edge of the daggerboard was sticking into the sail compartment. We'd hit so hard it had pivoted that fin so that it burst through the trunk, luckily above the waterline. I opened the side watertight compartments. They were dry. Yet I heard water sloshing somewhere.

Rush back through the boat, climbing through the bulkhead hatches, closing and dogging them behind me to seal all ten watertight compartments, into the cabin, then the cockpit. OK, we're still steering, sort of, good enough for now.

Back to the transom, look closely at that kicked up rudder. Is it intact? Can't tell. Climb over the lifelines, our safety perimeter, and onto the stern sea-level shelf, waves now sloshing over my seaboots in the dark. I hooked my harness tether through the lifelines to the mainsheet. If I fell overboard, this short leash might help re-boarding. I aimed my LED headlight at the rudder, looks ok, hmmm, oh-oh, maybe not there on the rudder post. I leaned out over the water, feeling the post with my hand. Oh-oh, splinters of carbon. I leaned further to grab the rudderblade and wiggle it. It wiggled, and it shouldn't. The rudderpost was broken.

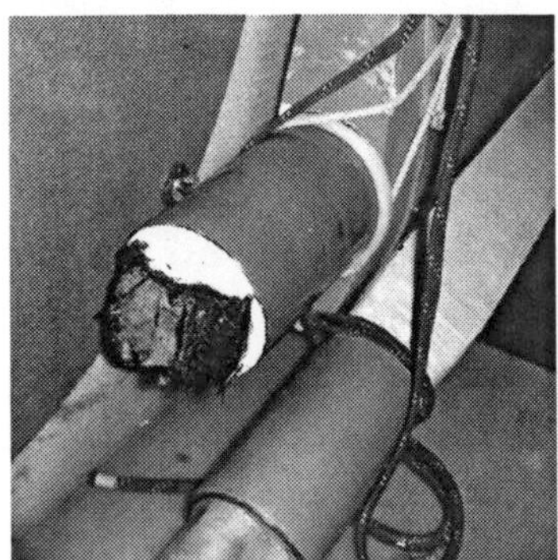

Broken Rudderpost

I had a spare rudder aboard, yet had never changed a rudder on this, or any other, boat. Well, here goes, and better get on it right now, can't wait for daylight or a nap, as there's no telling how long King Neptune will give us this reasonable weather.

I wrapped the rudderblade with a sling and strung it to the end of the main boom that I had lashed above the rudder structure as a makeshift crane. Kicking at the blade with my seabooted heel, it finally came out of the bottom roller bearing, was suspended by the boom, and saved for further study. I unbolted the hinged cassette that housed the two bearings that had held the rudder post, and hoisted it by my crane into the cockpit. Then, carefully so as not to ding it, I wrestled the spare rudder out of the stern compartment, halfway through the transom hatch, held it with one hand and managed to tie the sling around it with my other hand, without losing the rudder overboard. I hoisted it into the cockpit. After pulling the broken rudderpost out of its bearings, I lined up the new one to go into the same two roller bearings in the cassette. It wouldn't go in. I took a hammer to the cassette against the post. The hammer wasn't big enough. Then a big pipe wrench – nope. Then our huge channel lock pliers, and started whaling on it. If I couldn't get the new rudder's post into the rudder bearings, I couldn't replace the rudder. Each blow moved the mating by a millimeter. Ten hours now since the collision, almost noon, and drenched with sweat, I had the assembly together.

I hoisted it with my makeshift halyard on my makeshift crane up over the lifeline, and tried to line up the single connecting hinge bolt. The boat was moving, the waves were rocking us, the boom was moving, the suspended cassette and spare rudder were swinging, and I needed to line up a single bolt to a single bolt hole. Three hours later, I got the bolt in, reconnected the steering system linkages, and lowered our new rudder into the water.

After fourteen hours of effort, with only a 15 minute break mid-way to inhale for calories my favorite French pastry, Gateau du Pruneau de Bretagne, and to rest on the floor of the cabin, I had replaced the rudder.

Distraught, exhausted and fearful at the time, I would come to regard this episode as an important confidence-builder: I had made a major repair at sea, alone.

We continued westward. During the rudder replacement, I had made several forays forward, to try to find the source of the sloshing water sound. Finally I echo-located to the forward ballast tank that can be filled with seawater to weigh the bow down when sailing upwind. This helps reduce the horrific pounding of the flat-bottomed Open 60 when it leaps off waves. The daggerboard must have sliced back through the hull, tearing it open to the outside ocean. Good that Bernard Nivelt had designed the daggerboard trunk to go through this ballast tank, so that the hull leak was contained within the tank. The same scoop system used to fill and drain intentional ballast water could also drain unintentional leaking water. Over the next 18 hours, I gained confidence in the new rudder and we sped up to 10-12 knots. Best to get off the North Atlantic, with all deliberate speed.

Four days later, napping in the leeward bunk, the boat got knocked over to 50 degrees in a squall. Struggling upwards out of the bunk, I reached the chart table with my left fingertips and tried to do a one-armed chin-up to drag my body out of the bunk. Nearly out, the boat lurched, my fingertips slipped, and I fell backward heavily, a one-point landing on my spine on a cornered square of wood used to mount the autopilot's remote control when the skipper is in the bunk. Searing pain crumpled me to the floor.

I sailed the next four days in agony, and changed my destination to Portland. Brian Harris at Maine Yacht Center would manage the re-fit and changes, but after a summer of practice in Marblehead, that was the plan. With the broken rudder and daggerboard, we had to get to Brian now.

Despite these problems, we arrived in Portland after 13 1/2 days, my fastest passage ever across the Atlantic. In a flat calm at 4 am, and just as the navigation computer died, I tied up at the dock. Three hours later, a knock on the deck roused me, and Brian stepped aboard. I showed him straight to the daggerboard trunk, and he began a serious look. An hour later we calmed a Customs agent irate that Brian had come aboard before they had cleared the vessel into the country. I fudged, "I thought we were sinking."

My first solo passage aboard was completed. We had a hole in the boat, a broken rudder, a broken daggerboard, a cracked bow, and a month later an MRI showed that I had fractured my T-7 vertebra in my fall. Welcome to Open 60 sailing.

§

Sheared Daggerboard

We took the boat to Lyman-Morse shipyard in Thomaston, Maine. They hoisted the deep draft boat out of the water by shortening the lifting straps on their TravelLift, then dug a pit for the keel so that the hull would be closer to the ground. The remains of the sheared off daggerboard were jammed immovably in the hull. A railroad spike was driven upward by sledgehammer into the splintered daggerboard's wooden core, a tensioning come-along was lashed to the spike and chained to a back hoe, which backed up to loosen the jammed piece. The boat moved, but not that daggerboard remnant! Finally the yard cut it out of the boat by Sawzall.

Over 6 weeks the shipyard made a skilled and solid repair of the daggerboard trunk and hull, and repaired the fractured bow.

We sailed the boat gently in Marblehead that summer, not wishing to risk the rudders. Without the daggerboard, there was nothing to keep the Open 60 from slipping sideways, except the rudder, which is not engineered to take that side-load. The keel doesn't help much, since if the boat heels 30 degrees, and the keel is canted at 40 degrees, the keelfin is at 70 degrees to the vertical thus offering little lateral resistance.

Brian Harris

In the fall, we sailed back to Brian. His shipyard's dock was not deep enough to haul the Open 60. So at a nearby yard the mast was craned out, then the hull was picked up in the air, the keel was unbolted and stood on the pier, the hull was lifted higher off the keel and put back in the water, then the mast was laid and lashed lengthwise on her deck. We motored to Brian's yard where he pulled the boat out on a long trailer; the four-ton keel was delivered cross-town by flatbed truck.

Inside the shed, *Solidaire* was dis-assembled.

§

Old electronics were replaced by new. Lifelines were raised from 600 to 800 millimeters high to give more security on deck. The two 200 amp batteries were replaced by five x 100 amp units for more capacity and reliability. The 27 horsepower Yanmar diesel was shipped to the manufacturer for service. A rigging company came to measure for new PBO shrouds. Halyards came out; sails went to the sailmaker for chafe inspection. A new desalinator was fitted. A fifth solar panel and wind turbine were ordered.

Hinged Keel

An ex-U.S. Coast Guard welding inspector acoustically surveyed by oscilloscope the welds within the fabricated steel keelfin to U.S. Navy standards that permitted cracks or gaps no larger than 0.4 millimeter. He found only one. Chantier de l'Atlantique, the shipyard in France that built the keel, had built *Queen Mary II*. Clearly, they knew how to weld.

We installed the pedestal in the cockpit, linked by sub-cockpit floor tubes, to three of the five winches. Clutches engaged or disengaged the desired winch. The mainsail reef control lines were led from the mast along the deck to the cockpit so that I could reef more safely from there. For a half-day, I walked back and forth from the cockpit floor up two steps to the deck, forward to the mast, and back again, observing precisely where my foot placements would most naturally fall. We left those footprint areas as clear as possible of ropes and deck hardware to reduce the chance of tripping, slipping or falling. Ultimately, 51 control lines came to the cockpit.

Installing a roller furling system for the staysail eliminated the need for that halyard winch on the mast since that sail would now be lashed aloft permanently. We replaced the keel winch with this former halyard winch, since its model could be motorized. The keel was the only loaded item on the boat that race rules permitted to be powered by electricity. If the motor, drawing 200 amps, failed, I could still move the keel by grinding the winch manually, a valuable safety feature.

Electronics expert Mark Wylie came from England to install new autopilots, electronic compasses, computers, networks, routers, and instruments. The yard installed a new GPS, radar, desalinator, interior LED lights, battery monitor, and interconnected rotary switches so that if the 165 amp primary alternator failed, the 50 amp alternator for the engine-starting battery could charge the house bank, and vice versa.

I took a three-day required course in offshore emergency medicine, a two-day required course in survival at sea, and a two day course in diesel engine maintenance,

A late spring trauma. The rigging company's December quote had been subject to whether their cable end fittings, called thimbles, and around which they would wind individual PBO fibres, cable end to cable end, would fit in our mast's spreader tip openings. We got the word in April – they wouldn't. We would have to cut off the carbon spreader tips and build new ones - a modification of the mast to fit their cables! It was a big job, and now a rush job, with no guarantee that we would have the same structural integrity and strength as before. Couldn't they have done this calculation five months earlier?

We knew that Cedric's rigging would fit – it had before, but we thought the American company's sealing of the PBO from water and light was superior. In a panic, we sought builders who might undertake the spreader tip re-build. We also asked Cedric for a quote for his rigging.

In disbelief, I tackled the calculation myself one night, our spreader tip measurements in one hand, the rigging specification manual in the other. Five bleary-eyed hours later, I thought I had a solution. It required turning two of ten cables end-for-end, and sanding one millimeter of paint off two of four spreader tip openings.

In the morning I went through it with Brian and he concurred. I then called the company's chief engineer, who acknowledged that their non-engineer customer had solved the engineering problem for them. Expert now in their hardware, I asked if the thimbles on each individual cable, custom-wound for length and design load, would be completely filled with fibres? No, they will not be. Could they then wind 10% more fibres to each cable to add safety margin? Yes. A solo sailor's reliance on him- or herself starts on land.

Brian solicited bids from several builders for a new daggerboard, we selected one, and ordered it on March 15, accepting their proposed June 15 delivery date in time for our July 1 launch.

I met with Doyle Sailmakers and a representative from Dimension Polyant (DP) of Australia about a Vectran D4 mainsail. These DP high-tech sail panels, a layer of Mylar film with Vectran fibres laid arcing along the load lines, and sandwiched between thin layers of chafe resistant Dacron, would be laminated in Australia at 100 psi. Doyle would design the sail shape, send the design files to DP who would manufacture the panels and ship them to the U.S., where Doyle would glue them together, add the batten pockets, and finish the reef attachments.

Brian's right-hand man Will Rooks' observant eye noticed a problematic elongation of the hole that held the 1" diameter stainless steel pin for the critical headstay that holds up the mast at the bow.

Upon request, Thierry sent the bow's construction drawing. Incredibly, the 1" pin had moved under load across 64 layers of epoxied carbon cloth! Will reinforced the entire bow with carbon laminates and stainless steel bars to ensure that that hugely loaded pin would migrate no more. I noticed a delamination of the mast base structure that held the boom; Will re-built that too. And to add protection to the skipper in the cockpit, he extended the 6 inch cuddy overhang by 12 inches to provide a roof overlapping the single seats on each side forward in the cockpit.

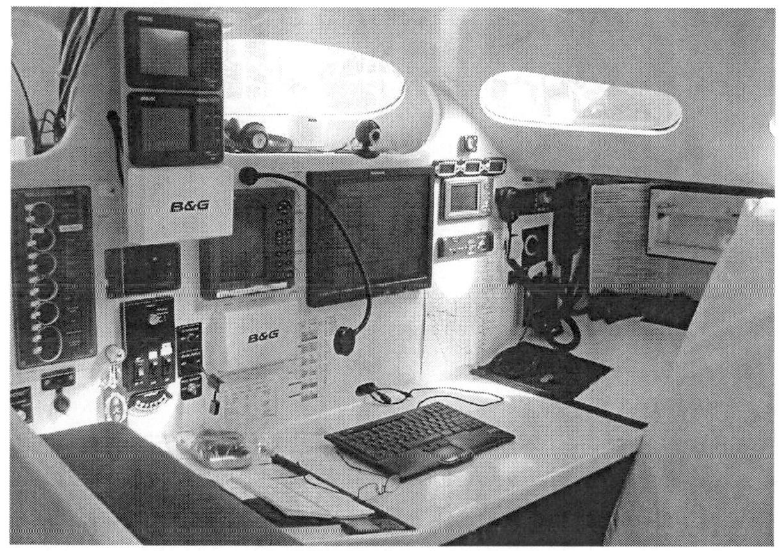

***GA3* Chart Table**

The ten-foot by eight foot cabin, that would be my living room, office, kitchen, and nap station for 100+ days at sea, was completely renovated. As I was taller than Thierry, out came the bench and chart table. Will built new ones, each 6.5' long, to accommodate my extra length for sleeping. Built in thirds, the outside sections were angled up 15 degrees, so that as the boat heeled a third of the chart table and bench would be nearly horizontal. A sink and one burner propane gimballed camping stove was installed in a new galley, with foot pumps for freshwater and seawater. The head was left unchanged: a bucket with biodegradable bags.

Will, an artist like Walter Greene, made each repair and rebuild strong and beautiful.

She'd gone into Maine Yacht Center as *Solidaire*, and eight months later, re-fit, renewed, and elegant in her new and pristine Cloud White paint, she emerged proudly as *Great American III*.

§

***GA3* 90° Test**

Dr. Stephanie Merry, an official Open 60 Measurer, flew from England to perform the harrowing 90 degree test that would certify *GA3* as an Open 60. A diver puts a sling on the keel bulb and leads it to a crane. The crane pulls the keel up, tipping the boat on its side, the mast parallel to the water. A load cell is fixed between the dock and the top of the mast, the sling is let off and the force generated by the keel and hull shape to right the boat are measured at the masthead.

Harrowing to see in person, especially since the newly lashed rigging hadn't yet been loaded, nevertheless it was reassuring to see how high the boat floated when on its side, a configuration that Open 60s take from time to time at sea, and that no water then came into the cockpit.

Subsequent calculation determined that we did, indeed, have adequate righting moment. We were a qualified Open 60.

§

As my solo passage to the U.S. had been disallowed as a qualifier, I had to race one of the two qualifiers left: a returning solo race from Brazil to France in December 2007 after the doublehanded Transat

Jacques Vabre (TJV) race, France to Brazil, in November 2007; or The Transat, UK-USA, in June 2008, a normally brutal upwind race that would be hard on the boat and skipper only 5 months before the Vendée Globe start. We selected the former and planned to sail for France in October.

I invited Mike Birch, a Canadian multihull sailor, legendary on the French shorthanded sailing circuits, to sail the return passage to France, and race the TJV to Brazil. I knew Mike through his close friendship with Walter, whose Greene Marine shipyard had maintained our trimaran *GA2* through the years. He accepted, an honor for me. We needed to sail a 500 mile qualifier for the TJV. Although the transatlantic passage to Le Havre could count, we decided to sail to Nova Scotia and back before departing for France, to have our paperwork completed early.

In September, three months after the promised delivery date, having lost an entire summer of practice, our new daggerboard had still not been delivered. I was past desperate. Twice, the builder brought the new one to Maine, twice it didn't fit in the trunk. Wanting to qualify for the TJV, Mike and I departed gingerly for Nova Scotia without it.

We proceeded cautiously, trying not to load the boat too much, yet we paid the price of the rudder alone taking that lateral load when, in the middle of the second night, hand-steering in the moonlight, the boat started turning into the wind. I pulled the tiller to turn us back – nothing. The rudderblade had broken off as feared. We turned around and limped back on our other rudder.

The American vendor who didn't deliver didn't understand consequence. The lost ten weeks of practice dramatically increased my personal risk at sea, for my upcoming qualifier and the Vendée Globe. And now we had to buy a new rudder. The builder's indifference angered me.

We needed two rudders now, a blow to the budget, to have a backup. These were re-engineered for increased strength forward and laterally. A different builder, Alfresco Composites, took on our rush order, and delivered. The daggerboard arrived again, finally to fit. We sailed for France immediately.

Mike Birch

Arriving there, Mike was fêted by the organizers, racers and press on the occasion of his 76th birthday. One of the greats of French sailing, the glamorous Florence Arthaud, who had won the 4,000 mile solo transatlantic race Route du Rhum (France to Guadeloupe) in a 60' trimaran against the top men, asked me with kind curiosity – "How did you get to sail with Mike Birch?" I explained about Mike's friendship with Walter Greene, and how Walter took care of *GA2*, our trimaran, and was a mentor to me, and how I knew Mike through Walter. She replied simply, "Walter Greene and Mike Birch, the history of multihull sailing."

Seventeen Open 60s set off for Brazil in the TJV fleet of 60 boats. We left the dock last because the adoring French crowds wouldn't let Mike through. We completed the race safely in 23 days. Mike was disappointed in our next to last place finish, yet I wasn't, as my real goal lay ahead, the solo transatlantic qualifier back to France for the Vendée Globe.

Michel, the winner, graciously came to see how it had gone for us. To my question for winter work in France after the qualifier, he helpfully offered: "Perhaps we could take the boat at my *Mer Agitée*, or my brother Hubert could take the boat at *CDK*." I had seen his personal kindness before. After the Transat 2004 from Plymouth to Boston, the skippers were invited to Marblehead for lunch. Michel, the winner then also, sailed his 60' trimaran *Geant* to the event. I invited Mom. When Michel looked for a table, he saw my 88 year old mother and immediately sat with her and introduced himself. Michel Desjoyeaux: champion and gentleman.

Hugues and Flo combined a vacation to Brazil with being in Salvador for our finish, to help prepare the boat and me for the return race. Ellen came from the U.S. over Thanksgiving to lend moral support as the stress of the re-fit, the daggerboard disaster, the two completed transatlantics, with one to go, in three months, was wearing on me. The culminating fatigue moment, which prompted no end of hilarity from Flo and Ellen, was my falling fast asleep while getting a haircut from a Brazilian beauty barber, jump-suited in one-piece, skin-tight, Lycra.

Discovering that a starboard PBO shroud had been chafed by a tubular batten in the mainsail, cutting an estimated 20% of the core fibres, I took a risk to race to France. The three-day turnaround offered no time to get a replacement from the U.S. over Thanksgiving. I took some reassurance from Mike Golding who said that he had finished the last Vendée Globe with one PBO cable chafed nearly 50% through. Nonetheless, Hugues and I lashed an unsightly sister cable of Spectra along the damaged cable, as tightly as we could from the bosun's chair. We hoped that if the damaged one broke, this backup would keep the mast from breaking. That side would be the windward, loaded side on the race back, and I would have to nurse it, the boat, and me home.

We did all three, sustaining a major December gale in the Bay of Biscay, which broke Dee Caffari's mast. When a cresting sea shocked the windward rudder, riding high out of the water, it broke the fuse and the rudder kicked up. I went to the stern shelf to push it back down against its bungee, and tap in a new fibreglass rod fuse. Kneeling on the shelf only six inches from the water, another cresting sea hammered the boat, knocking it, the boat, into my head. Dazed and wobbly, I vowed henceforth to wear my helmet on that stern shelf.

GA3 and I finished in Port la Foret, France four days before Christmas, to a reception of Hugues, Flo, and Benjamin, progressing well after a bone marrow transplant the previous summer. What a joy to see him! I flew home to have an emotional Christmas with Mom – who knew how many more she would have? And what if I were lost at sea in the Vendée Globe and never had another one with her?

Returning in January to haul the boat at Hubert's yard, I realized that we, the American team, were in exactly the right place, as Port la Foret was headquarters for not only Michel, but also Vincent Riou and Jean Le Cam, winner and runner-up in Vendée Globe 2004. Like flies on the wall, we'd watch, listen and learn from these, the greatest solo ocean racers in the world.

Hubert and I agreed on a set of repairs and changes. *GA3* was hauled and the mast and rigging disassembled. We had the chafed PBO cable, plus its undamaged twin, pulled to destruction in the rigging manufacturer's test facility. The damaged cable broke at a higher load than the undamaged cable! Strong and odd stuff this PBO! I flew home to Boston to continue developing our sitesALIVE! program and to train hard for the main event ten months away.

Hugues Riousse **Rick Williams**

When I returned to France on July 1, Marblehead friend Rick Williams came to help. Hugues took a six-month leave of absence from his job to be chief *preparateur*. Flo found us a rental house in Port la Foret.

Hubert had completed our job list. The boat had been moved out of the shed to the keel pit, where the keel had been attached, and *GA3* was ready to be launched. Yet our new set of PBO rigging had not been shipped from the U.S. for its July 1 delivery date in France. Daily calls to the rigging company in the U.S. resulted in: "We're working on it."

Brian, who knew *GA3* better than anyone, had scheduled a visit in late July to check her when she'd be launched, rigged, and sailing. With the boat still sitting on the pier, he postponed. Given his shipyard and family duties, he could not re-schedule, so this delayed equipment delivery cost us his confidence-building review. Practice time was lost again; risk was added again.

The rigging arrived in late July, we lashed the cables with Cedric's thirteen loops, launched the boat, then stepped the mast. Michel's new *Foncia* waited patiently to be hauled out into our spot. Even in this instance, where we Americans were in the way, nothing was ever said. Always, we were welcomed into this port, this community, and this race.

§

We made many friends in Port la Foret: the harbormaster, the *boulangerie*, the marine supply stores, the welder, the sailmaker, the ice cream store owner with a twinkle in his eye.

We'd work all day on the boat. In the evening, I'd call newspapers in the U.S. and around the world to urge them into our sitesALIVE! program. Our house rental requirement for Internet connectivity was semi-filled – by broadband in the garden shed!

Twice weekly, I would get out Marti's gear, tackle a hard workout, and email her the results. I ran sets up a steep quarter mile hill for my quads and lungs. I began to lose weight with the stress of the boat's preparation, sitesALIVE! program development, and impending Vendée Globe. As my numbers were holding up, she concluded that I was not yet losing strength.

I returned to the U.S. in September for a last visit with Mom before the race. Two years before she had been diagnosed with a slow Alzheimer's. She had excellent care at a retirement community, yet I was haunted by the thought that I really shouldn't be doing this, that I'd be away from her in this important time of her life. Friends suggested that she, the original adventurer, would not want me to not sail the Vendée Globe because of her. Intellectually, I understood; emotionally, it didn't curtail my distress.

Returning to France on a six-month round-trip ticket, Hugues and I prepared to sail overnight to Les Sables d'Olonne. The fleet was required to be there three weeks before the start; we went a week early to get settled before the fleet and public arrived. The night before our departure, ten Open 60s assembled in Port la Foret for a final three-day practice session, that would be videotaped, with briefings, de-briefings, and maneuvers critiqued and coached. I marvelled at this. In the U.S., ocean racers rarely practiced for Newport-Bermuda, Marblehead-Halifax, or the TransPac(ific). The French practiced.

Every flight to France had included duffel bags of food which were now organized, then sealed into 17 weekly garbage bags. Ellen's home-baked granola on my Mother's recipe for breakfast, Bumblebee foil-packed tuna, salmon, or chicken with pita bread for lunch, freeze-dried meals for two for dinner, and a midnight pasta meal with instant oatmeal and raisin appetizer, formed our core four daily full meals every six hours. Dried fruit, cashews, granola bars and a daily sleeve of Fig Newtons (825 calories) provided snacks. Gatorade, powdered Ensure and Nestlé's Nido Whole Milk, plus canned liquid juice concentrate provided hydration and calories. Deemed too disruptive of sleep, no chocolate, coffee or tea came aboard.

Hugues and I sailed overnight for Les Sables d'Olonne, arriving before dawn within the two hour window either side of high tide needed to get into the narrow channel. Motoring carefully in the dark, Hugues shouted to a man walking his dog on the quai: *"S'il vous plaîtes, monsieur, ou est le ponton pour le Vendée Globe?"* We followed his answer, wrapped around a corner, found the pontoon and tied up.

§

With the skilled, experienced, imaginative and relentless help from a myriad of people, *GA3* had made it to the starting line. This voluminous wealth of effort and knowledge from so many, combined with Bernard Nivelt's design and Thierry's original strong construction, would be what would get us around the world. I would guide, sail, and occasionally repair *GA3*, but fundamentally she would have to defend both me and herself on the open oceans of the world.

Halfway home, the decimation of the fleet amply demonstrated that fact.

"Alone, alone, all, all alone, alone on a wide, wide sea,
And never a saint took pity on this soul in agony..."
...Rime of the Ancient Mariner, Samuel Taylor Coleridge

Chapter 10: Alone in the Pacific

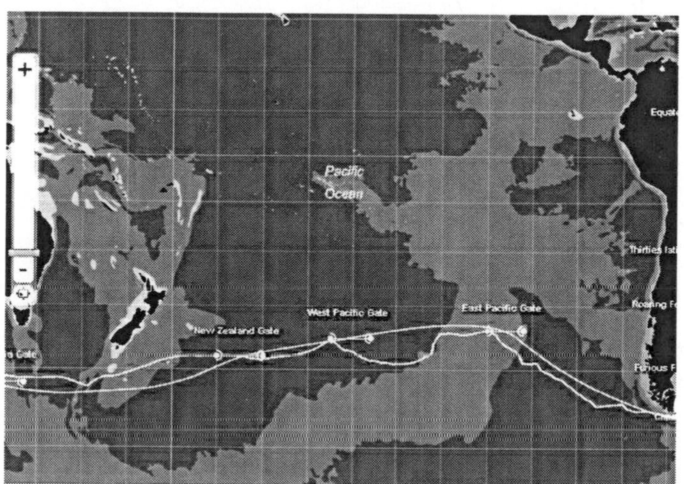

What a place to be on New Year's Eve! 51° 17' South, 145° 03' East, 450 miles south of the tip of Tasmania, 750 miles south of the Australian mainland, 900 miles north of Antarctica, making 11 knots eastward, jib and two reefs in the main, and an astonished "SMOOTH SEAS!" written all-caps in thc logbook. Make those easy miles that Walter Greene told me to make.

A New Year, a new ocean, but also the anniversary of Dad's dcath 23 years ago. His detailed mind showed me how to prepare a boat, and it was paying off. Fourteen of thirty boats abandoned, we're still racing, I think that he would have liked this project with the live school program. I called Mom to wish her Happy New Year and we reminisced at length.

Murray later called from New Zealand with New Year's greetings. He'd voluntarily written extra essays for sitesALIVE! and our young students. Flying to Singapore in ten days to command again the *M/V Cape York*, he would be out of touch until settled aboard. Our sitesALIVE! students would then be connected to a ship captain, captaining his ship at sea!

On New Year's Day, with the East Australian Ice Gate in our wake, we pushed east toward the longitude of New Zealand. The Indian Ocean had reduced the lead pack from 10 over a hundred miles to 2 over 75 miles, and 5 over 700 miles; the disparate second group was intact; our third group of five was now two, Jonny and I. Trailing us was the fourth group pairing of Raphaël Dinelli and Norbert Sedlacek.

Talking daily, Jonny and I had struck a wonderful Iridium friendship. It helped us both to know that another was being pummeled by Mother Nature and King Neptune, not that I wished it upon him, nor he upon me, but we both had a comrade similarly suffering and struggling nearby, day by day, hour by hour, in the endless Vendée Globe.

A skipper telephoning another skipper would call at mid-day, to lessen the chance of waking the other. One night, 2:30 am, the Iridium rang. I was resting in the leeward bunk with *GA3* tearing along at a 30 degree heel. Fearing bad news from home, for someone to call in the night, I scrambled upward through the cabin and lunged across the chart table to grab the phone before it stopped ringing: "*Great American III*".

"Have you seen the latest weathermap? We're going to get hammered again." It was Jonny, our friendship marvelously confirmed by his feeling free to call in the middle of the night.

What a race! Across the Indian Ocean, I was desperately trying to catch Jonny, closing often to 75 miles, and he was trying to bury us in his wake, pulling then away to 150 miles. But that was the race. We competitors were also new friends, and most importantly fellow mariners, where mutual safety was paramount. What sportsmanship in this race and these sailors! This was how all sports should be.

And one began to think other sports comically easy in physical endurance and mental persistence. Could Michael Schumacher stop his Ferrari and repair it by himself on turn 3? With only the tools he had brought from the start? Then rejoin the race? And be competitive? Could the New England Patriots, whose three hour pro football games consist of 10 minutes of actual action, play for 21 hours straight as Michel Desjoyeaux had hand-steered, sail-changed and sail-trimmed, during one 24 hour stretch in the South Atlantic when catching the lead pack? And then do it again the next day? And the next? And the next? Could Ronaldo play the entire World Cup schedule back-to-back, right through the night? The Vendée Globe fleet had done that before exiting the Bay of Biscay! Even the Boston Marathon, that I had run four times, and had once considered the pinnacle of endurance, now seemed a simple afternoon jog.

South of New Zealand, startling news from Jonny: he was considering abandoning. His mainsail was delaminating, falling apart before his eyes, just like Dee's. He didn't know if the remaining skeleton would last until France. Without solar panels or a wind turbine for backup, he wasn't sure that he had enough fuel to generate electricity for his autopilots, desalinator, navigation, lights and communications at his likely reduced speed to the finish.

Cold, Tired, Bandaged

I tried to talk him out of it, altruistically for him, and selfishly for me. "Jonny, we've got 5,000 miles to Cape Horn, we'll be 21 days. If we get there OK, we'll be close aboard the coast of South America, and you can drop out anytime, but maybe you can nurse the boat home and finish." Through the gales and destruction of the south, the fleet chatter had changed. Four boats out in the Bay of Biscay, two out in the South Atlantic, eight abandoning in the Indian Ocean. Only a handful of boats could now win; the goal for all was to finish.

For myself, I was alarmed. If Jonny dropped out, I would be alone crossing the huge Pacific in the deep south. The nearest three boats were Steve White, 900 miles ahead, and Raphaël and Norbert, a thousand miles behind. In the Pacific, no islands lay halfway across, like the Kerguelens in the Indian Ocean. Only one ship weekly sails from Australia/New Zealand around Cape Horn since shipping to Europe normally transits the Panama Canal. If what happened to Yann happened to me in the middle of the Pacific, it would be a week before a Navy ship could get there from New Zealand or perhaps Chile, not two days, as it had been with him.

Jonny and I endured another gale. Then, heading deeper south on starboard gybe favored by wind direction, another 40 knot squall with another hailstorm decided it for me - I'd had enough of the south. I gybed *GA3* northeast, early, tactically speaking, for the next ice gate which lay to the east of the South Island of New Zealand. I was tired; I was cold; I was very alone and very apprehensive. If Jonny dropped out, the nearest human being on Planet Earth would be nearly a thousand miles away, not counting the astronauts in the International Space Station, two hundred miles up.

Gybing early aimed us close to the four Auckland Islands, 250 miles south of the South Island of New Zealand. I studied going north or south of them, then squeezed to the south. Into the evening, a haunting dark against dark silhouette appeared ten miles away, Adams Island - Land Ho! The first land seen since the Canaries, 48 days ago. I zoomed on the electronic chart. Albatross icons dotted the south coast - the island must be a rookery. I zoomed further and scrolled northward - Coleridge Bay! So, did Samuel Taylor Coleridge visit Adams Island and then write the Rime of the Ancient Mariner? Or did a voyager who had read the poem name the bay after the poet? When *Radio Vacances* called that day for a live interview, I posed that question, then spontaneously recited the first four stanzas, memorized long ago:

It is an ancient Mariner,
Who stoppeth one of three.
`By thy long grey beard and glittering eye,
Now wherefore stopp'st thou me?

The bridegroom's doors are opened wide,
And I am next of kin;
The guests are met, the feast is set,
Mayst hear the merry din.'

He holds him with his skinny hand,
"There was a ship," quoth he.
`Hold off! unhand me, grey-beard loon!'
Eftsoons his hand dropped he.

He holds him with his glittering eye,
The Wedding-Guest stood still,
And listens like a three years' child,
The Mariner hath his will.

The substitute radio host was lost - this was supposed to be a sailboat race, not English class! Too bad Andi was off that day – he would have LOVED it!

The Vendée Globe includes everything, even poetry. And here near New Zealand had occurred one of the epic, Homeric, Vendée Globe efforts which helped to create its legend.

§

Yves Parlier

In the lead pack in 2000, Yves Parlier had broken his mast in the Indian Ocean. Somehow retrieving the two long, heavy, awkward broken mast pieces hanging over the side, he set a small jury rig, sailed to Stewart Island south of New Zealand, and anchored. He sawed shorter the two pieces, and filed and fitted the ends to mate exactly. He epoxied an internal connecting tube insert and an external sleeve, both of carbon, to make a 58' mast out of his 86' mast. During the days of the repair, a gale blew the boat to drag her anchor until she washed ashore on the beach; he got a second anchor out and pulled the boat back to floating vertically. Knowing this ten day effort would leave him short of food, he scrounged in the seaweed ashore for mussels to supplement his nutrition now. He re-cut rigging, then, astonishingly, re-stepped his mast by himself at anchor! Re-cutting his sails, he departed, sailed across the Pacific, rounded Cape Horn, then sailed the Atlantic to France to finish the race officially.

I'd briefly met the modest, soft-spoken Parlier after the Transat 2004. So when I saw him on the dock in Les Sables d'Olonne I invited him aboard *GA3*. A French rigger amidships, clearly awed, began to back away across the boat when Yves and his daughter climbed over the lifeline. We chatted, I showed him the cockpit and cabin, where he suggested rigging a net to catch me if we got knocked over, then they left. I exclaimed to the rigger how amazing that was, to have Yves Parlier come aboard. He replied "Yes, we call him E.T., the Extra-Terrestrial!"

To live up to Yves Parlier, to live up to Pete Goss, to live up to Desjoyeaux, MacArthur, Riou and Le Cam, to honor the race and its legends, that was what every skipper strove to do.

§

Later that day, Jonny called with his decision to abandon. He would sail for New Zealand. From there, *Artemis* would be shipped home to England. He wanted me to know right away, and asked me to keep the news private until his sponsor had issued a press release. I said of course, and that I was really going to miss our Iridium chats and chasing him across the oceans of the world. He gave me his land mobile number, said "call anytime", and meant it.

Hanging up, I slumped, back against the bulkhead, the full weight of Jonny's decision sinking in. Norbert and Raphaël were sailing within a hundred miles of each other, Steve White was isolated up ahead, but not with as much a margin in front of him as mine. Yann had been 800 miles south, a two day run from Perth's Naval Base. In 1996, Tony Bullimore had been rescued after four days inside his boat at a position 1200 miles south of Perth. In the middle of the Pacific, we would be 2500 miles from land, beyond the range of patrol aircraft to drop liferafts if need be, and a week at least for a ship to reach the position. To competitors, we would have a thousand mile gap. *GA3* and I would be truly alone.

It took no time at all for this to sink in as I'd known about the Pacific's hole of coverage for three years, except the current gap to competitors on either side, which could not have been foreseen. Nonetheless, we were faced with yet another "OK. Here we go!" Vendée Globe moment.

I was physically and mentally spent from the seven gales in the Indian Ocean. My ear hurt from being hurled against the bulkhead from the bunk. My eye and head hurt from the big gash under my left eyebrow. The constant cold was debilitating. The erratic wind instruments forced substantive use of the alternate compass steering for the autopilots, drastically increasing the risk of a potentially catastrophic accidental gybe. 5,000 miles to Cape Horn. Without Jonny's presence lending Dr. Chauve's "emotional support". Alone. So, here we go.

Remembering Michel's blog from the South Atlantic, "If you're too cautious, you lose confidence", I determined to push hard into the Pacific. The gales of the Indian Ocean had put us on defense; in the Pacific, we would go on offense. Hopefully, the extra adrenaline would get us across faster and safer, and soften my fears. We carried more sail deeper into squalls, canted the keel a few degrees more for more power. I mentally overrode my natural, internal safety margins. We would sail hard for Cape Horn, three weeks away.

Past New Zealand, I called Murray, explained the situation, and asked him if we could chat every other day until he departed, for company and confidence. "Of course!"

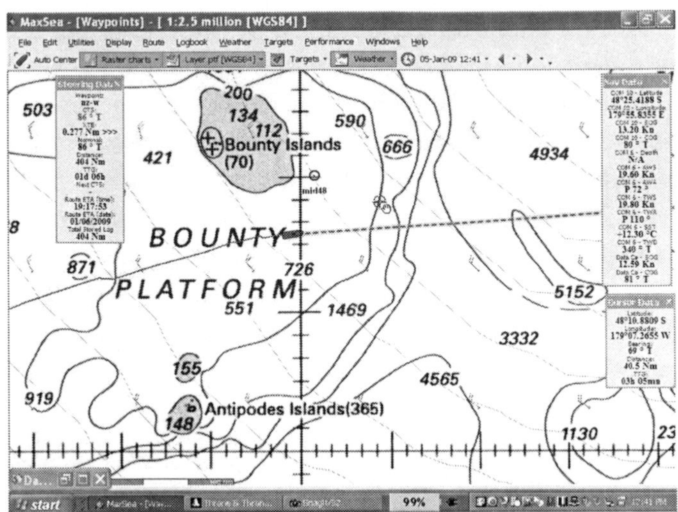

Captain Bligh's Neighborhood

A huge moment, January 5, crossing the International Date Line. I videotaped the E turning to W on the GPS. We had counted up in East longitude degrees to 180, and now would count down in West longitude degrees to the finish. The Bounty Islands, discovered by Captain Bligh, lay to port; the Antipodes, globally opposite in latitude and longitude to the Greenwich Observatory, the spiritual and cartographic center of global navigation, lay to starboard.

Neal sent Marti's NIE essay entitled "Overcoming Physical Limitations." We'd scheduled her for halftime in the race. She wrote about my persistence in enduring the excruciating pain of the broken ribs early on and about our rigorous training as preparation. And as I'd gained confidence from Michel's encouragement, I gained similarly from Marti, and needed to continue pushing hard to live up to her kind words and her example as an athlete. I also knew that her skill in training me had a huge amount to do with the fact that we were still in the race after the physical beating of the first eight weeks. Without Marti, as without Brian or Brien or Hugues or Rick or Mark or Jean-Yves or Michel or Hubert or Ellen or Mom or Clarke or Bob or Michael, or a long litany of others' best efforts, we may have fallen by the wayside long ago.

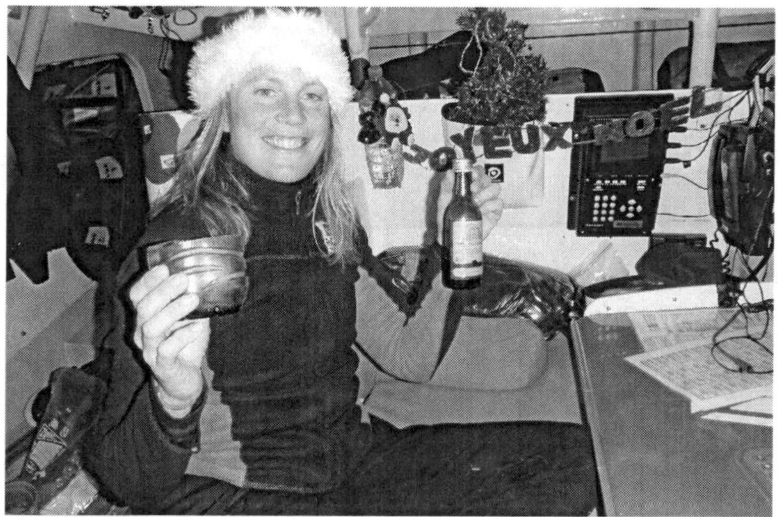

Samantha Celebrates Christmas at Sea

Two days later an email arrived from Samantha Davies, far ahead near the front of the second group. Samantha was a force of nature, always upbeat, loving the gales, truly happy at sea. She had done it all right. An Englishwoman, with a university degree in mechanical engineering, she had moved to France, learned French, had a French boyfriend, and trained with the organized French Open 60 skippers. She was sailing a mesmerizing race with her *Roxy*, a boat of legend which, although the same generation as *GA3*, had won both the 2000 Vendée Globe with Michel Desjoyeaux and 2004 Vendée Globe with Vincent Riou. She was sailing impeccably and doing exactly what the French public had asked, to tell them at home on land what life was like at sea. She posted a multitude of photos and videos, all with a delighted narrative.

We had arrived in Les Sables d'Olonne a week before required, to get the lay of the land before the fleet and crowds showed up. Tied up to the Vendée Globe dock was a beautiful wooden schooner, *Ninita*, a replica of the famous *Nina*, winner of the 1962 Bermuda Race. A couple was aboard, my age, and each day, walking to *GA3*, Hugues and I would say hello, and they'd say hello back. One day, I asked if they'd like to see *GA3*, figuring that it was interesting for cruising sailors to see an Open 60. They said yes, thank you, and came aboard the next day. I showed them how we'd led the mainsail controls to the cockpit, to reef from there, "Oh, yes, good idea." And then how we'd installed the pedestal to drive 3 of the 5 cockpit winches, "Oh, yes, that will help I imagine." And then in the cabin, satellite telephones, computers, instruments, "Oh, my", then into the engine compartment to show the keel winch leading to our 10:1 rope purchase controlling the keel's angle. "Oh, Sam has hydraulic!" "Sam? Sam Davies?" I said bewildered. "Yes, she's our daughter!" So that's where Samantha's modesty came from!

Samantha's email read:

Hi Rich,
I see you've lost your last running mate from your group. It won't be much fun to sail the Pacific alone, so I'll be your 'virtual running mate' and check in with you every couple of days.
Bises,
Sam

A wave of emotion. What a wondrous thing to have a competitor looking out for you like that, a satcom version of 'going to the aid of a mariner in distress.' An astute observation by this young and skilled skipper, now friend, and better yet, she acted on her observation. She did check in every couple of days as I made my way across the Pacific, and it helped me enormously.

Coincidentally timed to Samantha's email, and similarly astute was Laura Mirabella's NIE essay describing "Women in the Maritime Industry". Herself a SUNY Maritime College graduate and tanker broker, she acknowledged the challenges of being the lone woman working within an all-male industry, yet also described the fascination of a job in the original global business – shipping. Dee, Samantha, Marti, Laura, our two Davas and Lorraine, my Mom, Ellen, Flo – our Vendée Globe and sitesALIVE! project was graced with amazing women.

We pressed for the New Zealand Ice Gate, respected that mark by being north momentarily, emailed a photo of the GPS to the Race Office, then aimed at the West Pacific ice gate, a week's sail away. With the different ice gate locations for this 2008 race versus the 2004 edition, our official distance would be 24,840 nautical miles versus the previous 23,680. We get an extra 1160 miles, or 4-5 days. Glad I brought plenty of food.

The destruction of the lead pack continued.

Jean-Pierre Dick, having repaired his starboard rudder two weeks earlier after a collision, now hit something else, with his port rudder this time. He rushed to the stern just in time to see the whole structure break off his transom and sink before his eyes. Stunned, he abandoned and headed north toward the Polynesian Islands.

Then news that made everyone hold their collective breath - again.

§

No Bulb on Keel of *VM Matériaux*

Jean Le Cam, runner-up in the 2004 Vendée Globe, was in trouble off Cape Horn. He'd been in third place sailing his 2004 vintage *VM Matériaux* with his customary magic. Talking on the Iridium with Vincent Riou aboard *PRB*, in 4th place behind him, Jean commented to Vincent that something seemed suddenly strange with the boat. He then called his shore crew, who heard a partial report, then the satcom connection went dead. An underwater collision at high speed had torn the bulb to dangle from *VM Matériaux*'s keelfin. When the bulb then broke off, she immediately capsized.

Remembering our own Cape Horn capsize, Jean's struck me hard. He had also prepared in Port la Foret, but we had not communicated much, partly because I was in awe of him, partly because he and his team spoke less English than the others, and my French was inadequate. Yet after a September Vendée Globe press conference in Paris, where each skipper spoke briefly to the 500 journalists assembled, and I'd described our school program, I saw Jean on the dock looking at Sebastien Josse's new *BT*, and he came over to me and worked his best English: "I...like...your...school...program." Cloud nine for me.

In that day's ship's journal for sitesALIVE!, I wrote my last paragraph in French out of respect, and finished with *"Je pense de Jean"*. I alone in the fleet had been similarly capsized off Cape Horn and though his weather was currently moderate, it could change in a heartbeat.

The global COSPAS/SARSAT Search & Rescue system relayed Jean's EPIRB distress signal to the Race Office. The signal showed that Jean was inside and alive, but no one knew if injured. A coastal tanker, alerted, altered course to stand by in moderate conditions. Vincent, trailing, closed on Jean's position, arriving 10 hours later. Armel Le Cléac'h, in 5th place aboard *Brit Air*, arrived next. Vincent and Armel took turns circling Jean, one hour on, one hour off. Several hours later, Jean emerged from the transom escape hatch, designed to be above water whether the boat is right side up, or upside down, in his survival suit with a length of line. He tied himself on the slippery bottom between his two rudders.

Vincent sailed past close aboard and heaved a line to his childhood friend. He missed. He arduously circled - and the immense effort of maneuvering with a tack and a gybe an Open 60 alone at sea must be appreciated - approached again, threw, and missed again. He circled, sailing closer, threw the line and missed again. The fourth time, Vincent, desperate for his friend, sailed desperately close, threw the line, got it to Jean who quickly and awkwardly in the survival suit tied a bowline around himself under his arms. He then jumped into the water 200 miles off Cape Horn, and Vincent winched him across to his boat and aboard.

Hugging in the cockpit, they then noticed that Vincent's deck spreader, a carbon tube extending outboard from the deck's edge, which holds the stays that hold up the mast, had struck the keelfin of Jean's overturned boat in the close, successful pass, and had cracked. Vincent's mast was sagging 30 degrees to the other side. Together, they hustled to stabilize it with halyards, and proceeded slowly toward a Chilean port. The next day, in a seaway, Vincent's mast fell into the sea, and he was out of the race.

The International Jury correctly decided to award Vincent Riou a 3rd place equivalent finish, the position he had been in, when he rescued Jean Le Cam. Vincent Riou, defending champion from Vendée Globe 2004, had sacrificed his own race to save his friend.

§

Five days of hard sailing later, *GA3* approached the West Pacific Ice Gate. I had been warily watching a depression far to the north, Tropical Storm Heta. The fact that it was named demanded attention as it moved east to west, south of the equator. Forecasts indicated that the storm, two thousand miles to our north, would slowly dissipate as it turned southwest into colder waters. Yet although losing intensity, Heta retained her circular organization, and I thought she might re-energize.

A Moonlit Night at Sea

En route, on a beautiful night with the moon rising and casting a moon river of light across the swells of the Pacific Ocean, I remembered Jean-Philippe Guillemot, Michel's right hand man, on the dock in Les Sables d'Olonne the day before the start. Perhaps the most technically savvy person on the dock, one might have expected him to inquire about our instruments, rigging tension, sails or my satisfaction with autopilot settings, but no, he implored me otherwise: "Rich, you will be at sea, we will be stuck on land, you must tell us what it's like at sea! You must tell us of the birds and the stars and the gales in the south. YOU MUST TELL US THESE THINGS!" So I videotaped the scene and narrated, in my best effort French:

> *Bonsoir à tous, de l'autre côté du monde de Great American III. Les étoiles brillent, la lune est pleine. C'est une nuit belle pour la navigation. C'est incroyable. J'espére que tous de vous étaient ici avec moi pour voir cette nuit. C'est incroyable.*

Posted to our and the Vendée Globe websites, a flood of emails came in via Neal, mostly from the French, thanking me for the beautiful view from the other side of the world. The moment of beauty and peace had been captured and delivered from far away.

§

I mused back on the human and romantic French, and their warm welcome of me, our team, and *GA3*.

In Port la Foret, when people would come to the dock to look at the boat, I would engage them if they didn't engage me first. I would speak my poor French slowly – I couldn't speak quickly! Though appreciative, after a few minutes, they would get frustrated by the slow dialogue, and would start speaking English, to help me. Nearly always, their English was better than my French. I learned to say *"Non, monsieur, s'il vous plaîtes, c'est nécessaire pour moi à parler en Français, pour l'exercice!"* They would understand and try to help, correcting my grammar and teaching me new words.

I invited many to come aboard, stand in the cockpit, walk the deck, and come below to see our cabin. *"Vraiment?"* "Really?" They were astonished. Understandably, the top professional sailors didn't invite folks aboard randomly. After all, Michael Schumacher doesn't invite just anybody to sit in his Ferrari. Yet our pressures and purposes were different, so we invited anybody we wanted. I and they enjoyed this immensely. The friendship between the French and the lone American team grew.

Ellen had taken a vacation week to come in mid-August, gallantly lugging more duffel bags of food through Charles de Gaulle airport. Her superior skills in French made her a hit with our dock visitors.

One Friday night in late August, a power outage at our rental house rendered the electronic locks inoperable. Rick had returned to the U.S. after the bulk of the preparation was done, Hugues to his home in Vannes two hours away for the weekend, so I returned to the boat to sleep aboard. I saw an older man on the dock whom we had seen often, but never talked to, as he'd been shy, always standing a hundred feet away to watch us work. I asked him how to find a telephone number for our landlady. He said he would try to help. He drove home thirty minutes, looked her up in his phonebook, then called me with her number. I connected with her, the problem was sorted, and I went home. Jean-Jacques Le Goff, a friendly, bright, slight man, became a regular now alongside *GA3*, and we'd chat while we worked.

Another day, an elderly pensioner in worn clothes appeared on the dock. Speaking a mile-a-minute in French, I couldn't understand him. "*Je m'excuse monsieur, je ne comprends pas. Plus lentement, s'il vous plaîtes.*" He presented his papers to show me who he was, still talking rapidly, then reached into his pocket and pulled out a fistful of coins, and thrust them through the lifelines to me. At first I didn't understand, then slowly realized that he wanted to help us in whatever way he could toward our dream of the Vendée Globe.

When we moved *GA3* to Les Sables d'Olonne for the start, the welcome and encouragement had continued.

We settled into a new rental house and rented a car. Rick returned with three weeks to go. A local commercial diver inspected the bottom and offered to teach me to use our required emergency scuba tank in our rental condo's pool!

Despite my affection for the French, I was unaccustomed to their rich food or late dinner hours. Concerned about my weight loss, I tried a restaurant called Buffalo Grill, a French chain despite the name. At an early 6 pm, I could order a Pony Express: hamburger (no bun), baked potato (no sour cream or butter), salad (no dressing), glass of milk, mini creme-brulee and a sugar cookie. *C'est parfait!* I returned every night for the three weeks before the start, stabilizing my nutrition and weight. Moreover, befriending every waiter, waitress, and manager, I became Buffalo Grill's *de facto* Vendée Globe skipper.

Other friends had arrived for the start who spoke enough French to help solidify the *GA3*/French bond: Col. Griffen had been stationed at the U.S. Embassy in Paris early in his Marine Corps career; my sisters Eleanor, Anne and Sarah; and Paul Tamburello, a teacher who would end his daily fourth grade class with a Churchillian exhortation of "remember kids, it's a big world out there, it's not who you are on the outside that matters, but who you are on the inside, be brave, be strong, *corraggio*, have courage, see you tomorrow."; and Ellen, whose French and warmth had befriended vendors, race managers, competitors and the press.

And those of our group who didn't speak the language were so friendly, excited and obviously happy to be there, as to invite English from the famously pro-French-language French! Bob Metcalfe had come with his and our friend John Sculley, former Apple CEO; Trip Lowell, my initial colleague in our original NIE and Prodigy partnerships came with George Gibson, my closest friend since the ninth grade, their quiet, steady, "always there when you need them" support showing once again; Bob's father-in-law Bob Shotwell came, and Scott Hamilton, our Expert from Everest.

An email arrived from Frenchman Jacques Adlée of the American Battle Monuments Commission, a U.S. Government entity that maintains the cemeteries in France of our fallen soldiers from the two World Wars. Tears welled as Col. Griffen read to our group Jacques' description of our fallen soldiers who had lost two lives: the one they had been living; and the one they would have lived. Would *Great American III* carry around the world an American flag with which they decorate their cemeteries on Memorial Day? We'd be honored.

Fabienne Mollé came from our American Embassy in Paris. I had called their Cultural Affairs office to ensure that they knew that an

American was entered in this big French sports event, and to urge them to use my participation however they wished to promote good relations between our countries. Fabienne was happy to be there with the lone American team.

How could I thank the French publicly for their friendship and encouragement? Invite my cousin Rick Simpson, an accomplished opera singer, to sing *"La Marseillaise"* from the cabintop of *Great American III.* A thousand people on the dock sang and cried during his three marvelous performances that prompted a French newspaper headline: "*Rich Wilson Aime la France!*"

The Buffalo Grill set a table for thirty for our final dinner. Then photos and autographs with patrons and staff. After my usual Pony Express and speeches, including a Paul Tamburello variation for me on his Churchillian theme, and Bob Shotwell's presentation to me of his late beloved wife's Leatherman tool, the time came for a last sleep on a steady bed. As I rose to go, our table, then the wider room of French patrons, stood and applauded soberly. They knew what I knew: that tomorrow, the great oceans of the world awaited. And they wished me well.

§

A critical repair loomed. Our central "utility" winch, essential with 25 lines leading to it, was losing its low gear. If lost, I wouldn't be able to hoist to the full mainsail, or tighten the various reefs those last few inches, or give myself a fatigue break from 2nd gear when needed in the appalling physicality of sailing this monster day in, day out.

Another difference between the old boats and new. The new had carbon winches, with big drums, fewer moving parts inside, and recent engineering. Our winches had 100,000 ocean miles on them, and through that wear and tear, gradually had lost smoothness and added friction. For the same sail maneuver, I would have to work harder. This was known and accepted, and forced an envying wishful thinking.

A scary task. Once I took that winch apart, I couldn't reef the mainsail, rollerfurl a jib, adjust the daggerboard, or move the traveller. On a wind stable morning, I went at it. Take off the drum, a big plastic tray to hold the gears, springs, washers and pawls, try mightily to remember the sequence of parts, toothbrush with diesel fuel every bearing surface, then lightly grease. Now to the base plate, to get at the 3rd gear, unbolt six of the eight bolts, three in the cockpit, three through the deck into the stern lazarette, needing to be in two places at once, and substituting a locked vice-grip on a nut for one of me below. What to do about the last two bolts that were buried in the bulkhead, inaccessible to a vice-grip?

I called Brian in Maine. We'd never imagined that I might have to take that winch base off by myself. I could turn a screwdriver from deck, or hold a wedged screwdriver against the nut from below, yet not both simultaneously. Brian suggested epoxying the nut in place, using fast-setting hardener, then unscrew the bolt from above. I tried, yet, 30 minutes later, the epoxy didn't hold the nut. Every extra minute risked a wind change when I'd have to get that winch re-assembled in a HURRY.

As I cleaned the 3rd gear shift lever, a fear began to gnaw that I might not be able to re-assemble this Rube Goldberg contraption. What if I couldn't? Disaster. I'd have to lead every line to the off-duty running backstay winch - smaller, lighter-duty, inconvenient - and unable to be driven by the pedestal handles. I better stop cleaning now and start to re-assemble. Gears, springs, spindles, roller bearings, washers, the boat is charging along at 12 knots, greasy hands, deck slippery with WD-40, which washer goes on which spindle between which gears? An hour later, the winch functioned as it had before. Brian called with the idea from a winch specialist to pour boiling water into it to loosen built up grime. Three tea kettles of boiling rinse water helped. Low gear was better, not perfect, but we'll take it.

Onward.

My fear of Heta proved spot on. She turned southwest, then south, then southeast, strengthened, grew enormously in size, and as if a friend that hadn't seen us since our last Indian Ocean gale, set a course to meet us at the West Pacific ice gate.

The gap ahead and behind had maintained. At the ice gate we would be 2500 miles to Chile or New Zealand. My going on offense changed instantly to going on defense. How to deal with Heta? I studied dozens of weathermaps. Beyond the West Pacific ice gate, a course toward the last East Pacific ice gate, would take us in front of Heta, upwind into 40 knots of her clockwise rotation. We had managed that and more in the Bay of Biscay, but it wasn't good for the boat, and had broken my ribs. Here, I judged us too far from help to tempt fate.

Here's an idea, touch the ice gate, gybe southeast immediately, and let Heta pass us to the east on her parallel path southeast. Going faster than us, she would soon be past, then we could cut behind her in her wake, where we'd get following winds.

A good plan. We touched the ice gate, I emailed a GPS photo to the Race Office, then gybed southeast. A good plan - if only Heta had agreed and done her part! She stalled north of the ice gate, elongated, and began to spin off secondary depressions across our path. I downloaded every new weathermap, searching for an opening. There were none.

As the system expanded, a confused calm in front of her overtook us. Napping at 12 knots, I awoke going 3 knots, sails slatting. We headed up momentarily to speed the boat and calm the sails to a bizarre heading of SSW. We gybed back in the generally correct east direction as the secondary low overtook us. A day later, another low came off as Heta stayed in place. Finally, we bit the bullet and sailed into this tertiary low, just as the main part of Heta started to move. Météo France sent a weather warning, the first of the race. We were the only boat in Heta's path.

We got hammered again, 40 knots upwind, not as bad as the Bay of Biscay's 50 knots, but here in the deep South Pacific, aiming at the East Pacific ice gate, we were scarily alone.

Satellite sighting of three icebergs in the vicinity had caused this last ice gate to be moved farther north. I emailed the Race Office asking for the latest forecast for iceberg drift. Julian promptly responded with the file showing those icebergs to be drifting slowly. I replied my thanks immediately.

We crashed upwind into Heta, trying to get to the calmer center. The staysail is too big for going upwind in these conditions, but the storm jib seems too small.

I heard water sloshing in the back of the boat. When you hear water, you go, now. Donned the helmet, crawled back through the cramped portside tunnel. Remember the scene from the movie *Apollo 13*, after the explosion, when the capsule is going through uncontrolled gyrations, and violently? That was the back of the boat. Next time, elbow pads and knee pads, along with my by now *de rigeur* helmet. Lots of sharp, metallic edges and corners back there. I bailed a couple of buckets from the sealed compartment underneath the cockpit - how did water ever get in there? Maybe from the winch repair dislodging sealant from the bolt holes. I'll have to keep a close eye on that, because that compartment is where we mounted the two electronic compasses for the autopilots, thinking it was the safest, driest place on the boat.

We took our pounding, reached the calmer center of the low, and tacked to head out the other side toward the last ice gate. A terrible thrashing in 18'-22' crossing and breaking seas ensued, beating the boat and me to a pulp. Helmet on at the chart table. More water under the cockpit. Safer than going into the stern compartment, I drained it through a drain hole into the main cabin, then bailed it into the sink. What a mess. I'd diligently worked to keep the cabin as dry as possible, for comfort (!) sake. Now I'm purposely draining a leaking compartment into it to avoid being killed while bailing in the back of the boat.

Next, four buckets bailed from the forepeak. The Pacific Ocean - hah! Magellan must have emerged from his Straits on a flukey calm day 500 years ago to name it that! Seems to me the "Pacific" bashes every boat into a leaking sieve.

Inmarsat-C showed a message: "Cannot Acquire Synchronization of Channel". What now? Oh, OK, that's not so bad, it's lost the satellite for POR (Pacific Ocean Region) and has logged on to the satellite for AOR-W (Atlantic Ocean Region - West). That's the link we'd use near Boston, so we're in the same satellite footprint, a bit of hometown familiarity! What longitude do we have? Ah, south of

Fairbanks, that's good, we're in a USA time zone, overlapping a bit of U.S. land, and where Mom had gone for her amazing adventure. We're making progress.

Scab from the eye gash wound finally fell off, three weeks after the accident. Looks good underneath, nothing permanent, good guidance from Brien. My black eye is gone too.

Wearing helmet full time below, even sleeping in it. Boat taking a horrendous beating, her full open port underside exposed to these cresting, breaking monsters, just crushing her – how can she take it? But we have to go to the ice gate. 1 hour slept in the last 40.

From the ice gate to Cape Horn I hoped for an uneventful passage, to eat more, sleep more, stay warm, charge the batteries, make extra fresh water. I knew what Cape Horn could do, and we had to be ready. King Neptune smirked, and threw three brushback pitches instead.

Touching the ice gate, I set up to gybe for the Horn, 1700 miles southeast. Luckily I noticed that the top leeward running backstay had hooked around the top spreader. If I'd gybed and winched the backstays in, it would have broken the spreader and the mast would come down. I pulled the backstays forward to the shrouds tried to swing them out from deck level, to unhook it 65' overhead. An hour of futility. I unlashed the backstay from its group to give my swinging more arc. No go.

I devised a new plan. Roll up the staysail to reduce forward loading of the mast. Lower the mainsail to the 3rd reef, trim it hard on centerline so that the sail supports the mast. Now do what you're NEVER supposed to do downwind on an Open 60: release the windward running backstays.

The problem aloft was that a piece of bungee cord connected the windward and leeward sets of running backstays around the front of the mast. The windward tight side pulled the bungee aft, which around the mast then pulled the slack leeward group forward toward the mast to control it. However the cord, likely degraded through UV exposure, had stretched, allowing that leeward top backstay to hook the spreader tip, and was now pulling to keep the hooked cable hooked. Only if I released the windward cables, would it release the bungee, which would release the leeward cable from the spreader tip. This was appallingly scary to do, but it worked, I got the leeward running backstays free, and could gybe.

The problem identified, only two solutions existed. Either I had to never make that mistake again all the way back to France, or, I had to go aloft to cut the bungee. I didn't relish either.

An email from Dee ahead, who with her group had just missed a cataclysmic storm at the Horn, in which Météo France had issued their second weather warning and urged those nearby to stay put until the storm moved away, and not risk engaging it:

Hi Rich,
I felt for you having such a hard time getting to that final ice gate. Still now you are pointing at Cape Horn and will be there before you know it. Better luck than us getting round it. That storm was quite spectacular, fortunately we missed the worst of it but even so not a nice place to be as only you know oh too well. I forgot how cold it was in the real south and for two days around the Horn it was freezing. Time flies though after the corner and I have already taken off the mid layer. Keep going you are making America proud.
Lots of love
Dee

I re-read and re-read her email and Samantha's, what kindness, what generosity, what caring, the traditions of the sea being upheld continually. My palpable resultant emotions urged me on.

§

Inauguration Day, an inspiring day for the USA, an African-American to be President. Surely the country wouldn't all turn to milk and honey, but it was an undeniable sea change from watching convoys of school buses with black students be escorted to Hyde Park High School by a phalanx of motorcycle policemen.

In Les Sables d'Olonne on Election Day, just four days before our start, the French had asked about the election. They were intrigued with Barack Obama, and were not big fans of George Bush and Dick Cheney. And who could blame them? They'd been pilloried, even after no WMDs were found, for not supporting the Iraq War. And then Congress insulted them by childishly renaming French Fries as Freedom Fries in their dining room. Did we all forget who our only ally was in the Revolutionary War? And who gave us our Statue of Liberty?

Often people would ask how I voted. I demurred, saying that in the U.S., a person's vote was a private matter. They would ask again, how did I vote? I would repeat myself with a smile. Finally I understood: they weren't prying into whom I had voted for, although they hoped Obama, and I did, they were asking about the mechanics of voting: how did I vote in a U.S. election from France?!

I explained about our absentee ballots. I had filled it out with my voting choice, and then mailed it from Les Sables d'Olonne. *Vraiment? De la poste ici?* Really? From the Post Office here? Yes. They were very pleased with that.

§

After reading President Obama's inspiring inaugural address, and setting aside our daily flag for him, King Neptune heaved his next brushback pitch.

Sitting on the chart table bench, athwartships, leaning against the bulkhead, I dozed off. KLONK! What happened? I was on the floor in a heap and my head hurt. I'd tipped sideways, pivoted at my hips over the bench edge, and fallen three feet directly downward to land squarely on the top of my head. It felt like getting hit with a baseball bat. I was scared again. Does everything still work? Wiggled fingers, toes, seems OK, called Brien, got right through, and explained. We walked through it again:

"Any tingling in your toes or fingers?"

"No."

"That's good. Does your neck hurt?"

“Yes, feels like it really got scrunched. And it’s hard to turn my head in any direction.”

“Any sharp pain?”

“No, just a dull ache.”

“OK, a sharp pain would indicate a fracture. More ibuprofen for now, and watch for any tingling that might come on.”

“We’re out of ibuprofen.”

“OK, well, that’s OK.”

“Brien, this could have turned out a lot worse, right? What if I’d hit off center, rather than straight vertically?”

“Well, the human body can, in fact, take about a one meter fall directly on your head, without serious damage, if it’s all lined up.”

“Guess I’m glad that I lined it up properly.”

“Me too. I’ll call back in 8 hours.”

Neal recorded and posted on sitesALIVE! an Iridium discussion arranged by Lorraine between me offshore and Jean Pennycock, a schoolteacher on leave 800 miles south on Antarctica studying penguins. Near the Ross Sea Ice Shelf, she was probably the closest human being to me on earth. Add Jean to our amazing women list.

An odd thing had happened across the south. Three Radio Shack digital clocks, velcro’ed to the chart table wall, told Boston time (for sitesALIVE! and friends at home), our local time by the sun for our ship’s time zone, and Paris time (for the Race Office, and an hour off navigational GMT). Turning east from the South Atlantic, we entered a new local time zone every 3 days, requiring a change of ship’s time. Sleep-deprived by the gales in the Indian Ocean, I couldn’t make the calculations relative to Boston and Paris as to what time it was on the boat by relative time zones. Finally I just said to heck with it, and didn’t bother to change ship time. So then the sun rose at 4 am, then 3 am, then 2 am, ship’s time. The International Date Line was an incomprehensible final exam – what weekday, what date, what time was it? I finally just went with the GPS date and time. Making that calculation by myself simply wasn’t worth the mental effort.

Since pondering the Vendée Globe three years before, my single greatest apprehension was going aloft alone at sea, and especially in the south. When the bungee problem was identified, the weather wasn't conducive to try to go up. Today offered an opening: downwind, 2 reefs and the staysail, 8' seas, broad reaching at 11 knots, 53° South, 90° West, time to go.

We'd practiced at the dock with two systems. The first, a webbing ladder, was stiff and painful to hold, and it was hard to insert your feet into the flexible steps. The second, a chair with jumars, seemed awkward, and you only advanced a few inches at a time. The third system I devised on my own. I'd asked Scott, my Everest friend, and he'd asked his climbing buddies. They didn't like it, which gave me pause, yet it still seemed my best option.

I'd brought hiking boots for the occasion, and strapped on two foot ascenders, jumars for your ankles. A friend of Hugues' was a French Army paratrooper and had lent me his crotch-to-shoulders para-gliding harness. Two carabiners, a safety jumar, and a GriGri rappel descender rounded out the climbing gear. I hoisted 3 lines on our spare main halyard to the masthead, tightened two hard to the deck, leaving the 3rd a bit loose. I locked the foot ascenders on the two taut lines, the descender on the 3rd line and acting as a safety on the ascent, a carabiner high at chest level around the taut lines to keep me vertical, with the safety jumar above those on the ascent line. Two short lines with small carabiners were tucked inside my harness to secure me to the mast when aloft. It was awkward.

I'd spoken earlier with Brian Thompson on *Pindar*. He'd had to go aloft, halfway up, to make a repair. He ascended OK, repaired the lazy jacks, but then couldn't come down. The ascent and descent lines had different stretch characteristics, so when he transferred to the descent line, it stretched so that he couldn't detach the ascent jumar from the ascent line. He swung around, crashing repeatedly into the mast, twisting in the wind, struggling 50' in the air, for 25 minutes, before solving it and coming down.

I remembered Conrad Humphreys' tale from the 2004 race. He'd ascended similarly on lines, and the mast motion swung him a dozen times around a shroud. Squeezed by this accidental tourniquet applied to his harness, he thought he would never get down. He finally devised a procedure to unwrap himself. Ellen MacArthur went aloft in 2000, the boat accidentally gybed and the mainsail trapped her against the shrouds - until the boat accidentally gybed back.

Mountain climbers have a big advantage: the point where their ropes are attached isn't waving around in the sky!

Heeding Brian's story, I practiced. Ascend eight feet, then descend to the deck, to make sure I could. Adjust my harness, and the strops to the jumar, and rappel devices. Try again: up 15', and come down. Detach, go below to reduce the keel cant to increase the boat heel, so that I could lean against the mainsail more on the way up, and eliminate one dimension of swinging. Don the helmet, Lexan visor down, elbow pads from a friend who had played for an NHL team, kneepads, and gloves. Hook up again, time to go.

I didn't look up, didn't look down, just worked the problem. 8" steps, right foot slides up, slide the GriGri up the descent rope, move the safety jumar, shift weight to the right foot, left foot slides up 8", move the GriGri up the descent rope, then slide the safety jumar up, shift weight to the left foot, then slide the right foot up. Repeat. Continue. Work the problem. I was sweating like too long in a steam bath. Right, left, right, left, don't look up, don't look down, feel the sail on my back, try not to let the waving mast twist me. Keep going, work the problem in sequence. Midway up the span, a lull in the breeze, the boat straightened up, swinging me away from the sail, I spun 360 degrees, twisting the lines on themselves. Back against the mainsail, I was able to untwist, and continued. And then, *mirabile dictu*, there it was, the second spreader, 65' up. I struggled within the constraining harness to get to Bob's wife's Leatherman tool. Open the knife blade, cut the bungee, watched the two pieces fall to the distant deck, close the knife, pocket it.

I stood on the two foot ascenders, to get the GriGri high on the descent line, then sat back down, to put my weight on that rappel device on the third line. The moment of truth. Pick up each foot in turn, and detach those ascenders from the ascent lines. Left, OK free; then right, OK free. We're hanging now on the rappel device, with the safety jumar on one of the ascent lines as backup. I'd made sure that was loose before undoing the foot ascenders; it came off easily. Dangling 65' up the mast, *GA3* charging along a thousand miles short of Cape Horn, my life hung on one rappel device on one line.

Work the problem. Open the lever to let us slide down 12 inches - NOT TOO MUCH - or we'll slide 10 feet and maybe it will come off the line and I'd crash to deck. Open again, another 12", making progress. Another 12", and another. A little bit, a little bit, a little bit. Sort the feed line. Focus. Can't see from my left eye for the sweat. The helmet's Lexan visor is fogging. Keep going. Finally to the deck, a 30 minute roundtrip. My left hand's effort to control the rappel device's lever had exhausted it to cramped paralysis.

I unhooked myself, carefully maneuvered my spent body to the cockpit, collapsed in the seat under the cuddy, and drank a quart of Gatorade in one swig. I had to rest: my legs were shaking and my left hand was seized up. Then back to the mast, disassemble the climbing rig, stow it in the forepeak, then again to the cuddy for Baby Bels, Fig Newtons, and Nestlé's Nido Whole Milk. Well, I thought, I'm proud of that, that's an exclusive club I just joined. More importantly, the leeward running backstays were less likely to get caught and stuck around the upper leeward spreader and threaten the whole mast.

With albatross still with us, Dr. Ioannis Miaoulis, President of the Museum of Science, wrote a fascinating NIE essay "Learning from Animals", on how animals had solved many engineering challenges for themselves by evolution. The high aspect ratio albatross wings, like high performance glider wings, showed the point. Every Expert's essay thrilled me with what it might do for the kids.

And on our approach to Cape Horn, a place of intense memories, who more fitting than my 1990 rescuer Murray Lister to write. Having earlier written an extra piece about that rescue, to be sure it was in our students' minds during the voyage, he now wrote "The Gulf Stream" for our Forces of Nature activity – from aboard *Cape York* in the South China Sea!

Our Pacific crossing had brought a New Year and a new school semester, even a new illustrious President. Through it all, our own illustrious Experts had satisfyingly continued.

A piercing autopilot alarm cut short my reverie. Neptune is playing with us. The wind instruments, erratic since the Cape of Good Hope, had triggered the alarm. I laboriously switched to the backup pilot and its backup masthead unit - no wind direction input. OK, back to the primary pilot and connect it to the backup masthead unit. Nope. OK, the backup pilot connected to the primary masthead unit. Nope. OK, back to primary pilot, since it has the stronger hydraulic ram, and the primary masthead unit, now showing only windspeed and not direction. Program the pilot to steer in compass mode.

The last time this happened, the backup had wind direction. Not so now. The pilot is back on, steering by compass. We're OK for now, but I knew the stark implications.

If the wind shifted substantively while I was asleep, the pilot, steering a compass course, couldn't follow the shift, and the boat could accidentally gybe or tack. In a strong wind, this could be catastrophic, crashing the mainsail across the boat into the running backstays, which could load the carbon mast tube into an explosive compression failure. If the keel was fully canted, the new side would be the wrong side, and the boat could be knocked flat.

The only way to minimize that risk was to go into the cockpit and look with my own eyes at the masthead windvane to check for changes in the wind direction. If the wind shifted, I'd then adjust the pilot's compass course. For safety, I'd have to do this every 20 minutes. Whatever little sleep I had been getting, 45 minutes now and then, would be destroyed. 20 minute naps, until we got to France, or until the masthead unit magically cured itself. In that, I had little faith.

Looking aloft hurt my scrunched neck. Bend backward at the waist, neck locked in place, look up, did that little 6" windvane 90' up move any? All the way to France...

But first, Cape Horn.

"When you get to Cape Horn, you will be tired, and the boat will be tired."

...Jean-Yves Bernot

Chapter 11: Cape Horn

The Horn is the Horn because it's a bottleneck. The Chilean Andes sweep south and the Antarctic Peninsula sweeps north, with only the 500 mile wide Drake Passage between. The mountains funnel the weather systems; the coastlines funnel the wave systems.

A further geographic reality for a mariner is that the tip isn't a long pointed peninsula, where from east or west you dash south, round the point, then dash north to safety. Across the continent's rounded bottom, you're pinned and exposed south of 55° South for 400 miles. From our Pacific side, once past the Horn at 56° South (the southern equivalent of being 1,000 miles north of New York), you must sail 150 miles ENE past Staten Island before turning North.

Eerily, as if the fine hand of the "Wizard of Oz" was tuning the cosmos behind the curtain, the wind shifted twice in the last 500 miles of our approach, necessitating two gybes, which led us through 55° South, 79° West, the spot where we had capsized nearly two decades before. Across the Pacific, I had hoped for a wide berth of that dismal memory; King Neptune sent a reminder instead. The memory flooded my mind.

§

30 days out of San Francisco, 2,000 miles from Cape Horn, Steve Pettengill and I, aboard the 60' trimaran *Great American*, encountered a storm worse than any nightmare I'd ever had of going to sea. On Monday before Thanksgiving Day 1990, in 45 knots of wind driving 30' seas, we surfed down a wave at 16 knots with only a small corner of the staysail poking out and the mainsail down and furled on the boom. Fearful that if we buried the three flat-decked bows in the bottom of a trough, we could trip, and somersault the boat upside down, we deployed spare lines, about a hundred feet long each, to drag over the stern to slow the boat. We put out five; they did nothing. I pulled them back in, tied overhand knots about every ten feet to add friction, then deployed them again. No effect. I added more. When the eighth line was deployed, we reached some critical friction, and the boat slowed to a range of 8 knots up the seas and 12 knots down. We tried to stretch the boat down the seas to aid steering, front-wheel drive with the corner of the staysail to pull the bow forward, these "warps" to drag the stern back. Wind and seas continued to build.

Into Tuesday night, with seas surging to 40' and the wind to 60 knots, at midnight, the boat turned sideways on the cresting front of a monster wave, threatening to capsize us. The daggerboard grabbed jerkily as we slid sideways down the sea, making it harder for her to straighten to course. With the daggerboard pulled up as far as possible with our cockpit controls, I crawled forward to the mast to put a spare halyard on it and hoist it another eighteen inches, acutely aware that if the boat capsized when I was there, I'd be pinned underneath a 60' x 40' platform, in the cold and dark ocean. I made the adjustment, returning to the cabin to see that the barograph, strangely steady until now, had started ominously down. This already appalling storm was going to get worse.

Into Wednesday, the barograph continued to plunge. In the morning, we got sideways on another wave, threatening capsize, yet with the daggerboard slightly higher, we slid sideways more smoothly, and the boat straightened out to our intended course.

We took the seas about fifteen degrees off our starboard stern, trying to edge south to clear the tip of South America. If we headed straight downwind, slightly safer, we would close the coast faster, and we'd be forced later to make a more drastic and dangerous turn to starboard to get around the land.

On Wednesday night, our weather router told us by radio:

"You should see 54 knots of wind tomorrow."

"We have 70 knots already."

"We don't have any information on that."

At midnight, the barograph tracing pen went off the paper chart and dragged along the lip of the recording drum at 926 millibars. Steve deployed four more lines to slow our increased speed down these mountains back to our 8-12 knot range, fast enough to not be pooped by a sea, and to give the rudder good steerage, not so fast that we'd bury the bows, trip and somersault over a wave.

Early on Thanksgiving Day, I was in our one bunk, the boat got sideways again, grabbed, and threw me out to land 5' down flat on my back on the floor. I checked joints and bones, then forced myself to laugh to break my tension.

I heard Steve yell: "Something's wrong with the rudder."

Suited up, he rushed to the stern. A trim tab on our rudder (a mini-rudder on the trailing edge of the main rudder) had come loose and its leverage on the rudder threatened to overpower our hydraulic autopilot ram. Steve made progress on re-pinning it, then came back inside when he could no longer move his fingers in the wet ten degree wind chill. I went out and was able to finish the job, then retreated inside. A monstrous sea roared aboard, stripping the two wind generators, one of its blades, the other of its tail.

A few minutes later, with 85 knots of wind, and seas having built to 55' by our estimation, 400 miles west of Cape Horn, a wave hit the starboard stern, knocking us sideways to the next cliff of water, 40' wide on a 50' cresting sea face, the big trimaran heeled alarmingly, heeled some more, hung there, and then slowly capsized.

Scrambling inside, neither of us was hurt. We struggled into survival suits and then set off the emergency beacon. Looking out the main hull escape hatch, I could see that the pontoon and cross-beams on that side were intact, and oddly admired our tidy anti-fouling paint now facing skyward. The cabin door had been ripped off allowing the sea to surge inside, yet with the pontoons and cross-beams apparently intact and keeping us afloat, the water level on the cabin ceiling stabilized at shin-deep. The surges compressed and decompressed our large volume of air, producing agonizing pressure and release on our ears. We cracked open the escape hatch to act as a pressure release valve. As we'd capsized almost gently, we believed that the mast was still intact, and now acted as a 70' deep keel.

90 minutes later, in a first in maritime history, the capsized trimaran was violently re-righted by a wave that must have been far bigger than the first. Thrown against the floor overhead, I was knocked out momentarily, came to underwater, holding my breath. Flailing with my arms and legs, I found something with my feet, pushed off, and came to the surface.

Now neck-deep in the 41° F water in the main cabin, with the ceiling again overhead, I heard Steve yelling for me and went underwater through a door to get to him. We clambered into the cockpit, not knowing if the boat was sinking. The massively built mast was in three pieces and dragging over the aft starboard crossbeam, pinning that corner into the seas. The huge aluminum boom, lashed amidships to the low cabintop, and therefore close to the rotational axis of the main hull and unlikely to attain a high rotational velocity, was nonetheless in three pieces, with the welded gooseneck ripped off the mast stump.

Able now to reach the deck-mounted, solar-powered Argos positioning beacon, we pulled its magnetic plug to release an SOS into its data stream. Moving the flares, liferaft, and both emergency beacons forward to the sail locker, we pumped out the 4' of water there. We returned to the flooded cabin to find things we might need. Everything was sloshing everywhere. Saran Wrap came out of the galley, unrolled, and started to envelope us in an unbreakable tangle; we used all four hands to bunch it together and throw it overboard. In my eyeglasses phase when we capsized, my contact lens case conveniently floated by - I stuffed it into my survival suit. Next came an asthma inhaler - I stuffed that in too.

With the stern pinned by the overboard mast to face the seas, every wave came aboard filling the cockpit and surging through the cabin door. Back in the cockpit, standing thigh deep in the frigid water, I saw two waves advancing from the horizon. Far bigger than the others, I watched these majesties of the ocean approach. Beautiful and incalculably powerful, would we ride up and over them and survive? Or would we be rolled over again and crushed into the sea? No matter what happened next, alongside my fear was an odd yet complete joy to have seen these two magnificent waves with my own eyes.

Up, up, and up we rode, like looking up the stands of a stadium, then the top crested on either side of us and foamed away to the east. We were spared. Perhaps the dragged ropes had triggered an early crest to the sea directly upwind. Perhaps the ten tons of water in the main hull had stabilized us. A few minutes later, up, up, and up again, would we get over this one too? Yes, the pre-cresting happened again, and the mast dragging in the water may have played a role in disrupting the circular flow of the wave.

Having studied trade routes of the world at Wind Ship, I knew that the shipping route from Australia/New Zealand across the deep south Pacific and around the Horn into the Atlantic had only one vessel every eight days, so we ought not be discouraged if no ship showed up for a week. Retreating to the sail locker forward, we ate canned ham and Wasa bread for Thanksgiving Dinner.

Through the night, the wind blew, the seas came aboard sweeping the deck. Surging water into the cabin flexed the bulkhead protecting us – would it hold? If not we'd have to retreat to the anchor locker, our final line of defense. The surging seas blew air through wireholes in the bulkhead, screeching an annoying high-pitched whistle.

Fifteen hours later, in the dark of midnight, a new sound entered the cacophony. Was it the mast tube tearing apart underwater? No, it was low and uniform - it must be manmade! I opened the hatch, stuck my head up, and saw an outline of a ship. It looked like a sea-going tug - but what would a sea-going tug be doing out here? Then I could faintly see a square stern, a containership, and the stern was a very long way from the faint bow, a really big containership! I lit a flare so that they'd know somebody was still alive on board. Her lights were out presumably to aid the night vision of the searchers, yet by a lone light on the stack, I could read *New Zealand Pacific*. Good, I thought, knowing the Kiwis maritime prowess. Being only the 2nd ship that we'd seen in 32 days, obviously she was there to find us.

New Zealand Pacific

Undoubtedly she would stand off until the storm abated. She couldn't put over a boat - it would be lost; they couldn't come alongside in the seas that had by now diminished to 35'-40', they'd crush us. The wind had helpfully diminished to 55 knots. It was snowing. Suddenly, her lights were getting closer, 400 yards, then 300 yards, then 200 yards - they're going to try to come alongside! This was going to be interesting, and exciting – we would be spectators at our own rescue. A light appeared in the side of the ship - the pilot door had been opened. I could see silhouettes of two men working inside. Then the light went out, as the massive ship rolled the door underwater, and when it rolled back, the light and men appeared again.

Steve and I debated briefly about survival suits versus foul weather gear: survival suits were thick neoprene and awkward for a handhold, but would keep us alive for 24 hours if we missed and went into the water; foul weather gear would allow a better grip with hands and fingers – until they were numb, and if we went into the water would drag us down, not float us. We decided on survival suits. Coming out of the sail locker, we held on amidships as the ship approached - 50 yards, 25 yards, then two lines snaked through the dark - "Tie the lines around yourselves" shouted a voice. We did, then crawled to the pontoon and held on there, 10 yards, 5 yards, then the side of the ship kissed the side of the trimaran, perfectly parallel, and with the pilot door directly overhead. The next wave took us up the side of the ship and we had one chance to jump. I went for a rope ladder hung down from the door and Steve for cargo netting hung down from the deck.

I grabbed two handholds on the ladder, hung there, and struggled against the thick survival suit to gain one foothold on the bottom rung, then climbed for my life. Steve went into the cargo netting and likewise, climbed hard for the pilot door. We feared that the 20,000 pound trimaran with 20,000 pounds of water inside would come back to crush us on its next wave cycle. We got into the pilot door.

Four men were inside, with red lights on to safeguard night vision. No one spoke, we and they stunned that the rescue had succeeded in the appalling conditions. Then one crew spoke:

"Are you guys hurt?"

"No."

"Then you're going to Holland with us."

"We're going where you're going", I said.

***NZP* Chief Mate Murray Lister**

The Kiwi crew took care of us with food, clothes, hot showers, yet let us be without too many questions while we collected ourselves. After several days, having learned why we were out there, on a record attempt and connected to thousands of schoolchildren, they, being Kiwis, asked: "When are you going to try again?"

Regardless of why I was there, the eighteen days to Holland were some of the most interesting days of my life. *NZP*, aka “The Big Red Lady” for her red painted topsides, was the largest refrigerated containership in the world, 815' long, Panamax at 105' wide, refrigerating 1200 containers below decks, and another 1000 above decks. 36 crew were aboard, including 32 Kiwis and 2 women. Captain David Watt (a Scot) and Chief Mate Murray Lister were in command.

Captain Watt told me that it was the worst sea conditions he’d seen anywhere in the world in 40 years at sea, that they’d always considered Cape Horn overrated, with the Tasman Sea and the Bay of Biscay being the worst, but now they believed in the legend of Cape Horn. They described feeling the ship getting up on the face of a monster and starting to slide down it in a surf. Their logbook recorded wave heights to 65', confirming our estimates from *GA*. And one sea had pooped the ship, cresting over the stern and crushing the stern-most row of containers, the tops of which were 37' above the waterline.

The crew of *New Zealand Pacific* were rightly proud of executing the rescue, yet they were more proud to have lived up to the tradition of the sea: to go to the aid of a mariner in distress.

When Coast Guard New York received our second distress beacon’s signal, they found, from AMVER (Automated Mutual Vessel Rescue), a global database of tracked merchant vessels, *NZP* to be the closest. Fortuitously, the ship had a satellite telephone. USCG-New York applied the area code for the deep south Pacific and called the ship on the satellite telephone. Captain Watt answered in his office:

“New Zealand Pacific.”

“This is Coast Guard New York. We have a distress signal at 55° South, 79° West. We’d like you to go and investigate.”

Captain Watt, despite being in the most dangerous storm of his or his ship’s careers, replied simply: “We’re on our way.”

We were given full run of the ship. I worked on the bridge with the radio operator, and Steve worked with the Chief Engineer in the engine room. We ate with the officers, or the crew, or the cooks & stewards, each of whom had a dining salon. We continued reporting from our new vessel for our school program. When we had peeled off our survival suits that night, a crewmember had admired Steve's Leatherman multitool, a new device at the time. Via satcom one day when the radio officer "Sparks" had stepped out, I asked my mother to find 36 Leatherman tools and FedEx them to the ship's agent in Holland. Arriving Vlissingen, the agent delivered our package. We went around the ship to personally give one to every crew member. The Cook's Assistant was so moved that he turned on his heels and rushed away down the corridor. He returned a few minutes later, tears in his eyes, and gave me his favorite T-shirt, depicting a bright Kiwi. I still have it.

En route to Holland we learned of the trauma at home. My mother had been at my sister's house in Cambridge for Thanksgiving Day dinner. We were scheduled to call every hour on the hour from 4pm – 8pm. We didn't. In mid-evening, Mom drove home alone to Marblehead. She found three phone messages: the first, "this is Scott Air Force Base in Illinois – can you confirm that a distress signal from *Great American* is correct?"; the second, "This is Lieutenant Kranzien, Coast Guard New York, can you confirm that a distress signal from *Great American* is correct?"; the third from my friend and mentor Phil Steggall in Newport, "Mrs. Wilson, this is Philip, please call me right away." This is the potential agonizing trauma that sailors may inflict on their friends and families ashore.

Arriving in Holland, Steve and I took the train to Amsterdam, where our Embassy issued a new passport to me, we returned to Boston to a relieved and warm welcome by friends and families.

The solar-powered ARGOS beacon continued to transmit, so we tracked *GA* as she drifted toward the Chilean coast, then detoured southeast and sloshed around the Horn – without us. We engaged a Chilean tug for a salvage operation. The tug would be available on January 31, yet on January 25, the beacon stopped transmitting her position. Without an accurate position, we had to call off the tug.

Perhaps the beacon's batteries had died, perhaps there wasn't enough sun to charge them, perhaps it had washed overboard, perhaps *Great American* had broken up or sunk.

A year later, I received a telephone call from a sailor who had cruised to South Georgia Island, 1000 miles East of Cape Horn. They had found *Great American* washed up on the island's west coast, on the rocks and under a blanket of snow. Twenty miles south of where Sir Ernest Shackleton had landed in his famous small boat journey, she rested in good spiritual company.

§

Eighteen years later, now aboard *Great American III*, our forecast was 30 knots of wind with 12' seas. My plan targeted a waypoint off Diego Ramirez Island, 60 miles south of the Horn, to stay off the shallow, 600' deep shelf. Seas rolling from the west would pile up on the shelf like a beach, and get steeper and bigger. The moderate forecast induced a change of plan: to cross the shelf and save fifty miles.

Coming on deck at midnight, I saw a light, dead ahead, a ship! The first since the fishing boat in the Indian Ocean, the second since the South Atlantic ten thousand miles ago. The chart showed a stationary fisheries management vessel. When closer, they shone a powerful spotlight on us, to ensure that we'd seen them. I was too tired to call and chat.

At dawn, closing islands west of the Horn in limited visibility, we gybed offshore to the SE to be assuredly clear of hazards. Napping after this clearing gybe, my fatigue was so severe that when the Iridium phone rang and woke me, I didn't know where I was.

An hour later, the big moment, January 26, after 78 days at sea, I recorded on video:

> *There it is, after 19,500 miles, Cape Horn. Didn't think we were going to see it, I was rolling out the reef, going from 3rd reef to 2nd reef, another 165 grinds on the pedestal winch in the medium gear, by the way, and looked up, and there it was. Very gray,*

foggy, misty, rainy, overcast, still have that but, there it is, the legend.

The lighthouse is on the darker island, there in the middle, the lower left, can't see it unless close enough, did see it in 1993 when we came around going from San Francisco to Boston. A whole group of islands in there, named after Hoorn, the town of the Dutch Captain who discovered it.

Think who else has been here, Charles Darwin with the Beagle, the Beagle Channel is just up the coast there in Tierra del Fuego. The Magellan Straits, named after Ferdinand Magellan. We're in the Drake Passage for Sir Francis Drake, between Cape Horn and the Antarctic Peninsula. A lot of history here. Captain Bligh couldn't get around going east to west, spent a month, finally gave up and had to go across the South Atlantic and Indian Oceans to get to the Pacific, and the hardship and duration of that voyage contributed to the mutiny.

A lot of history here, there it is, that's the legend, Cape Horn.

A momentous occasion... My first rounding had been disconsolate on the nighttime bridge of *New Zealand Pacific* after losing *Great American* the day before; my second, at night aboard *Great American II*, we saw the lighthouse on Horn Island flashing white every five seconds; this third time in overcast daylight, after 78 days alone aboard *Great American III*. Would I ever be back to this outpost of grim majesty?

How many seaman had lost their lives here? How many ships had disappeared without a trace? How much hardship, cold, and fear had they endured? They didn't have our food or fresh water, our clothes, foul weather gear, or sleeping bags. They didn't have electronic navigation or satphones to call home. They didn't have winches, or batteries, or reliable rigging. But they persevered, they were determined, and they pushed themselves to new limits of endurance in their voyage quests. Just as one had to race the Vendée Globe with respect for those who had raced before, you had to sail Cape Horn for those who had sailed here before, who had tried mightily, some succeeding, some failing, yet none ever giving up.

My emotions now upon turning for home recalled my emotions upon departure.

§

The people in Les Sables d'Olonne had been amazing.

The lady security officer on the dock who greeted me warmly each day and gave me a teddy bear to take around the world. The middle school media class who intently interviewed me with cameras and microphones on booms in our cockpit. The France 3 TV piece recalling my email exchange with Michel, where I showed him *GA3*, and he showed me *Foncia*. The massive crowds arriving pre-dawn on start day, the access roads lined with parked cars for miles from the harbor, such that special police escorts were made available to the skippers to ensure they got to their boats. Seeing Ellen MacArthur on the dock early, and her looking up at me and saying "Remember to enjoy yourself!"

Our friends, *preparateurs*, and vendors, the organizers and inspectors, the press and politicians, and the people most of all, unknown but hardly strangers, they had wished us all so well and so fervently.

We sailed for them all.

§

Turning for home, we had to *boucler la boucle*, as the French would say. By no means out of danger, we were at least leaving the south. Setting course for the east end of Staten Island, the yellow mail LED shone: a message from the Race Director:

Hi Rich,
Congratulation on your fantastic sailing. Hope you had a great Cape Horn. And that you enjoyed it as I know that it is quite a great deal due to your past sailing in this area. For a press release, can you tell us the exact time of your rounding Cape Horn?
All the best
Denis

As I'd been unrolling the reef, I didn't have an exact time, so I approximated in my reply. An idea blossomed into a smile.

VROOOOOM! What was that? I jumped into the cockpit to see an airplane recede into the distance, having buzzed us at low altitude. The plane banked and came around again, a Chilean Naval Patrol plane. I grabbed the handheld VHF, turned on Channel 16, and heard the pilot calling. I replied, identifying ourselves, the boat name, how many aboard, where we'd come from and were going to, and thanked him for the contact. We chatted while he circled, then signed off when he headed north.

Disconcertingly, we had to gybe ESE to stay away from the continent's Andean wind shadow. The breeze lightened, calling for more sail, yet I found it hard to respond. The stress of the Indian and Pacific Oceans, of the 8 gales since Cape of Good Hope, of 7 weeks racing an Open 60 in the deep south alone, of crossing the Pacific without nearby company after Jonny had retired, had started to fall away; yet in that relief, in that draining of adrenaline, I couldn't muster an effective response.

The northwest wind was shockingly cold, colder than on the Pacific side, where it blew across the water and adopted the sea's 40 degrees. Here it blew down the Andes, and was frigid.

Emails poured in via Neal from friends ashore. Congratulations! Fantastic! What a relief! The occasional, well-intentioned "It's all downhill from here" was mistaken though, it was 8,000 miles upwind to France, and we were by no means home free. Still, engagement of people ashore, our primary goal, warmed my tired heart. Maybe this gigantic effort and risk had been worth it, but to modify Robert Frost, I had eight thousand miles to go before I would really sleep.

Sprinkled in were emails from those who knew best, from Dee, Samantha, Brian and Brien, and Hubert, whose CDK shipyard had nourished *GA3* in Port la Foret:

Hi Rich,
Great stuff to see you clear of Cape Horn. Only a few more miles before the big left hand turn. Nice work and it is great to have you back safe in the Atlantic. A milestone to tick off. Soon you will be

removing the layers and feeling the warmth of the sun on your skin and life will feel wonderful.
Take care
Dee

Hi Rich,
Congratulations for Cape Horn!! I hope it has been easier than your previous time. Enjoy the satisfaction of rounding the Horn after all that hard work in the South. It's an amazing feeling.
Take care, Bises,
Sam x

Congrats Rich,
SUPER !!
You must be really pleased
I know there is still a long way to go…
But you have just rounded Cape Horn
AMAZING
Soon you will point the bow of GA3 north and Homeward Bound!!
Well Done !!!!!!!!!
Brian

Hi Rich,
Congratulations on passing Cape Horn! Very well done! Following closely and will watch as you pass Staten Island. I assume that your neck is improving. I am wondering when you turn north and head upwind, will your instruments allow sailing to wind or will you still be dependent on compass steering and glances above to the windvane? Keep up your guard as I know you will. Calories, fluids and rest. Fantastic job!
Brien

Bonjour Rich,
Nous voyons avec plaisir que cette fois ci votre navigation ne s'arrêtera pas au Cap Horn. Bon retour dans l'Atlantique et à bientôt aux Sables d'Olonne.
Hubert et toute l'équipe CDK Technologies

A chart detail provoked a smile and an email to Dr. Barnewolt: "Fun task, find an atlas, look at group of islands 20 miles ENE of

Cape Horn." A few hours later came the happy reply to his discovery of Islas Barnevalts: "I knew I had land down there! I'll have to visit!"

A thunderous roar startled me, two steps to the cockpit to see a fighter plane streaking away low toward the horizon. I called on the VHF, no reply, but minutes later the plane returned shattering the relative calm, maybe a Royal Air Force plane patrolling from the Falklands.

Race Rules required skippers to notify Race Office at the time when each mark was rounded: the three great Capes to be left to port; the seven ice gates to be respected; and Antarctica to be left to starboard. This last was, of course, redundant. I emailed the Race Office:

Great American III wishes to report, per Notice of Race, Section 3, that we have respected the mark of Antarctica by properly leaving it to starboard. We cannot give an exact time for this mark rounding, just the last one or two months.

An email reply described the burst of laughter in the Race Office, and their subsequent banter on whether they should send the fleet ahead back to Cape Horn, since no one else had properly reported, per Race Rules, rounding the mark of Antarctica!

On our doublehanded voyage in 1993 we'd been 35 days from San Francisco to Cape Horn, and another 35 days to finish in Boston. This time I'd been at sea for 78 days, on a bigger, tougher boat, singlehanded, and 15 years older. By tradition of the sea, rounding the Horn under sail awards a mariner the right to wear a gold earring in his or her left ear. I'd earned that privilege on our earlier passage, yet this time I'd really earned it.

On our capsize voyage aboard *GA*, King Neptune had scowled. On our *GA2* voyage to Boston, he had smiled. On this voyage with *GA3*, he sent a reminder of who was in charge by sending us through our capsize position. I now asked him for a fast passage home, easy on the boat, and easy on me. Would he grant me this fervent wish?

At midnight we cleared Staten Island and turned north for France.

"The most grueling and dangerous prolonged competition on the planet."

...Garry Emmons, HBS Alumni Bulletin

Chapter 12: The South Atlantic...Again

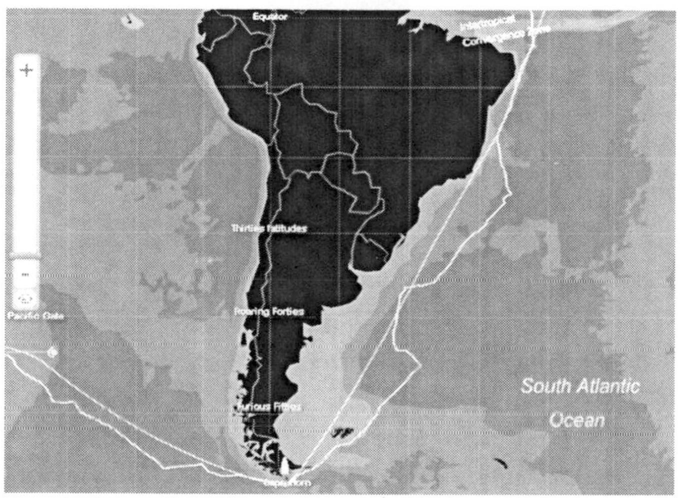

A hundred degrees of latitude, seventy degrees of longitude, another quarter of the globe to finish at Les Sables d'Olonne - here we go.

Hard on the wind on port tack, with frigid northerlies blowing off the Andes, we headed straight for the Falklands. If the wind shifted, we might pass to their west, if not, we'd ease sheets and sail to their east. After a day of hard winds, we approached in a lightening breeze.

Onboard, instead of rejoicing about passing the Horn, the computer decided to pout. Had we gotten a virus via the satcom system? Seemed impossible, but now I had to re-boot the computer several times daily. What a pain.

Since the wind instruments' failure, I'd tried their input several times to check for resuscitation. It seemed now that the primary anemometer and windvane had speed but no direction, and that the backup had direction but no speed. Without both, neither True Wind Speed nor True Wind Direction could be calculated.

Endlessly pondering a fix, I finally imagined one. If we had speed on the primary unit, and direction on the secondary, perhaps we could cross wire the two into the autopilot computer. Take the red, green, and blue wires from the primary bundle, and the purple, black, and yellow wires from the secondary bundle. But would there be enough voltage from the units to make it work, or too much voltage that would fry the circuit board in the pilot, now working properly on compass course? No answer in my head, so I called B&G, who called their electrical engineers – they'd get back to me promptly. I wondered if Tom Brady had to worry about voltages in his helmet headphones.

Zooming on the Falklands' chart, wavy icons dotted the south coastal waters. I scrolled for the legend – kelp! Bear off immediately and get away from those icons. That's the last thing we need - to get stuck in a kelp bed, as the ancient sailors had feared being stuck in the weeds of the Sargasso Sea. Samantha had written about huge kelp patches wrapping around her keel and daggerboard. She'd stopped the boat, then sailed backwards to withdraw from the entanglement. If that doesn't work, stop the boat, put on the wetsuit, get the 10 minute scuba tank, face mask, flippers, and the biggest knife aboard, jump into the water, swim under the boat, and try to cut a forest away. I shuddered at the additional exertion of either option. Best to not engage the kelp.

Jean-Yves was right, now past Cape Horn, I was tired and *GA3* was tired. Adding miles by sailing a snake wake past the Falklands would be worth it, if it saved the fatigue of dealing with a kelp snare.

A mast appeared dead ahead; the radar had not seen it. Relieved that I'd caught it visually, I called on the VHF, and chatted with the two couples aboard their 40' sloop as they passed 200 yards abeam. Past the Horn and Staten Island, with the Falklands close ahead, the lee of the continent seemed to imply that we were back in civilization from the desperation of the south, so it oddly didn't seem odd to see another sailboat. They planned to transit the Straits of Magellan, thence to cruise the west coasts of South and North America, to a final port stop in Vancouver. That sounded appealing!

Passing Port Stanley five miles off, I saw the distant, low silhouette of the rolling heights of East Falkland Island. A war was fought here, as much for pride as for any geopolitical advantage or resource. My wandering mind slid to politicians in my context.

You can't bluff, bluster, or bully your way across the Southern Ocean. To survive, you must be honest in your appraisal of the sea, your ship, and yourself, and humble in the face of nature's might. It's easy for politicians to rage with no personal consequences at stake; perhaps they all should be sent to the south for seven solo weeks of harsh personal reality. Then we'd see progress, if they survived. More likely, they wouldn't, so we'd replace them with those honest, humble, and brave enough who could.

On the other side of the Falklands from the squid fishery that "Fish" had alerted us to so many years ago, I wrote about Resource Depletion for NIE, comparing our boat resources being consumed en route to world resources being used up. Dr. Ambrose Jearld's piece "Sustaining Fisheries" amplified mine with his career-long authority. Not only a fisheries' expert, Ambrose was an inspirational role model for our African-American students.

A question from Lacella:

How did you become a National Marine Fisheries Service worker?

Ambrose replied:

When I was about your age, I lived on my grandparents' farm in the swampy southern part of North Carolina. I spent my days hunting and fishing with long cane poles to catch swimming creatures in ditches, long-standing puddles, ponds and swamps. In the summertime I loved going to the seashore in nearby South Carolina. There, my friends and I spent many hours looking across the ocean surface to spot what we called sea horses (dolphins) and flying fish.

In junior high school I liked science and decided to become a biologist. In college I studied fishery biology and earned three science degrees. After earning a Ph.D., I was hired as a fisheries scientist by my current employer, NOAA Fisheries.

I spent years doing science in the laboratory and in the field, studying the reproductive behavior of fish to understand their social and behavioral ecology and taxonomy. I removed scales and bones and spines from fish to determine their age – information we needed to determine the abundance of fish stocks. Now, as a fishery science administrator, I spend my days talking to people about how to develop educational programs, and going to conferences to meet young scientists, yet I do miss getting my hands in the water!

Out from the Falklands' lee, we were hammered again by 35-45 knots of wind and 15' seas. All downhill from here? Hardly. Flat-bottomed Open 60s hate to go upwind, the motion being that of a continuous car crash, and France was halfway into the next hemisphere, and upwind all the way. Could the structure survive the pounding? Could the skipper? It was violent outside; it was violent inside. I sat cold under the cuddy, to support my shipmate *Great American III* bashing her way north in severe upwind distress. I groaned in sympathy with every crash – UNHHH – UNHHH – UNHHH. What had she done to deserve this?

Nodding off, a crashing collision with a cresting wave hurled me out of my seat and across the cockpit; I caught myself inches before my face smashed into the metal lip of the jib sheet winch. Go below, it's safer there, you must leave your friend.

The next afternoon, still pounding upwind, I sat again under the cuddy, watching our wake. Something caught my eye, a black piece of rubber that cushioned the windcharger on its mounting post was creeping out...and then it was...gone...overboard! Before my very eyes! 80 days at sea had loosened the locknuts. The windcharger was askew on its post. I shut it down. If allowed to spin, the blades might strike the post and shatter.

With sheet rock screws and a screwdriver, I climbed onto the antenna platform aft of our transom and leaned over the water to the windcharger mount. Completely exposed, if I fell off, I'd be dragged along until drowned. The unit was aft for clear air, and to keep lines and fingers out of its whirring blades.

I screwed the screws upward between the charger and the post, where the black rubber had been, to solidify the mount. 30 minutes of struggle later, four screws were crookedly in. I returned relieved to the cockpit. The screws lasted five minutes before falling out from the jarring upwind sail. In the darkening afternoon, let's leave it until tomorrow's daylight.

In the morning, I tackled it again. Hmmm, yesterday I noticed that the three-lobed radar reflector, mounted beside me on the antenna platform, was loose. Its one big bolt would be easy to tighten. Yet I'd forgotten it when I finished with the screws. This morning, the radar reflector was gone, another victim of the incessant pounding.

Such mistakes worried me. Fatigue was chipping away at my logic and detail. With an active radar, and a radar detector, we could get along without the reflector, but what if I made a mistake on something critical?

No solution for the windcharger leapt to mind. Its sweet spot is upwind, i.e., from here to France. Put 25 knots of wind through it and it generates 12 amps, enough to power the whole boat - lights, pilots, navigation instruments, computer, low baud rate comms. The battery charging burden is now squarely on the engine and alternator, with the solar panels helping in the short segment of tropics, but not here now, nor toward the finish in the northern North Atlantic. What a dumb mistake that was. I should have a monthly maintenance list, where I tighten every bolt on the list. Then we would still have the radar reflector and a contributing windcharger.

Before Cape Horn, I'd hoped for an uneventful stretch, and didn't get it. Past Cape Horn, I'd hoped similarly, or at least for moderate weather, in the long upwind slog along the South American coast. King Neptune was in no mood to grant us that either.

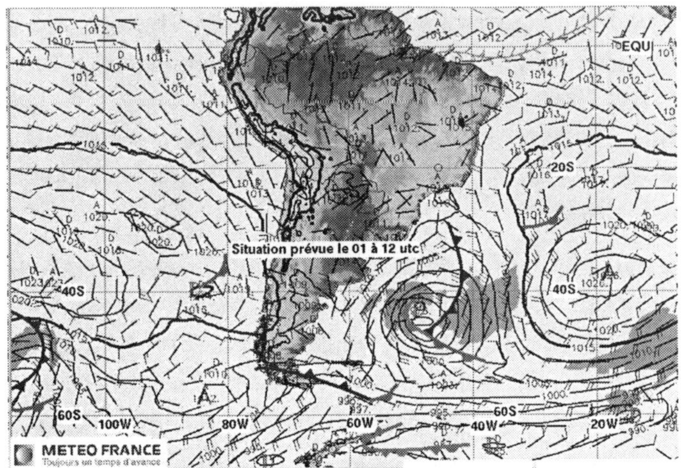

Intense Low off Argentina

Weathermaps showed a low forming over southern Brazil, forecast to intensify and move southeast across our path. No rest for the very, very weary.

Check the boat thoroughly. Plan a strategy as we converge. Eat, drink, nap, study alternatives. I was reminded of the movie title "No Way Out". That was us. The storm looked to expand to enormous size, to engulf the entire southwestern quadrant of the huge South Atlantic Ocean. 25' seas were forecast, driven by 50 knot winds.

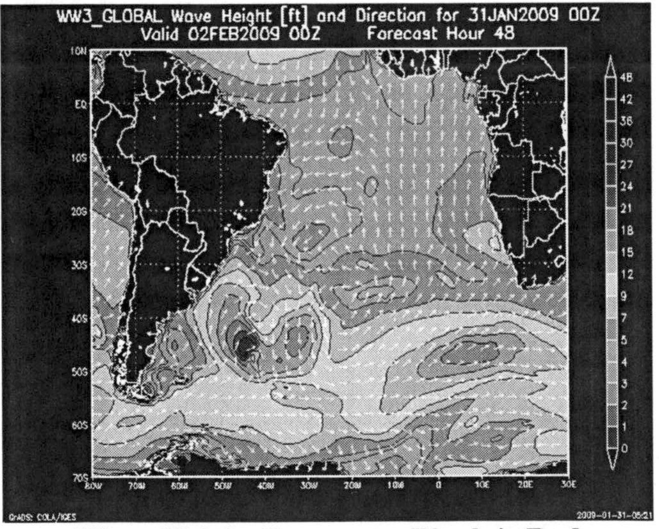

Wave Height Forecasts: Black is Bad

As between the first two gales of the Indian Ocean, which carried 60 knot winds each, I decided that discretion was the far better part of valor. Steve was still a thousand miles ahead, and Raphaël and Norbert were still a thousand miles behind. Unless any of us had breakdowns, the order would likely stay the same until France. So save the boat, save the skipper, and finish.

We'd sail into this monster until 30 knots of headwind, then tack to the west. The storm's center, with its lesser winds, would track over us. We'd come out the west side and be going downwind when we got the 50 knots. Into the gale, I sat up again with my friend *GA3*. Then remembering my close call with the winch, I went below, sadly leaving her side.

Since the start, I'd downloaded a dozen weather maps daily, always looking for changes that could ease our way. Brains over brawn, if possible. The maps were either printed maps, hand drawn by NOAA meteorologists, or MaxSea's digital GRIB files, that often understated wind speed forecasts, but had proven precise for barometric pressure by location. This latter acted as a positioning check for a forecast storm: if our pressure matched the map's pressure, we could confirm where we were within the storm.

Like homework checked for the tenth time, I calculated our entry into the system. Our ship's pressure and position didn't match those on the weathermap. The glass should be falling here, but it's steady. My trust in the data, gained over 84 days at sea, was shaken. I was bewildered and apprehensive. We sailed past our entry spot – where were we in the storm? We do not want to crash up the wrong side of this swirling behemoth, the downwind side will be to the west, time to tack even though something's amiss.

We raced west for 100 miles, before the pressure and wind dropped in the mis-mapped center, and then struggled in the sloppiness of no wind and a leftover sea to get out the other side to the southerly. We slatted along as the sun set, getting just enough wind to bear away to the north. When the southerly wind came, it increased rapidly into that ominous night. At 35 knots we went early to 3 reefs and the storm jib.

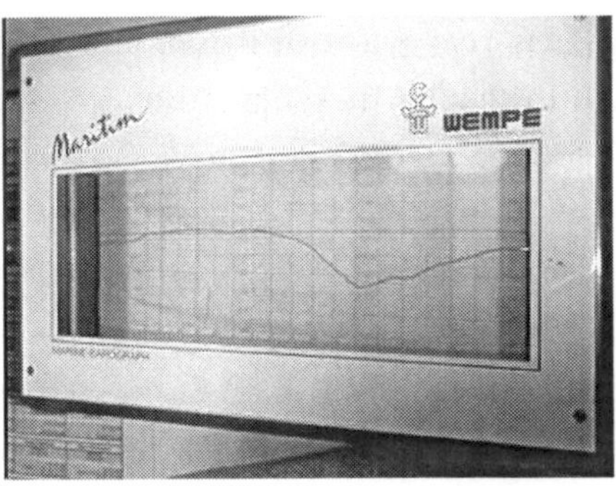

Barograph Plunges

We flew north. 35 knots became 45 knots, the seas rose to 20', then the breeze to 50 knots steady, and the seas to 25', approaching 30', and breaking. It was tumult outside, and cold, with the clockwise rotation of the system sucking air from the Andes. A swirling storm generates waves in all directions, and as the system moves, newly generated waves in one direction mix with earlier generated waves from other directions to create a maelstrom like a giant washing machine. Chaos, fear, and debilitating cold outside, nothing to be gained there, I stayed in the cabin, watching instruments, and hoping that the pilot, steering by compass, could hold her downwind.

Although 700 miles off the distant River Platte, I worried about logs and river debris in our path.

At 3 am, 50 knots of wind, surfing thunderously down huge cresting seas, I knew that our luck couldn't last. Zipping up my foul weather jacket to go on deck to reduce sail to storm jib only, I watched the readouts in horror as *GA3*, on port gybe, accelerated down a wave to 24.5 knots, the fastest speed of our race, and carved a turn to starboard. 20 degrees off, 30 degrees off, then 40 and I knew what was going to... HOLD ON …BAM! *GA3* crash-gybed, ...POP!...the mainsail boom preventer's fuse broke, the mainsail slamming across the boat, the boom hitting the rigidly loaded backstays to put a nearly infinite shock load on those cables and thus the mast. Is the mast still up? Is it still there? Or is our Vendée Globe over...

It got eerily quiet. The keel had been fully canted 40 degrees to port and now it, and the mainsail, were loaded on the wrong side. The boat stopped dead in the water and lay over at 70 degrees of heel, just sitting there. The pilot's alarm screamed at me – BEEP – BEEP – BEEP – as if I were unaware, that it couldn't turn the boat back to course. *GA3* lay stricken on her side, one rudder waving around 10' in the air, and the other nearly level with the water's surface, and offering insufficient bite to turn us back.

There had been no great explosions of carbon fibre, so maybe the mast was still up. Into the cockpit, carefully stand on previously vertical surfaces, turn and look. The mast is still there. My relief was religious. Could it sustain a crash-gybe back?

In the 2004 Vendée Globe, Patrice Carpentier had been similarly knocked over in the south. With no keel winch motor then, he had been unable to grind it back to center to straighten the boat. Mulling limited options, he climbed outside the lifelines, to the near horizontal surface of the topsides, crawled to the mast shrouds, then came in to the mast to try to pull the mainsail down so that the boat would be relieved of that weight and pressure, and straighten up somewhat. Amazingly, he succeeded, the boat straightened enough that he could winch the keel back to centerline.

I disengaged the pilot to quiet the annoying alarms, took the tiller and tried to turn the boat back. Nope. Of course not, that's not the protocol, the protocol is to center the keel, then the boat will stand up straighter thereby immersing the rudder to a better angle and depth. Go below, walk on the wall, the galley now underfoot, into the engine and keel area, stand on the wall there, get the proper control rope wrapped on the keel winch, now overhead, be happy that we'd charged batteries fully in the storm's lull, and push the button to surge 200 amps through the winch motor. Inch by inch, grind the keel to its center point, and feel the boat straighten to forty degrees of heel.

Back to the cockpit, take up the slack in the now slack mainsheet, so that when we crash gybe back, the boom would travel only a foot before fetching up harshly, less chance for destruction. OK, here we go, push the tiller over – are we turning? Can't tell. Keep it over, maybe we're moving, watch the red LED course readout, is it changing? Slowly, a degree, then a couple, is it just the random slop of the big sea? Don't know. Keep the tiller over, maybe, OK we're turning, watch the windvane lit at the masthead by the tri-color running lights. Almost there to a gybe, keep going, the mainsail becomes uncertain, OK...HANG ON...BAM – we crash-gybe back and the wind on the mainsail sheeted hard rounds us up into the wind and seas. The mast survived another one – YES – but refrain from silly land sports fist-pumps. Wrench us back down to course, engage the pilot, and take a breather after 30 minutes of cold fear. If the mast had come down, we were done.

My worst nightmare had been realized, crash gybe with the keel on the wrong side, in big seas and big wind, and lay over almost flat, all because our masthead instruments wouldn't input complete data to the pilot. In their on-again, off-again erratic behavior in the Indian and Pacific Oceans, I'd spoken with Mark a lot about options. I had a third wind wand, but mounting it would need climbing to the top of the mast, and precisely connecting the fifteen pin connector then screw fitting, a delicate and awkward job even in the calm of the dock, and very dangerous at sea. Furthermore, we didn't know if the instrument was the problem; maybe it was a faulty cable. I could take that big risk and perhaps not solve the problem. I'd bemoaned to him one day about why they didn't build these instruments stronger. He said that they'd measured the masthead G-forces of an Open 60 crashing upwind on her flat bottom at 9 Gs. Well, why not engineer them for 18 Gs to give a 2:1 safety factor? No idea.

Per our protocol of the south, we turned to sail into the 50 knots of wind and nearly 30' seas to drop the mainsail and tie it to the boom. It was wild and wet and cold and black. Oh to play in the Super Bowl with the Patriots just to take an afternoon off. Turning back downwind with front wheel drive from the storm jib, we sailed at 12 knots and under control, or as much as one could imagine in these seas, the worst we'd seen in the Vendée Globe.

The storm continued its southeasterly track, but it expanded, even to our northerly direction, lengthening the time we were in her grip. 24 hours later, the wind diminished to 40 knots, then to a sedate 30 knots. We'd dodged a huge bullet, two crash-gybes in appalling conditions. The mast had stood, the boom had endured, the skipper had survived.

Onward.

When the gale withdrew, a reprieve prevailed. A pod of whales crossed our stern. A solitary, errant flying fish flew south, and I yelled at him "Wrong way, warm water is this way, follow us!" No reply. I took a shower in the cockpit with desalinated water warmed in our one-gallon solar shower bag. My straggly hair would need to be cut soon. I re-read my notes on the South Atlantic from Jean-Yves Bernot, to refresh myself on what to expect. The Iridium phone rang – it was Jonny! My comrade through the gales of the Indian Ocean, checking in on his mate!

"Hi Jonny! How are you? Where are you?"

"I'm recovering in the French Alps. How's it going with you and *GA3*?"

"OK, got through a bad one last night, two crash gybes in 50 knots, but everything held."

"Good going, my friend. Wish I was still there with you."

"Me too, Jonny. Is *Artemis* on a ship going home?"

"Yes, she should be back in Southampton in three weeks."

"Good. Thanks for calling, and save some champagne for me."

"Will do, mate."

Then the best news of all from the race office. *Le Professeur, Mon Professeur*, Michel Desjoyeaux, having sailed through the lead pack in the south, had held on in the Atlantic to win the Vendée Globe 2008-9 in stunning fashion, going away, and having sailed his Open 60 *Foncia* at an unheard-of average speed of 14.0 knots. He was the best. Elated, I emailed him: *"Felicitations!"*

B&G had called back saying that I could do my imagined re-wiring without risking the pilot computer. I'd been just too tired to try. Lifted by surviving the storm I thought to do it now. Before starting, though, best to assure that one of the masthead units did actually have wind direction. I tried both into the instrument displays. Wrong; neither has wind direction. So even if I got all the tiny wires properly connected under their tiny screws, and giving myself an eyestrain induced headache after working with the 3.0x reading glasses for a few hours, it wouldn't work. A big effort saved vs. no pilot wind steering to France. I was too tired to be relieved by the former, or upset by the latter.

Onward.

Two days later, in the early morning dark, sitting under the cuddy to watch the boat, it got suddenly quiet. Why? What? The boat had turned away from the wind and seas - BEEP – BEEP – BEEP, the screeching autopilot alarm raced my pulse. Grab the tiller, disengage the pilot, turn her back upwind and re-engage, nothing. Gauge when to jump below to start our protocol to boot up the backup pilot. I got through it, pushed the Engage button, and, nothing.

A chill went through me. Without pilots, we were done.

I started over: boot up the backup compass, boot up the backup pilot computer, boot up the backup instruments and pilot controls, push the Engage button. Nothing. OK, back to the primary: boot up the primary compass, boot up the primary computer, boot up the primary instruments and pilot controls, push the Engage button. Nothing.

A worse chill. I can hand steer for seven or seventeen hours, but I can't hand steer to France. If I can't solve the pilot problem, we're done.

Try each again. Nothing.

I can't leave the helm and leave the boat to the mercy of the seas.

And I'm so tired.

What a silly word "tired" is. It's so inadequate. "Tired" - a joke of a word. Tired is if you have a bad night of sleep. Tired is if you had two bad nights of sleep. Our sitesALIVE! Expert on sleep, Dr. Chuck Czeisler had written that if you have 5 hours of sleep for a week in a row, your mental functioning will be comparable to a .1 blood alcohol level, meaning, you're functionally drunk. What on the planet earth is your mental functioning level after 12 weeks of 4-5 hours of forty minute naps? With the 6,000 calories per day physical fatigue of racing a 60' boat alone around the world thrown on top for good measure? This game has gone on now for 87 days, 2000+ hours, without a single break, ever.

To continue, I have to solve our most difficult electronic problem. Our three year project encompassing everything I have to offer - boat, school program, asthma awareness, everything - depends on it.

How do I leave the helm to tackle the problem? If I take down all sail, the boat will be thrown about randomly by the seas and something may break, including the skipper.

I remembered reading about a technique called "heaving to" when I was a kid. But I'd never tried it in any boat, let alone this Open 60. Well, no time like the present. If I could do it, it should stabilize the boat giving me a chance to solve the pilot problem. To start, lower the mainsail from the second reef to the third, and roll up the staysail halfway.

We'll backwind the staysail on the wrong side, to push the bow to leeward. Then trim the mainsail hard, to push the bow back to windward. Lash the helm so that the rudders are immovable in the water. Balancing the two sails is the key. Too much staysail, and the boat will circle clockwise ending with a crash gybe. Too much mainsail, and the boat will tack accidentally, sail backward, and maybe break off a rudder.

OK, here we go. Trim the staysail backward - NO, NO, NO, TOO MUCH! Steer the boat back up against that. Trim the mainsail, NO, TOO MUCH! Darn, the boat headed into the wind and tacked. I held the tiller to control the rudder as we picked up speed in reverse. Steer *GA3* backward and sideways to the wind to slow, stop, then move forward again, picking up speed to gybe, BAM, gybed. OK, try again.

Ninety minutes later, *GA3*, perhaps the first Open 60 ever to do so, was hove-to, taking care of herself, making 2 knots toward France, with no rudder input.

Eat, drink, here we go. I unscrewed the front plates of every junction box and every instrument box in both primary and secondary autopilot systems. With headlight and 3.0x reading glasses, I inspected every connection of tiny 22 gauge wires. Was anything disconnected, corroded, loose or abraded? I couldn't see anything amiss.

What about the two rams in the stern? Helmet on, life jacket on to pad my ribs like a quarterback's flak jacket, elbow pads on, crawl back there with headlights, flashlights, and the 3.0x reading glasses. Any wire problems there? No, the connections in that junction box are solid.

Has a ram locked? Is that why the pilot won't work? Detach the backup wormgear ram – push it – pull it - it moves. Detach the on-duty hydraulic ram, push that in and out, seems OK, not frozen, re-attach it. Wait a minute, something's wrong here but my tired brain can't put my finger on it.

Keep thinking. And don't get hurt back here.

After I pushed the ram in and out, it ended up at a different length. But when I re-attached it to the steering system, to the mini-tiller on the central post, THAT moved, and it's not supposed to. It's supposed to be rigidly connected, through the central post, to the lashed tiller above deck. So, either the mini-tiller below deck, or the tiller and rudder linkages above deck, are loose on that central connecting post.

Test the mini-tiller below deck. Watch with the reading glasses to see if the bracket is moving on the post. I don't think so, but it's hard to see. Move it a bigger move. Looks like the post is turning, and it's not supposed to be, because the tiller above decks is lashed. Maybe, just maybe I've found the problem.

Contort like Olga Korbut to get through the transom hatch onto the stern shelf. Reach back inside to push the ram to turn the post while watching it above deck. It moves, and it's not supposed to. Can you see the post moving inside the tiller bracket? That connection is underneath the mainsail track, what a pain. Look closely. Move the ram again - is the post moving? YES! OK, there's the problem. And it's a mechanical problem that I could tackle. With an electronic problem, you might never know what was wrong, or even if you did, never be able to fix it. A wave of relief swept over me.

There were three bolt holes, but only two bolts. The two were on either side of the central post and squeezed the metal tiller piece around the post to make a compression friction hold. There was also a hole where a bolt would go straight through the post for a mechanical hold. But there was no bolt in the hole. Seems there should be, but I couldn't remember.

Hugues and Rick had worked on this when I was studying with Jean-Yves Bernot. Back into the cabin, call Hugues' cell phone in France, explain the issues – was there a bolt in there? He couldn't remember for sure, but he thought probably yes, and it seemed logical to both of us.

Find a fistful of bolts from our spares box that look similar.

Back on deck. Two hours later, the bolt was in the unreachable hole under the mainsail track. A tube extension levering a crescent wrench honked down on all three bolts. With the system back together, fire up the primary pilot. Is it....? Yes it is, it's working.

Trim the aback staysail onto its proper side, roll it out fully, turn the boat to an easy reach for a rest, then slump into the leeward seat under the cuddy.

I had fixed it. Yet I had also been shown in the starkest terms how tenuous the Vendée Globe is. Far from being a triumphant repair, this incident marked my lowest point of the race.

In 85 days at sea, I had never felt this before. I was tired and beat up. And worse, I was demoralized and discouraged. I was just done. I ate and drank, then set the correct sails to continue crashing our way violently north, BAM, BAM, BAM, crushing blows of the flat-bottomed Open 60 leaping off seas and smashing against the troughs.

Remember the scene in the movie *Das Boo*t, running the straits of Gibraltar, where the Captain is on the conning tower grabbing the railings and screaming into the wind and storm as the spray and seas pelt his face and shoulders? That was us. Seven thousand miles to go like this. Could she do it? Could I do it? I wasn't sure.

When people have asked if I get lonely solo at sea, I've distinguished between loneliness and solitude. I don't get lonely, because with the satphones, I can call anyone, anywhere, anytime to talk. Besides, being lonely takes energy, and I had little of that to spare. Solitude is different. It's when things go wrong, like the spinnaker broaches, or the repair aloft, or the crash-gybe, you're the only one aboard to help. I'd never been lonely at sea before, but now I was beginning to feel it. I wanted this to be over. But it was a long way from that.

"Being over" meant finishing. It never meant abandoning the race; that thought never crossed my mind. It was the respect thing, I had to finish if at all possible, and so of course we push on, until the boat is so broken, or I am so broken, that one of us cannot physically continue.

I was worried about my physical state. My fingers hurt, my wrists hurt, my elbows hurt, active pain at every motion. The human body is not built for 4,000 average loaded revolutions on the pedestal or winches each day. I knew I could press on through that pain. Yet my mind and emotions worried me. How to get past that, how to keep fighting. I knew I would, but how to make it easier? I really wanted this to end.

35-40 knots again, upwind again, pounding again, three reefs and the storm jib again, can't we ever get a break?

Two days later – BEEP – BEEP – BEEP – the pilot alarms screeched again. The replacement bolt had broken. I hove to again, and replaced it again. It only took two hours this time. But it made me fearful. I only had three bolts of that length and diameter left, and we wouldn't make it if each bolt lasted only two days.

I called Brian in Maine, "Should I use one of the bolts without threads?"

"Yes, it's called a shouldered bolt, and it's stronger for the same diameter, without the threads cut into the metal."

"How much stronger?" He measured the threads as close as he could on a similar bolt and made the calculation of areas.

"It should be about 20% stronger."

"OK, thanks, I'll use that one."

"How are you doing, Rich?"

"Not so good. Very tired, very discouraged. Frankly, pretty demoralized."

"Well you're doing a great job, everybody here is glued to the race, and we're so proud to have worked on the boat with you. Look at all the big guys who've dropped out, and you're still going, and it's not just the boat, it's you too. You're doing it right, backing off when you have to, and pushing when you can, you're doing great, and we're proud of you and proud to be part of it."

I felt like crying, and maybe I did. My daily audio reports and ship's journal had begun to reveal the true story aboard *GA3* – the skipper was really done. As Bill Smith of WZLX had commented 20 years earlier, the audio reports, like radio, offered the "theater of the mind". People ashore could sense it in my voice, the skipper was on an edge. They knew my reserves were depleted, and they were chiming in to help, mostly by email, sometimes by satphone.

The official video of the 2000 race had shown Ellen MacArthur freely crying in the stress and fatigue of the gales of the deep south, yet she kept pushing through it. Before our start, the giant JumboTron at the dock had shown a clip of Michel Desjoyeaux, a week from winning that race, reduced to tears in his own stress and fatigue at a seemingly insoluble electrical failure which could snatch that victory from him.

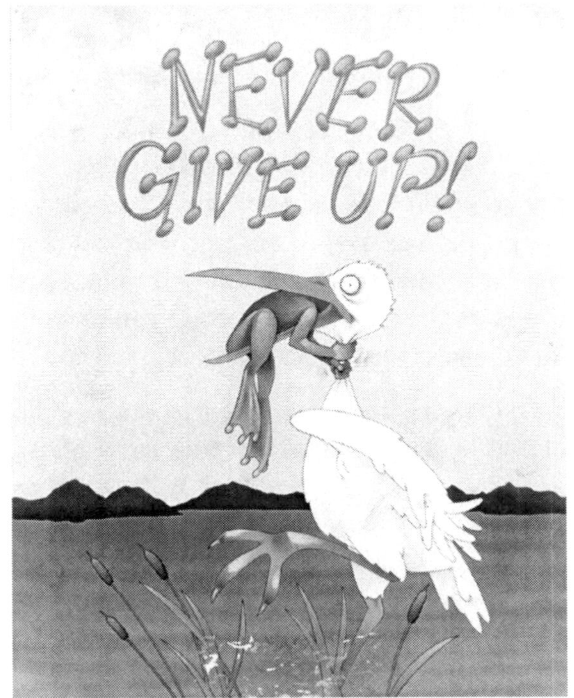

Philosophy Needed for Vendée Globe Skippers

Before an earlier voyage, a close friend had faxed a cartoon. It showed a big bird in a marsh eating a frog who was halfway down the bird's gullet. But the frog had his forelegs out and clasping the startled bird's neck, choking it so it couldn't swallow him. The caption read "NEVER GIVE UP!" That cartoon was taped to my chart table and defined the necessary default philosophy for a Vendée Globe skipper.

Certainly I wasn't the only one who had had problems. Michel had revealed that a rudder structure had cracked in the Pacific, he'd stopped the boat just before it broke off, which it then did and started to disappear under his boat. He'd lunged through the lifelines, grabbed it, pulled it out and secured it aboard. Then he scavenged a lifeline stanchion to insert as a new pivot axle for the kick-up structure. He raced on.

Roland Jourdain, the ever-smiling hero of young French kids, with his pirate costume eye patch and beard for Christmas pictures, in second place behind Michel at the Horn, had had a collision off

Argentina with a submerged object, possibly a whale. The keel, acting as a 14' long lever, had cracked the two carbon bulkheads which held it in the boat. He sanded the paint off, then epoxied and through-bolted carbon plate across the cracks to stabilize the bulkhead. An amazing repair. He sailed on, up the Atlantic, chasing Michel as best he could. Just short of the Azores, his keel broke off below the waterline. He caught the boat in time, didn't capsize, considered the risk of trying to sail 1500 miles without a keel through the Bay of Biscay in February, before deciding that although he desperately wanted to finish, discretion was the better part of valor. He abandoned to the Azores.

To come so close – he'd raced 27,000 miles - how could he stand the disappointment? Yet you knew that "Bilou" would shortly have his mile wide smile back, happy to be alive in this wonderful world.

The beginnings of another storm came out from Brazil requiring a dozen sail changes in the squalls and calms as we slid along its front for 24 hours. When finally released, looking at weathermaps, and about to download more, I fell asleep face down on the keyboard, out cold, for four hours. Awaking, I realized that the high-speed 56k Fleet 77 satcom had been turned on all that time. Usually, I only turned it on for 30 minutes to download weathermaps, then shut it off immediately. In the heat of the tropics, with an older secondhand unit, four hours straight – was it ok? No. The circuitry had overheated and the unit never logged on again.

I had wanted to record a video in French for the race website, and now I couldn't, because there was no way to transmit a big file. Several of Samantha's emails had been addressed for fun: "To the Great American". It alerted me to the chance that the French might think that the boat name meant that I thought I was a great American. I wanted them to know that our 1990 boat was named *Great American* by her previous owner. The name worked for our voyage between American ports of San Francisco and Boston, and for our school program for American kids, so we kept it. *GA* saved us, but we lost her off Cape Horn. Trying again in 1993, we had renamed another secondhand trimaran *Great American II* in honor of the first boat. This Open 60 was named in this line of respect – *Great*

American III. In my draining fatigue I became obsessed with recording this explanatory video, I just KNEW the name would be misunderstood, yet if I couldn't transmit the video, there was no point in recording it. Nevermind our multitude of new French friends, the boat name was an inevitable *'faux pas'* and I couldn't let it go, couldn't rationalize it away. It haunted me.

In the Indian Ocean gales, I had listened to the St. Benedictine Monk Chants to calm myself. I also had ten, inspirational, true sports story movies on my iPod. Needing inspiration in the south, I'd watched those on its tiny screen, unwilling to expend amps on the monitor: *Miracle, Chariots of Fire, Invincible, Prefontaine, The Greatest Game Ever Played, Glory Road, Remember the Titans, Coach Carter, The Rookie, The Express*. Long since memorized, I'd fast forward to the pivotal moments, then go on deck to try to urge me, and us, home. Now I watched double - and triple-features. When levity was needed, I watched *Cars*, Mater driving backwards across the moon, the tractor-tipping, Luigi, Lightning, Doc and Sally, anything to escape.

I sailed in some nether state between awake and asleep. No stark hallucinations with people aboard like my first transatlantic race. No memory blackouts as in Transat 2004 where I'd raced the first five days on ten total hours of sleep, slept through our 120 decibel Sonic Boom alarm clock for the hearing impaired, and awoke not knowing my name, that I was on a boat, or in the Atlantic. Something different was happening here, from the physical, mental, and emotional stress of racing this big boat for 90 days alone.

Somehow a notion took hold, from a dream or daydream, that I had to download a twenty-ton anchor through the satphone onto the boat. I didn't know why, I just knew that I had to. The notion continued when awake. The problem as I saw it was not that you can't download a physical object through the satellite, but that since the high speed 56k baud rate Fleet 77 was down, it was going to take absolutely FOREVER to download that huge anchor through the 2.4k baud rate Iridium. I struggled with that dilemma for eighteen wide awake hours.

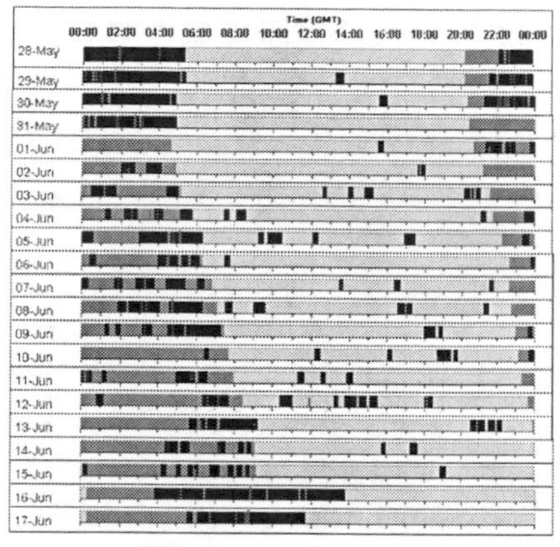

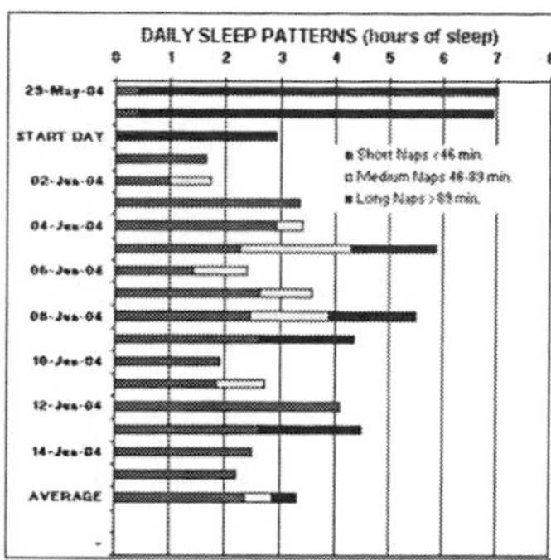

Transat 2004: Sleep Data from ActiWatch
On Left, Dark Gray is Night, Light Gray is Day, Black is Sleep

In Transat 2004, I'd worn an ActiWatch, a wrist-watch like device with an accelerometer in it. If your wrist is steady, it deduces that you are asleep. From that race, I gained confidence in the ActiWatch data. For Vendée Globe, two of Professor Newman's MIT students would analyze my sleep data. They would get special project credit; I would get useful analysis. Yet the software froze after the first two weeks, so none of us got the data. The students lost their credits, and I lost the corrections I might have made if I'd known what sleep I was actually getting.

I slept nearly always at the chart table bench, athwartships. Closer to the cockpit if an instantaneous reaction was needed, nevertheless, it wasn't quite as comfy as the bunk could be. Yet a challenge for sleeping in the bunk is that when sailing upwind, the boat heels more or heels less per the varying wind strength, so you can't sleep on your side, as you'll be rolled over one way or the other. My scrunched neck couldn't turn side to side anymore, so I couldn't sleep on my stomach. If on my back, a bit harder on my asthmatic breathing, I'd also need a pillow on my face to protect me from getting thrown up against the underside of the deck in the incessant, appalling pounding and crashing. As I knew from my eye gash episode, sleeping was dangerous.

Pounding our way past Rio, I spoke the bulker *Protector*, Captain Raz from India in command. She was bound for Santos to load

40,000 tons of sugar, thence to Durban for bunkers and Singapore for delivery. Our twenty minute chat helped.

A line of squalls drifted off the unseen Brazilian coast. Such towering thunderheads – who knew the sky was that tall? Up and up they went, I shook my head in awe.

Wonderful news from the Race Office. Armel Le Cléac'h, aboard *Brit Air*, had finished second in his first Vendée Globe. A young, friendly, and wondrous sailor, winner of the prestigious La Solitaire du Figaro (as Michel, Jean, Jérémie, and Kito before him), he had sailed fast, consistently, and had kept his boat together. He'd had similar pilot problems with failed masthead wind instruments, but whereas ours was likely a circuitry failure aloft, his instruments had been washed off by a wave when *Brit Air* was knocked flat in the Pacific! A final gale in the Bay of Biscay welcomed him home, with a sea coming aboard and ripping off the 12 foot wide sliding hatch that protected his cockpit, and sending it broken to the ocean depths.

The weather stabilized for this section past Rio. Time to focus on sitesALIVE! This stretch to the equator might be frustrating, but we were out of the dangerous storm area until we reached the northern North Atlantic.

Our Newspaper contracts were for 15 weeks, but clearly we wouldn't be finished by then. I would lose the motivating tool of my weekly essays for readers and students, so these last few had to be perfect. More drafts, wordsmith them, make them sing as best I can. And don't short the keyboard with dripping sweat.

This week's topic was Decision-Making, which surely defined the Vendée Globe. I wrote to support an essay "Decisions at Sea" by Rich du Moulin. A tanker owner and my shipmate for Hong Kong - New York, he described key elements of the process: experience, judgment, planning, preparation, and anticipation. That just about covered it.

The tropics became staggeringly hot. We crashed up the coast. More pilot alarms, more resets while I held my breath. Torrential downpours in squalls that darted around us, fat raindrops splashing and bouncing high off the water to create micro-rainbows at the ocean surface.

A spectacular full moon in the next dawn sky, and a visual on a ship dead ahead. Hard on starboard tack, we bore off to port and passed starboard-to-starboard, instead of the recommended port-to-port. Our radar detector had not been triggered; his required radar watch was off. Abeam at ¼ mile, his radar came on, as if he had just learned of our presence when alongside. Lucky I saw him first.

I called Dr. Barnewolt. "Brien, you got me through the ribs, the eye gash, and my scrunched neck. Can you turn into a shrink now and help get me home? I'm really done out here."

"Well, you're doing great, everybody is watching here in the ER. We can't believe what you've been through, and we've seen a lot. Try to get more sleep. That will help."

"I'll try, but it's pretty hard. We're along a coast, there's more ship traffic, and the crashing is beyond belief. My teeth hurt, my neck hurts, my joints hurt from grinding winches all day. We've still got over four thousand miles to go."

"Work on the sleep, that will help a lot if you can manage it. You're the only one on the boat, but you've got a lot of people rooting for you back here. And look, you're still going, and half the fleet has dropped out. Work on the sleep. Things will look better if you're better rested. Good job fixing the steering. I'll check back in a couple of days."

I called Brian Harris again. "OK, steering is hanging in there, but I'm not. I'm really tired. Can I call every couple of days, just to talk? You've been through this before."

"Of course, call anytime, day or night, I mean it. Alison and Jackson are following every day too, they can't believe it. Jackson asked at breakfast yesterday 'How's Rich doing?', it was so cute. You're doing great. You've got a good boat. You're sailing smart. Keep it going, and call anytime."

Off Salvador, I called Ellen to reminisce on *GA3*'s rapid turnaround between the TJV and the B2B qualifier. To inject levity, she reminded me of my falling asleep in the barber's chair. As the race progressed, my weekly calls to her had become several times weekly, and now were almost daily. Whereas Brian and Brien heard a lot, Ellen heard it all.

A half day patch of erratic light wind. I rolled up the jib, reefed the mainsail, shut off the pilot, and let the boat drift in circles while I went below to sleep. An hour, look around, another hour, look around, another hour. Force it, force the sleep, just as I've been doing with the food, maintaining strict rigor in that protocol, four meals daily, snack in between, eat before and after sail changes. Force the sleep.

I had noticed that the rigging, or maybe the lashings, seemed to have stretched, that when the mast was fully loaded, the unloaded leeward shroud was hinting at going slack. We have to do EVERYTHING that we think will help us get to the finish, even if it takes a huge effort for a miniscule improvement. A great mariner and boatbuilder, Waldo Howland once said: "You either put a vessel in a little better condition today than it was in yesterday or it will put itself in a little worse." So, we have to re-shim the mast.

Out comes the hydraulic pump, pressure gauge, hoses and two pistons. Out comes the 2" diameter steel pin that goes through the mast near the bottom. It's 100 degrees in the shade. Place the plywood and aluminum plate under the pistons to distribute the point load on the deck. DARN! Forgot about that. When we did this in Port la Foret, we had to unbolt the mainsail halyard turning block from the deck, because it sits where the port side piston should sit. But I can't take that block off alone. I can't be above deck to hold the bolt, and below deck to turn the nut, at the same time. And even if I could, I wouldn't want to, because then I couldn't lower the mainsail if we had a sudden squall. So I'll have to wedge the piston in alongside, a bit cock-eyed. With that block still there, the aluminum plate to distribute the load on the deck won't fit in its space. So take it below, clamp it hard in the vise, load a new blade in the hack saw, and go at it to cut off the corner to allow for the halyard block. 110 degrees and humid in the cabin, sweating fire hydrants, I sawed a three inch cut in the half-inch thick aluminum plate.

Back on deck, set it up. Get the pin through the mast without pinching the cables going to lights, radar, instruments up the mast. Pump the hydraulic arm, slow at ten tons pressure, slower still at twelve tons, pump little pumps now, gingerly, fearfully, hoping the imperfectly supported piston wouldn't break through the deck, the loads off the charts. We need 14 tons pressure. Tiny pumps now – carefully – carefully - we're there! Pull out the 2 millimeter fine-tuning shim at the top of the four 12 millimeter shims, and push the 3 millimeter shim under the mast now held up by the hydraulic pistons. Pump a ¼ pump, push the shim, pump a few pounds more, push the shim, a tiny pump, push the shim, OK it's in! Back off on the pump valve. OK, we gained 1 millimeter on the 90' tall mast. That's all I can do. Disassemble everything, put it away.

I just re-tuned the mast after 95 days at sea. Saw a problem, and tackled it. Proud of that. I'm doing what I'm supposed to be doing.

Our fourteenth NIE topic, "Defining Success", seemed premature. For me, *GA3*, and sitesALIVE!, this meant finishing the race and delivering excellent content to our school program. Complementing this, Lorraine wrote about how sitesALIVE! supported the school curriculum with exciting, live, real-world content. She'd helped her students, and us, connect beyond the U.S. Ahead of her time, we need a million Lorraine Leos in our classrooms.

That afternoon, as the sun set in the west, a full moon rose over the eastern horizon. It was big, and lingered. I got out the binoculars to look more closely. It was uniformly white and beautiful. But what? I don't get it, it's not really rising. Maybe an optical illusion variably refracting through the earth's atmosphere? It's not a ship, what is it? I watched for 15 minutes until figuring it out. A car carrier, a huge ship like a gigantic shoebox, with square sides, no silhouette of a normal bridge or sloped bow, just a big ugly box of a ship, no windows, no nothing on the side, painted white and perfectly reflecting the setting sun in the west. Mystery solved.

After midnight, hard on the wind but not fetching the continent's corner at Recife, we tacked offshore. It took the usual half hour to get squared away, with new sail trim, adjusted keel cant, re-setting the autopilot, checking course on the computer. Finally back to the chart table to rest as we raced east toward Africa. Sail 25 miles out, then tack back north and hope to fetch the corner.

The phone rang. "Hi Rich, it's Julian in the Race Office. Noticed that you changed course, just wanted to check in and see how everything's going."

"Hi Julian, thanks for the call. We're OK here, couldn't fetch the corner of the continent, so needed to get a few miles further offshore before trying again. How are things in the Race Office?"

"Pretty good."

"Hey Julian, how did you ever end up with the midnight to 6 am shift?"

"Oh, easy. In the first week of the race, as we were getting sorted out, all the press and politicians were coming by during the day and evening shifts, so I asked for this one, so I could get my work done without anybody bothering me!"

The next day, closing the equator, unbearably hot below, but with the sun sneaking under the cuddy, I sat on the cockpit floor to find shade by the side deck, anything to save a few degrees. Sticking my head into one of the open rope lockers under the deck overhang for shade, I noticed an oddity. We'd had so much water washing through the cockpit for so endlessly and continuously long, that we were growing a lustrous field of algae in the back of the compartment.

Fetched Recife at the corner of Brazil. Pounding, pounding, pounding, upwind, upwind, upwind. Steve had pulled further ahead. Raphaël and Norbert had made it around the Horn. Raphaël had been hammered by a gale like ours that came out of southern Brazil behind us. We had gotten a piece of it off Rio, but Raphaël got it all, a vicious storm, but he got through, and Norbert behind him too. Good going Raphaël; good going Norbert. We three old boats have to finish this race.

Through or around the Islas Fernandes? Pinch up to go east, no sense in getting tangled up in the shallows to the west. Close the Equator. Remembering my apprehension heading south, when I wondered, 82 days ago, what adventures and challenges would lay ahead before we crossed this line going north? Make that - if we crossed this line going north... We had had those adventures, we had survived, the two of us together, skipper and boat, shipmates, we.

Crossing the Line, we offered a toast to King Neptune with a pour from a Mount Gay Rum nip over the side, then to *GA3* with a pour on her deck. I toasted our competitors, friends, our newspapers, teachers, students and readers, and the French, who had dreamed up this incredible race, supported it with their hearts and souls, and welcomed me into it. Another pour for *GA3*, and the last for Neptune. A momentous occasion and a boost for tired spirits. In the home stretch now, only 4,000 miles to go.

But what a home stretch it would be.

"New Storm, Storm, Developing Gale, Gale, Developing Gale, Gale, Gale"

...North Atlantic weathermap en route to finish

Chapter 13: The Northern North Atlantic

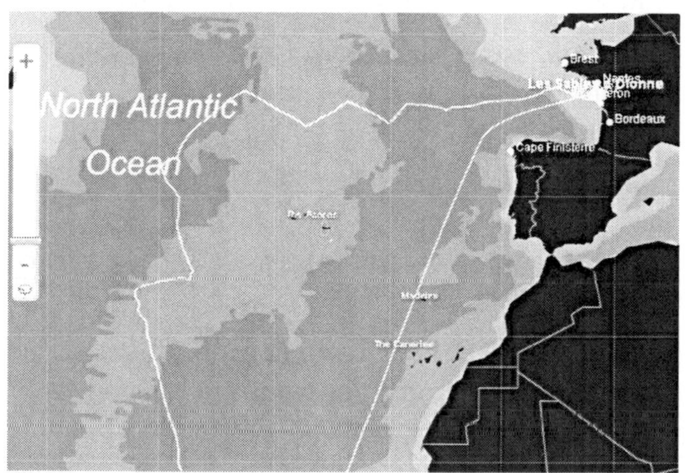

One more ocean to go.

Spoke the Norwegian flagged *Grindanger*, a smart looking ship with cranes collected aft that roll forward over her holds. She sailed south to load 40,000 tons of Brazilian newsprint for Belgium.

Tracking north across the ITCZ, we slowed to 7 knots, but never stopped as we had southbound. Instead of the normal northeast trades, that would let us sail north fast in the path of the fleet ahead, a small low formed off northern Brazil and sat privately on us. We logged 16 thunderstorms in the morning: rain, wind, no wind, 50 degree wind shifts, sails up, sails down, heading for Morocco, heading for Mexico, pounding, crashing, cant the keel, uncant the keel, start over. The violence knocked the windcharger off its mount, to dangle by its three wires. I lashed it upside down to minimize self-inflicted damage.

How to explain this violence to those ashore? I wrote a description. Take your house. Sit or stand in it. Get a crane to lift it 10' off a solid concrete slab. Then drop it, with you in it. How did that feel? How did the house do? Now lift it up again, and hover it over a concrete slab tilted to 45 degrees. Drop the house again from 10'.

Now when it crashes, it also bounces violently sideways, and out from under you. OK, how did that feel? How is the house doing? OK, do that another thousand times. Don't forget to eat, sleep, write, make sail changes, analyze the weather, charge the batteries, bail the forepeak, drain the cockpit compartment, and oh, be really careful brushing your teeth, so you don't stab yourself down your throat.

There were no options, except, as always, to continue, as best we could. In my crushing fatigue, frustration multiplied. I screamed epithets at the wind gods to vent.

In the night, a light appeared, unmoving. Closing to a mile, I saw decklights and her profile and called on the VHF, Channel 16, the channel required to be monitored, to chat. No reply. I called again, no reply. A stationary ship - a research vessel? A mystery.

Then her lights went out. She showed as a target on the radar, but no lights, a mystery ship, or... I turned our lights out too, turned off the radar to send no signals, and watched warily from the cockpit. In my studies of piracy in the South China Sea, the International Maritime Bureau's piracy website had included beginning activity off Venezuela. A high alert chill in the heat of the tropics until we were an hour away.

Finally, the hard normalcy of the trades, staysail and two reefs in the main, 30-35 degree heel, keel fully canted, crashing and bashing once more. Checking everything daily for chafe, cracks, any sign of things going wrong. "You will be tired, and the boat will be tired", Jean-Yves had said, and that was for Cape Horn, 4,000 miles ago. 4,000 miles remained.

I wrote my 15th and final essay for our NIE program on "What I'll Miss". It wasn't appropriately timed as we'd be at sea for two more weeks. In the 1980s, a phrase came into vogue pertaining to environmental issues: "The best and highest use of a resource is..." The best and highest use of me is to be offshore, hanging on by my toenails in a gale, and writing for schoolkids. So I wrote about the beauty of the sea, the sky, and the wildlife, as well as the hardship of managing this big boat in storms and the accompanying fears and frustrations. Our final Expert, Scott Hamilton, wrote similarly, about finishing expeditions, and then recuperating, physically and mentally, but nevertheless being lured to start planning his Next Expedition after a few months in civilization.

Although extremely satisfied to have constructed and completed this fifty newspaper feature series, I knew that not reaching that wide audience would reduce my motivation. I was wary of that as we headed north, into winter.

A flurry of boats were finishing. Third in was the amazing Samantha, her time adjusted for her diversion toward Yann Eliès. Two days later came Marc Guillemot. His diversion to Yann was longer, and his resultant bigger time allowance nipped Samantha by 80 minutes, after 3+ months! Yet nary a hint of disappointment from modest Samantha for the narrowly missed podium; nor did it stop her from giving Marc *"deux bises"* and a big hug, as his race had been astonishing.

After standing by Yann, he'd resumed racing. A section of mainsail track pulled away from the mast. He sailed to empty Enderby Island, 250 miles south of New Zealand, anchored, climbed the mast, drilled and tapped new holes, re-bolted and epoxied the track, returned to deck, hoisted anchor and raced on. Across the Pacific, the repair didn't hold. Past Cape Horn, he anchored off Port Stanley to make a new repair. Racing up the Atlantic, he chased those ahead. Past the Azores, where Roland Jourdain had abandoned with a broken keel, he sailed for the finish. BOOM! What was that? Let the sails out, the boat seems unstable, look over the side, his keel was gone too. Fill the ballast tanks for stability, reduce sail to storm jib and third reef to give low centers of effort, contact the Race Office and shore crew. The designer sent a new stability curve: if *Safran* heels to 28 degrees, she will capsize. So smiling Marc Guillemot held the mainsheet in his hand and sailed the last 1000 miles with no keel and no sleep.

Later that morning Brian Thompson finished fifth aboard *Pindar*, having continually repaired his boat around the world. In the afternoon, Dee Caffari finished sixth aboard *Aviva* to achieve her goal to be the first woman to circumnavigate solo non-stop in both directions. She had nursed her disintegrating mainsail home from the far side of the world.

On our 100th day at sea, a *Radio Vacances* session with Andi Robertson. Approaching my mother's February 25 birthday, family and friends planned to celebrate with her early. My voice quavered in my tired telling to Andi: yes, it's the greatest sailboat race in the world; yes, we have a global school program with a quarter million kids; but it's my Mom, she'll be 93, I shouldn't be here, I should be there, with her. Andi was wondrous, letting me talk and my choking emotions run. When I slowed, he brought on a friend, Merf Owen, who had designed Dee's boat *Aviva* and was in Les Sables d'Olonne for her finish. Hearing his voice brought me back from my abyss: "Hi Merf! How are you? Dee did GREAT with your boat. Give her a big hug for me. Really well done to you both." After we signed off, the phone rang again, it was Merf calling back on a private line. We chatted some more. Months later I asked him why: "I was worried about you, mate." The Vendée Globe: the friendliest, hardest, most caring race in the world.

The overcast, grumpy trades now turned to the Caribbean brochure trades: white fluffy clouds, blue sky, sunshine, white cresting foam against the royal blue seas, 25 knots northeast wind, dry air, flying fish, barograph rising. Our crashing continued - but at least it's pretty out.

Spoke the bulker *Sea Hamery,* in ballast, from Portugal for Brazil to load 140,000 tons of iron ore, 25 crew aboard, a good-looking ship. Had a bout with diarrhea, not sure why. To assure our fresh water, I cleaned the desalinator with biocide to prevent growth from clogging the reverse osmosis membrane and possibly contaminating the output. Turned off the computer and monitor to save amps. Transferred three jerry cans of diesel into our main tanks via our pumping system. Made a hash on the fourth by turning the valve the wrong way and pumping main tank diesel back into the full jerry can, thus overflowing its diesel into our portside compartment. What a mess. My mental mistakes were increasing.

I called Dr. Barnewolt. "I'm really beat, everything hurts, and I'm not sure how to pull myself out of this. I'm thinking that if I had something concrete to look forward to after the finish, so that this won't seem endless, do you think that would help? Maybe schedule a vacation?"

"Yes, great idea, do that. It will give you something positive to look forward to."

I called Ellen and told her the idea, and asked if she'd want to go to the Caribbean in May for a week. Yes! Keep thinking about that. It offers a bookend to this race, and makes the pain finite.

Staysail and two or three reefs in the main. Heeling the boat more so that she crash-lands on her side, to cushion the blows. The forecast is complex. The Azores high, rotating clockwise, had allowed those ahead to wrap around it, and sail downwind for France after getting through the NE trades. Not for us though. The high is forecast to dissipate, and re-form off New England, forcing us upwind on a longer route, where the others were downwind on a shorter route.

Twelve knots boatspeed, 35 knots across the deck, staysail and three reefs, likely going to storm jib. All decisions are toward what is best for the boat. I desensitized the autopilot settings, so that she'd steer less, to reduce wear on that critical bolt. We've come so far, we must finish. Don't miss handholds, make precise foot placements, talk out loud through every sail maneuver.

Thirty years ago, we sailed *Holger Danske* Canaries to Barbados, downwind in these trades. I was impressed by how steady they were. Now, I am impressed by how erratic they are, 12-28 knots of wind, +/- 25 degrees. With the pilot steering a course on compass, unable to follow shifts in the wind direction, when the wind did shift forward or aft in angle, the sails would be either not trimmed enough, or too trimmed, and would be aerodynamically inefficient. Since Cape Horn, this had plagued us and slowed us, and would until France.

I got into the bunk for the second time since the Horn, and slept for 60 minutes. Have to get more rest before the northern North Atlantic, and before we negotiate the abnormal and complex weather pattern ahead.

A celestial boost from the night sky as we regained familiar Polaris.

Frequent windshifts as we approached the high, which began to dissipate as forecast. With the pilot on compass course, I was awake constantly. After a painful nap at the chart table, I awoke with the boat at 50 degrees of heel in light winds, what's going on? A windshift had accidentally tacked the boat with the partially canted keel on the wrong side. I'd caught almost all the windshifts, but not that one. Go through the protocol, sort the boat out, continue, NEVER GIVE UP!

The good side of the dissipating high is that the sea calms, the bad side is that you make no progress. Trying to get past the calm, I gybed eight desperate and exhausting times in the night. I set the pilot to steer very little, both to save the bolt, but also to reduce rudder action which would slow us. Twice in the night the little bits of breeze caught us aback setting off the pilot alarm when it couldn't steer us back to course. Sorting those episodes out, along with the intentional gybes, was finishing me off, even with the wind down.

More complexity from the weather gods. With this high dissipating, we would have to sail 600 miles further north to meet the next high descending out of Canada, to wrap around that before heading for France. I screamed at the wind gods and turned north. A dark line and black clouds on the horizon, uh-oh. Full main to first reef, jib to staysail, first reef to second reef – hurry - second reef to third reef – hurry! BAM! The squall line hit, 5 knots of wind went to 40 knots and knocked us silly. *GA3* shuddered, then composed herself. I raged at Neptune - could we never get a break?

A day into pushing north to the next system and I couldn't stand it – hard on the wind on starboard tack we're sailing at right angles to France! I knew it wouldn't work, that a tack would not fetch the finish and would put us parallel to the next system, creating worse headwinds in the foreseeable future, but I had to try it anyway and tacked. I just had to try, just this once, to actually head for France. As suspected, we headed for Gibraltar. I tacked back north tired and depressed.

In mid-Atlantic, we crossed paths with four tankers. We spoke the first three, but the last gave concern in not answering as we converged. Finally he did. I asked if he planned to go under our stern. Yes, he was changing course now, and what were we doing out there sailing in the North Atlantic in winter? I explained, and could hear in the background gasps of disbelief. You're doing what? Around the world? You've been at sea for how many days? Alone? A chuckling "Oh my goodness!"

An encouraging but cautioning email from Unai. A 100 knot gale had demolished the giant A-frame building at the Race Village, generating 45' seas in the Bay of Biscay.

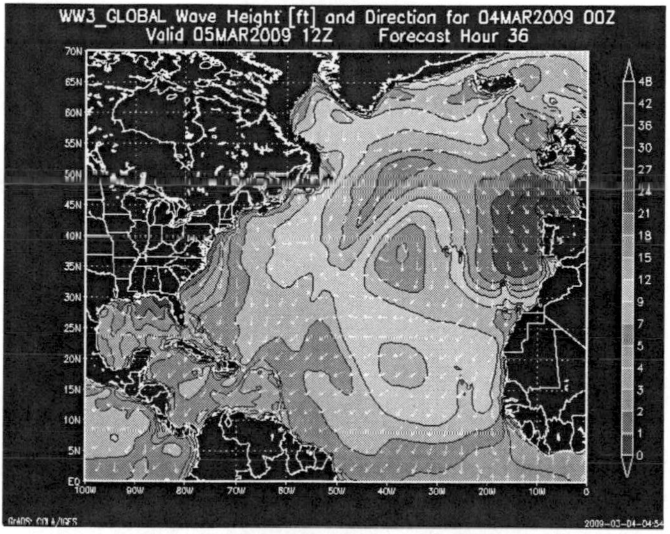

Big Seas in the Bay of Biscay

In our slog up the endless Atlantic, our fleet sequence had seemed unlikely to change. Now, I wasn't so sure. Whereas we had to head north for three days to get to this next system, behind us the dissipated high was re-forming, and Raphaël would be able to turn early and cut the corner. He was gaining 100 miles a day, heading for France while we headed north. In the last three days we'd made only 400 miles toward France. I became frantic, screaming at the weather gods in conversations with Ellen. I tried to cry to dissipate the tension but couldn't.

I wasn't so concerned over 9th versus 10th place, but that our stories, developed over four hard and human months at sea, would change. The story would become "Dinelli catches Wilson at finish". That would be a silly sports story, and a waste of the two more important human stories. Our story was the lone American, the oldest skipper, the asthmatic, the big global school program. Raphaël's story was solar panels, a big vertical windcharger, and racing the Vendée Globe using only renewable energy and no fossil fuels. These were two great stories, and both would be lost if he caught us.

Samantha emailed from her whirlwind post-Vendée Globe PR tour for *Roxy*:

Hello Rich,
SORRY I have not been in touch for AGES. I wanted to send you some encouragement as I can see that your race is continuing to be pretty tough, and I can imagine that you must be impatient to get there now. Not much longer to go, and I hope that the wind will be kinder to you soon so you can enjoy the last few days of your adventure. So, hang in there, you are about to make the USA proud with your great result.
Go the Great American!!!
Have fun, take care, Sam x,
PS I hope to be there at your finish....

North, north, north, head to intersect the new high with 1042 mb pressure forecast. 1042 millibars? Is that even possible? I'd never heard of pressure that high. There will be NO wind anywhere near that. Should I try to cut across its path upwind? No, we won't make it. Sail for the center, let it pass, then wrap around its slow clockwise rotation.

Can't we catch a break? The high stalled right in front of us. Our barograph read precisely 1042 millibars, impossible, but true. We've been heading north for Newfoundland, not east for France. Dead ahead is zero wind in the stalled high. How to get around it? Head northwest for Nova Scotia to go around the no-wind center. Two knots of wind, one knot of boatspeed, heading for Halifax, I'M GOING TO SCREAM! Can this get any worse?

Forget it, roll up the jib, reef the mainsail, turn off the pilot, go below. The boat drifted in circles while I tried to sleep per Brien's instructions. My anger and frustration wouldn't permit it. Emails arrived from people who understood what was happening:

Everyone from office assistants to my dentist are cheering for you. The struggle you have had all the way up the Atlantic from the Horn is truly amazing. It seems that head winds seek out GA3. You are due a break and the odds say you will get one.

And...

What an epic journey, like something out of Homer. It never seemed like you caught much of a break in any part of the world yet you proved you are as tough as they get.

Some tried to encourage with humor...

Rich, you realize you're 500 miles closer to Boston than France?

I was in no mood for humor, no matter how well-intentioned. YES, I REALIZE THAT!

A catspaw in the distance, then another, then a puff across the calm. OK, jib, full main, course NNW, France is perpendicular to our course north. Through the afternoon, slowly, slowly, slowly, we wrapped our course first gaining N, then NNE, then NE, and sailing downwind. Dr. Barnewolt emailed from the ER.

I see that you are turning the corner. This is OUTSTANDING! Talk to you soon.

He called later, and as we talked, my anger and frustration exploded at the weather gods who wouldn't give us a break. Brien had seen me through three serious injuries, and had regularly called through the Atlantic to check on both the physical and mental health of his patient far offshore. He let me rave for many paragraphs, then when it was spent, he urged sleep and a feeling of accomplishment. I calmed and reverted to a steely – NEVER GIVE UP!

Autopilot alarms. Boot up the backup, it works. Go back to the stronger primary, alarms, log the Data Error number from the readout and call Mark Wylie. "That error indicates a ram problem, it's not moving as far as it should for the voltage applied. Often that's air getting into the cylinder. It's been working a long time. It's a sealed unit, so you can't add hydraulic fluid, but you do have that replacement ram that I replenished in Sables d'Olonne." Get out the third ram, two hours later it's in place, go back to the primary pilot, keep going. As Jean-Yves had warned, *GA3* was tiring.

An email muffin arrived:

Dear Rich:
Sounds like you are in the home stretch now and it is time for the penultimate blueberry muffin. What an incredible accomplishment. I am sure you are tired, lonely, and SICK TO DEATH OF THE WHOLE THING. But we have all been following your trip so closely and thinking about you throughout. Your mother may be the first adventurer in the family but you may be the most ambitious...and the most successful. So sad to think that your father isn't around to see this...he would be so proud. By the way, those blueberries are FRESH! And the muffin is warm.
All the best,
K

The mention of Dad caught me aback. No matter the normal father/son differences that we'd had, he *would* have liked this one: a huge, real world K12 program, in the hands-on image of MIT; and a huge adventure at sea. When we'd finished San Francisco – Boston in *GA2*, a power boat came alongside with John Kiley at the helm. In primary school together, he'd known my Dad. He shouted over simply "Richard, your father would be proud." My warm blueberry muffin had the same emotional effect.

On the northern side of the high, we were dead downwind for France. The system started to move with us. We couldn't get in front of it, even a bit, to get northwesterlies and head straight east for France. Just as you can't sail directly upwind, but have to tack back and forth, zigzagging into the wind, you can't sail straight downwind, you have to gybe back and forth, taking the wind at 30 degrees off the stern. When we engaged with this new system, our hoped for course perfectly due east, but with the wind perfectly due west, we had to gybe back and forth in front of it, first for Norway for a day, then gybe for Morocco for a day, then gybe for Scotland for a day, then gybe for Portugal for a day. In utter exasperation, I wrote a piece for the website explaining the trigonometry of our course, with sines and cosines, and that our unavoidable zig-zag added ~40% to our distance to France, and that the press forecast ETA was wrong.

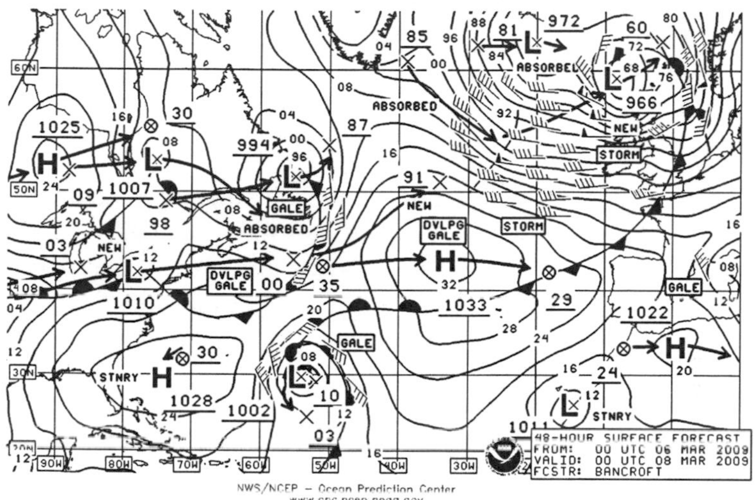

The North Atlantic in Winter

The weathermap showed seven depressions in the North Atlantic, all moving, all interacting, all changing daily. We were making progress – KEEP AT IT, AND BE CAREFUL IN THE GYBES. It would be stupid and embarrassing to lose the mast now.

Arnaud Boissières and Steve White finished 7th and 8th on sisterships from our generation, great efforts both. When a New York Times article had finally mentioned us in the Vendée Globe when we were off Buenos Aires, they published a photo of Arnaud, his young child, and me. I'd sent the weblink to Arnaud via Denis Horeau, he sent back happy thanks. Across the Pacific, Steve and I had several solid Iridium conversations. Ellen had sent me his superbly written reports, including the hilarious one about seeing an albatross who, every once in a while, would drop a leg, and shake it, as if it was cramped from too much time in an airline seat! I'd burst out laughing, shouting "I've seen that bird!" What a marvelous effort Arnaud and Steve had made. Keep going *GA3*. Fend off Raphaël, now closed to within 600 miles, but at last we're moving again, and generally toward Europe.

Then terrible news from Raphaël. He'd broken his boom. In a monumental effort, he'd gotten it off and down below, and made a major repair with fibreglass, epoxy, and carbon, then got the boom back on deck, mounted it, got the mainsail back on. A job that would take 4 crew at the dock, Raphaël did at sea, alone. In his resultant fatigue, he was thrown across the cabin, and broke ribs, as I had done four months ago. He slowed, but persevered.

A huge storm was brewing north of Scotland and looked to expand south over the region. The Azores High had re-established itself to our south and would now slow Raphaël. We zig-zagged on the edge between these two systems, tiptoeing a tightrope toward the Bay of Biscay.

Our radar detector alarmed. I turned it off and scanned the horizon. Nothing. Turned it back on, it alarmed again. Turned it off and scanned again. After two hours, from its slow overtaking of us from astern, I saw a big containership paralleling our course and usually hidden by the big Atlantic swells. We spoke the ship, German, 3,000 TEUs, from Philadelphia for Rotterdam: "Captain, what speed are you making?"

"18 knots."

"Isn't that slow for your size?"

"Yes. We're waiting for the 35' seas at the mouth of the English Channel to subside before we go in."

An email from Unai reinforced the point:

Hi Rich,
Nice to see you sailing back near Biscay Bay. Keep going!
Remember race finish on the marina berth! not before !!
BIG AND SINCERE CONGRATULATIONS !!
BEST REGARDS
UNAI

I kept checking the boat. An adjustable tensioning line on the staysail stay was fraying. I interlaced a fixed Vectran lashing in support. I cut the three electric wires to the windcharger, one at a time so as not to short any circuitry, brought the unit below, unbolted the blades from the hub and stowed the pieces. I bailed the forepeak and bow compartments. I made sure the daggerboard was down halfway – we didn't need it for lateral resistance, yet it would offer some sacrificial protection to the rudders against collisions with submerged objects.

An email from rock-steady Ellen who had heard it all for four months: "Denis forecasts a big crowd for your Sunday arrival. He wants to know what music you want when you walk up the dock, and what you want for your first meal, they'll cook anything for you." I replied that both questions were premature and tempted fate. If Denis needed answers, could she please provide them? Furthermore, I would never arrive by Sunday, likely Tuesday morning - what weathermaps were they looking at? Had they not read my piece on trigonometry?

Nearing the Bay of Biscay, the chart indicated defined shipping channels from Cape Finisterre at the northwest corner of Spain to L'Ouessant at the northwest corner of France. We encountered the southbound lane first: five ships in single file. We altered course for the first two, then sailed across the lane in a gap before the third.

Twenty miles further east, we approached the northbound lane: four ships in single file converging from the horizon. The first three crossed our eastbound path easily, the fourth might be an issue. Rather than follow on radar, I sat in the cockpit, under the cuddy on the port side, eating Fig Newtons and watching the ship converge with our course.

Then I woke up.

The ship wasn't there anymore. I leapt to my feet and looked forward. There it was, a mile ahead off our port bow. I thought, but couldn't be sure, that she had passed in front of us. How bad would that have been, to get run over by a ship in daylight 24 hours from the finish.

Keep pressing. We're sailing onto a lee shore now. The massive 966 mb system north of Scotland extends to the middle of the Bay of

Biscay and will expand down the coast. The weathermap labelled it "New Storm". Our wind is shifting to pull our course toward it. Where we are says "Storm", and behind us says "Developing Gale". Yet it's starting to feel like home - we're aiming at Port la Foret, where we prepared *GA3*, where we lived and made friends. Yet remember the inscription of Dr. Francis Wright's book Celestial Navigation - "Constant Vigilance!"

An email from Scott, with good counsel from a veteran expedition leader:

> *As you get closer to the coast the excitement will build and the temptations will also increase to just "get there". They call it "get-there-itis". Many bad outcomes are the result of a series of bad decisions, skipping checklists and taking shortcuts in a rush to "get there". Just a reminder to keep your focus on the game until you and GA3 are safely across the finish line and tied up in LSDO. Same thing goes for nutrition and hydration. 350 miles probably doesn't sound like much after 28,000 or so that you've already sailed. Stay aware and keep being cautious and safe until the fat lady sings. She will be singing soon!!!*
> *Scott*

Onto the edge of the Continental Shelf, our tiptoeing between systems offers a moderate breeze and sea. A few hundred miles to go. Full on high alert as best you can.

At dusk, gybe south along the shelf aiming to pass west of Plateau de Rochebonne, an area of shoals and rocks fifty miles west of the coast, before a final gybe for the finish in the morning. Beware fishing boats tonight in these shallower waters at the shelf's edge.

As the sun set on what would likely be our final night at sea, a pod of dolphins came alongside, leaping in our bow and stern waves, and amidships, a welcome and emotional escort home. Bill and I had had the same reception closing Cape Otway on our final night at sea coming into Melbourne aboard *GA2*. Now, as then, I shouted and banged the winch with a handle in communication. "Thank you, thank you, thank you, we needed this, great to have you with us, great to see you, thank you, thank you, thank you!" One more night, maybe

I was going to make it, maybe I was going to finish the Vendée Globe.

Watch the fishing boat lights through the night, alter course to go west of Rochebonne, easier and safer then trying to pinch downwind to the east of them, and though shorter, force us close to the rocks. Check three GPS units to confirm our position. See a couple of fishing boats trawling on the banks. Once well past, a final dawn gybe, maneuvered ever so carefully, toward the finish, 50 miles away. A fishing boat exiting the banks southbound crossed our bow a hundred yards ahead. Heed Unai's warning: pay attention until tied up to the dock.

As the big North Sea storm expands down the coast to greet our arrival, it will be blowing hard at the finish. Study the chart. The finish line is .4 miles from the beach. There will be no time to celebrate, we'll have to have the staysail ready to be furled instantly, and no more than three reefs in the main. Per multiple planning emails, Hugues and Flo will be on a Zodiac and will come aboard after the finish buoy. The Race Office will put an inspector aboard to check seals on the propeller shaft and extra jerry cans. At the channel entrance, the Harbormaster will take us in tow. Ellen will come aboard once we're in the channel, which we can't enter until 1 pm for the tide.

I loaded the staysail furling line on a winch to be ready. I overtrimmed the mainsail so that I could set up the new running backstays to be ready for a gybe after the finish. Keep those three reefs, no bravado now.

The phone rang, it was Andi from *Radio Vacances*. Mistaking this last interview as a personal call, a flood of emotions spilled privately out, about how tired I was, and how utterly endless the Atlantic had been. I'd described in an earlier interview that although I could remember factual details of our race pre-Cape Horn, I couldn't remember it emotionally. An odd sensation, but true, the Indian and Pacific Oceans seemed five years ago. The ascent of the Atlantic had needed every bit of my emotional capacity, and had pushed out everything else.

For me and for others, the Vendée Globe is comprised of two halves: pre-Cape Horn, and post-Cape Horn. Although 2/3 of the race by mileage and time, the Horn was only halfway emotionally and physically on the accumulated fatigue curve. The endless Atlantic, mostly upwind and 9,000 miles now for us, took its toll on all.

I couldn't extend our conversation, I needed to keep a lookout. Yet it was good to hear his voice. A satphone friend for four months, Andi was part of our team too.

After hanging up, I returned to the cockpit, to check everything again. I went to the forepeak, found a short line, and rigged a bridle at the bow for a towrope when we got to the channel. Back to the cabin, the phone rang again. It was Brian Thompson, calling from the UK. "Great job Rich, enjoy the finish, you won't believe the reception you're going to get. Take it all in. Be proud, you did a great job finishing a tough race."

"Thanks Brian. It's a long way from the little trimaran, for both of us!"

"It sure is", he agreed.

"And great job yourself sailing that monster boat."

"Thanks, she was a handful."

Off the port bow, flecks on the distant horizon, hints of buildings grew slowly more distinct – Les Sables d'Olonne! We'd been alone for four months, just the two of us, *GA3* and I. This fantastic boat, now four times *"autour du monde"*. At the start I'd been right: she couldn't do it without me; and I couldn't do it without her. Yet together, we, yes we, would finish the Vendée Globe.

I patted her cuddy in affectionate thanks. On the horizon, splashing bow waves streaked our way.

"BRA-VO! BRA-VO! BRA-VO!"
...French crowd cheering at finish

Chapter 14: Finishing Among the Amazing French

Six Zodiacs, bouncing and splashing, with official green flags snapping in the wind, swooped alongside to establish protective escort positions: two forward, two amidships, two aft.

"BRAVO RICH!"

"MAGNIFIQUE!"

"SUPERBE!"

Thirty minutes out, we closed the finish rapidly, the breeze increasing, our speed surging toward 15 knots. I stayed in the cockpit, no exulting yet, heed Unai, the race isn't over until we're tied up to the dock. I had zoomed the digital chart to watch our track, and tried to discern in the distance the finish line marked by the Nouch Sud Buoy.

Press boats with photographers and TV cameramen aboard jockeyed for position alongside. A Zodiac with a huge American flag on a pole inserted itself between the cameras and *GA3* providing a patriotic foreground. A passenger ferry paralleled us with hundreds of spectators lining the rail. *GA3*, flying now, began to leave the slower motorboats behind. The seas built from the shoaling, the increasing wind, and the power boat wakes.

We were surrounded by humans, the first seen in four months! But we can't engage them yet, we're not finished.

I checked the cockpit – were we ready? The staysail furling line was loaded on the utility winch, locked into third gear for high furling speed, and the pedestal clutch was engaged. The GPS was tracking on the computer screen, but we can't see the buoy yet. More vessels join our parade as *Great American III* races toward the coast.

Warm wool stocking cap, sailing gloves, foul weather gear, still have some sailing to do, don't get distracted. At this speed and course, the beach is two minutes past the finish, so we'll have to get sorted fast. We'll bear off downwind to slow, roll up the staysail in the mainsail's lee, then gybe and head away from the harbor until the Race Office boards to check the seals. Then we'll gybe back and sail on 3rd reef alone toward the harbor entrance. There we'll get a tow from the harbormaster. That's the plan.

There, a half mile ahead, the Nouch Sud Buoy (46°29' N, 1°47' W). I'd dreamed of this moment for three years, a huge project, with grave but calculated personal risks, undertaken for onshore effect. Yet to succeed onshore, we had to succeed offshore, and we nearly had.

Check the computer screen, dash below to zoom and get the buoy markings to check as we go by. Back to the cockpit. *GA3* is flying now, 15+ knots boatspeed, the breeze and seas are up as expected, heed Unai, heed Scott.

Closing the buoy, a flood of emotions. Just like the start - talk out loud to allay the emotions. Around the world, alone, my faithful shipmate *GA3*, almost there, watch the fleet around us, make sure we have clearance on the buoy, watch ahead, and watch us, not the spectators and well-wishers who are shouting congratulations and pointing innumerable cameras, pay attention until the finish and until the dock.

A hundred yards to go... Fifty yards... Almost there...

BWAAAAHHHH! The Race Committee blasted its horn.

WE'D DONE IT! *Great American III*, 121 days at sea, 28,790 miles on the GPS, had finished the Vendée Globe 2008-9 in ninth position, with two boats still at sea, and nineteen abandoned. I banged on the cuddy, *GA3* and I, we'd done it, together.

Get to work. Bear the boat off, re-set the pilot on the new slowed course, grind the pedestal to furl the staysail, bear off further to slow further. Grind. A Zodiac with Hugues and Flo aboard bounced alongside. Keep grinding. They were trying to come aboard as we sailed toward the beach. Another figure climbed first over the lifelines, leapt into the cockpit and smothered me in a bear hug and a huge smile – Thierry Dubois! He'd built the boat himself, and when we'd bought her, he wasn't sure about me, an older American, who thought he could sail the Vendée Globe – so there had been doubting tension as I sailed his baby away. But not now. Now, for the first time in three tries, his boat had officially finished the Vendée Globe, the hardest race in the world, and he was ecstatic.

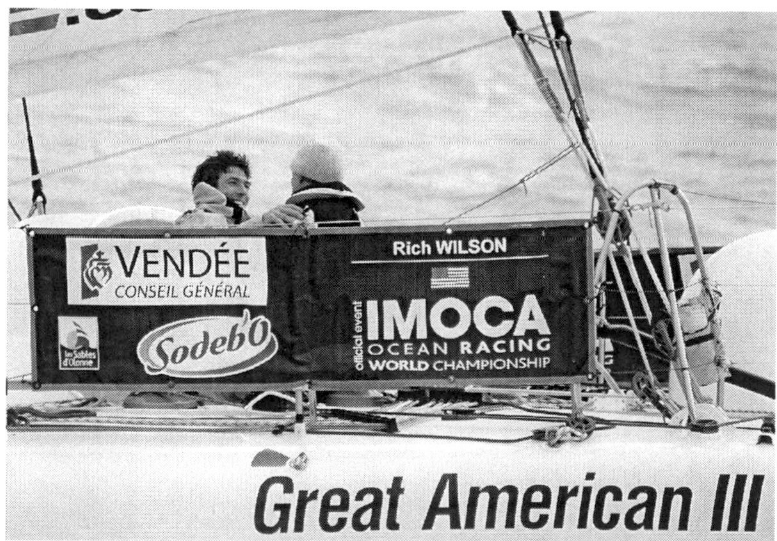

A Happy Thierry Dubois

Hugues made the bouncing transition next, with Flo alongside. I hugged our long-time Wilson family friends and *GA3*'s chief *preparateur*. A fourth jumped aboard whom I would soon befriend, Papo, recommended by Samantha to help us sort the boat after finishing.

With the staysail furled, I said let's gybe, and was momentarily concerned that with all the people on board, we'd be casual, get it wrong and make a problem, especially with the wind and seas up. I waved to the Zodiacs and spectator boats where we would turn, they accommodated the big white sixty-footer that had just sailed the world, and moved off to give us space. Our new crew aboard gybed attentively, we were OK, and *GA3* headed down the coast.

A Zodiac brought Race Official Joël Gâté alongside, Hugues helped him aboard.

"Felicitations, Rich, superbe, absolument superbe."

Then Hugues led him below to show the intact seals. We were legal. Hugues fired up the engine, we gingerly gybed again, and headed under third reef alone upwind toward the harbor a mile away. It was blowing hard now, the escort fleet had stood off for our two gybes, and now closed ranks as we neared the harbor entrance.

A bouncing Zodiac surged alongside *"Felicitations, The Great American, très bien fait!"*

It took a moment to recognize the smiling face of Samantha under her big stocking cap and foul weather jacket collar. *"Merci, Samantha, merci, c'est incroyable."* My "virtual running mate" who had helped me across the Pacific had returned to Les Sables d'Olonne to see *GA3* and her skipper come home.

***GA3 Returns* Home from the Sea**

The tide was high enough for us to enter the channel. Approaching the entrance, we rounded up and lowered the mainsail, our engine working but inadequate in the wind and seas. Hugues went forward to receive a tow-rope from the Harbormaster and tie it to the bridle. The Harbormaster clapped his hands high overhead to signal his congratulations. With a load taken on the towrope, for the first time in four months we were not on our own. We entered the calmed waters of the channel, finally protected from the open ocean. Thousands lined the breakwater to cheer and clap: *"Bravo Rich!" "Bien Fait!" "Bienvenu aux Sables d'Olonne!" "Bon retour!"* It was overwhelming.

Another Zodiac alongside, Ellen climbed over the lifeline, big hugs and kisses. She'd seen the entire project for three anxious and stressful years, had encouraged all the way, and never questioned why. Without her, would we have made it?

Hugues said "go forward and wave to the crowd". I couldn't imagine leaving my shipmate's cockpit, but reluctantly did.

A smaller version of "YES U CAN", which had dramatically draped the pier at the start, was held high overhead by a spectator. We passed the Harbormaster's office and dock, turned to starboard into the marina and toward the Vendée Globe pontoon, more people on boats and the docks, cheering, applauding, shouting their whole-hearted *"Felicitations!"*

The doctor had been right so long ago when I went for a flu shot before the start: *"premier ou dernier, vous serez un vainqueur, et la publique sera la pour votre retour."* And there they were, in warmth and in spirit. They had only asked our best effort, to tell them about life at sea, and to come home safely. They knew what it had taken; they knew how hard it had been. No matter that we were foreigners; now we were family.

Someone steered. I stood on the bow waving. A mass of people jammed the sturdy dock. Then we were alongside, docklines being tossed to welcoming hands. I saw my sisters, Anne and Sarah, tears in their eyes, then cousins Judy Fletcher and Paul Simpson, whom I had not known were coming. Then Andi with a handshake and "Well done, Rich, welcome home".

Race Director Denis Horeau

Then Race Director Denis Horeau – what a joy!

"Ah, Denis! Je l'ai fait! C'est incroyable!"

"Bravo Rich, you have done it!"

Kisses on two cheeks from both of us. Denis had loved our school program because the newspapers had brought this incredible race, not only to our students, but also to a large family readership in America. He'd always said that the Vendée Globe is a race of human stories, and he liked ours.

The Deputy Mayor of Les Sables d'Olonne, in his best French-accented, deliberate English, handing me a magnum of champagne with a handshake: *"Rich - wonderful race - everybody here is proud of you. This is for you - you deserve it - quite a lot."* I replied *"Pour maintenant?"* He indicated yes, and I pulled the cork, shook the bottle, sprayed the crowd, and took a giant swig, the unfamiliar champagne tickling my throat happily to a cough.

The huge American flag from the Zodiac was passed through the crowd. I gave it a giant wave overhead, inciting a cheer from the French.

Over the lifelines for the first time in four months, I turned to give several hardy slaps of affection and appreciation onto *Great American III*'s deck. I didn't want to leave her. What an amazing boat. We had been through so much together: the broachings under spinnaker, the gales in the south, the crushing seas, the dangerous, accidental gybes, the incessant pounding up the endless Atlantic from Cape Horn. She had hung in there, older and with many miles on her, persevering, while so many new boats faltered, and giving me a chance for this moment. We had done this together. She couldn't do it without me; and I couldn't do it without her. We, yes WE, had done it.

Denis and the Deputy Mayor, with security guards leading the way, escorted me through the crowd on the dock. A French woman, in a dress sewn solely of American flags for my arrival, gave a kiss and a hug. Alain Gautier, winner from '92-'93, and now the Safety Officer, congratulated me: *"Bien fait, Rich, très bien fait."* My unsteady land legs were supported by Denis' helping hand under my elbow. Ray Charles' "America the Beautiful", Ellen's happy choice (the French love Ray Charles) in response to the Race Office query for the occasion, provided appropriate background music for this especially moving moment. A big hug of thanks for Neal Skorka. He had managed our sitesALIVE! program, satcom to the boat, fifty newspapers and live website ashore, communications to our 15

Experts, for 121 days straight, through weekdays, weekends, nights and holidays. Seamlessly, smoothly, and calmly, Neal had delivered the critical shore component – the goal of our Vendée Globe effort. Up the companionway to firm land, inching through the crowd, all extending a handshake, or a slap on my back. They wanted to say *"Bravo, Rich"*, and make eye contact, to be sure I received their sincere good wishes.

Denis delivered me to the steps of a stage, I mounted them alone. An interviewer waited to get the very first thoughts and emotions of the skipper who had just sailed singlehanded around the world and finished the Vendée Globe. At the top of the steps was Julian, who had called on his graveyard shifts to check on us. He reached out his hand with a big smile, I took it and pulled him in for a back-slapping hug of thanks, then on to the interviewer.

A Chance to Thank the French

The multi-thousand crowd began a rhythmic chant *"BRA-VO! BRA-VO! BRA-VO!"* A translator was on stage with the interviewer. I asked to say a few words before his questions.

In 1980, when Phil Weld had won the solo transatlantic race, he had said that as he approached the finish, not knowing if he was 1st , 2nd, or 3rd, he'd thought about what he would say if he was first and had the chance to speak. From that good idea, I'd thought a lot about this moment, and what I would say if I finished and had the chance. I resolved to thank the French, for their welcome and encouragement, and I would try in their language (see page 292 for English version):

Pour moi, ce Vendée Globe était deux Vendée Globes. [a wondering murmur].

Un Vendée Globe en mer, très dur, très difficile, le plus stimulant dans le monde. Et avec les navigateurs incroyables – [pause] beaucoup des Français navigateurs incroyable [appreciative chuckle] - et plusieurs des autres pays aussi.

[Big exhale from me] Golfe de Gascogne, l'Atlantique du Nord, du Sud, Ocean d'Indien, le Pacific, Cap de Bonne Espérance, Cap Horn [I shook my head at the thought, evoking sympathetic laughter], l'Atlantique encore...sans fin [murmurs of understanding].

Mais aussi, le Vendée Globe sur la terre est l'autre Vendée Globe. ...Notre... [I stumbled].

Sur mon approche à Cap Horn, dans Les États Unis, nous avons eu un nouveau Président...c'est bon [a cheer for our new president and the departure of our old]. Mais il y a beaucoup, beaucoup des ans, notre troisième Président, Monsieur Thomas Jefferson, qui a écrit notre Declaration d'Independence, avant qu'il était notre Président, il était notre Ambassadeur à France. [Knowing nod from the interviewer.] Et dans Paris, il a dit que 'tous les hommes ont deux pays: son pays, et la France'. [Big cheer, the French love Thomas Jefferson.] Et je pense qu'il était absolument correct. [Intrigued smile from the interviewer.] Parce que pour moi, cet expérience ici en France était incroyable. Toujours, toujours, vous m'avez donné votre encouragement, pour trois mois dans Port la Foret, et un mois ici aux Sables d'Olonne, et je l'apprécie beaucoup.

Dans le futur, quand les choses très difficile sur la mer – les tempêtes, les tempêtes, la fatigue, pas dormir – sont perdu de ma memoire[interviewer nod for my correct grammar], je me souviendrai cet autre Vendée Globe, ici, sur la terre, en France, avec vous. Merci. [Huge roar of approval and applause.]

Ten minutes of Q&A onstage with the interviewer, a local TV host, and then across the compound to a tent for a Press Conference. The big lot seemed empty, and it was. That's where the huge A-frame had stood that housed the sponsor and education exhibits, blown down by Unai's 100 knot gale.

A half hour press conference, with the public and schoolkids in attendance, then autographs, pictures with classes, hugs from Samantha's parents. Then across the street to the Race Office, to sign the required Race Compliance certificate, and have my first meal, knowingly ordered by Ellen on my behalf, that of an American roadside diner, cooked to order by the French: two eggs scrambled, home fries, toast, bacon, milk, orange juice.

An interview with a French medical magazine about my asthma, then home to our rental house for a shower and change of clothes. Later to our favorite restaurant – the Buffalo Grill – whose Vendée Globe mascot we had become when I dined there nightly before the start to stabilize my nutrition. Greeted as a homecoming hero, we took photos with their entire kitchen and wait staff, and signed requested autographs for diners and their kids. I ordered my usual Pony Express: a hamburger, baked potato, salad, glass of milk, mini crème brulee and a sugar cookie.

Plus a glass of champagne.

We were home from the sea.

"2012 ou 2016?"
...question from the French public

Chapter 15: Prizing-Giving Ceremony

Emotional Man on the Dock

The next splendid day, with sunshine, warmth, a light breeze and blue sky, we returned to *GA3*, looking calm, beautiful, and content tied up to the Vendée Globe pontoon. Denis Horeau came by and joked that the boat looked so good that perhaps we had anchored behind nearby Île de Yeu for four months! Bags of croissants and the magnum of champagne sustained our group in the cockpit.

All day on the dock, a rotating group of well-wishers, 8, 12, 4, 18 people, surrounded the boat to chat. They wanted a picture with a finishing Vendée Globe skipper, or an autograph, or their child to ask his or her shy question. I loved to talk to them about dreams and challenges, the cold and gales of the south, of Cape Horn and Crossing the Line, the demoralizing autopilot problems in the South Atlantic, the mesmerizing albatross and flying fish, the new stars in the south, the breath-taking reception in Les Sables d'Olonne, and the hardships and joys of preparing for, and then living and racing their French Vendée Globe.

Toward the afternoon's end, I noticed a man standing apart fifty feet down the dock. He was looking at the boat, but not joining the group, even on its periphery. Occasionally, I caught his eye. When the current group disbanded, I walked toward him to say hello, and as I approached, tears began to stream down his face. In the emotion of our moment, my tears flowed too. From Grenoble in the center of France, he was in Les Sables d'Olonne on business. He had followed the race every day, and was overwhelmed and honored to see a boat that had just sailed around the world and to meet her skipper.

His tears flowed freely. The skippers had had their role to play – to sail alone around the world; and he and the onshore public had had their role to play too – to live and breathe every triumph, travail, fear and joy of every skipper every day at risk at sea. His emotion poured from the fact that it was we, humanity, in these two roles, together, who had sailed around the world in the Vendée Globe. He was proud to be a member of this remarkable species homo sapiens who, together, had accomplished this feat.

Raphaël Dinelli, Norbert Sedlacek, & Me
Comrades & Competitors

Four days later, Raphaël finished in 10th, and Norbert the next day in 11th. Norbert was the final finisher, but he was not last, as nineteen boats had fallen by the wayside en route. We three had a great reunion, and the fondness and true affection between Vendée Globe racers was evident. We had been both competitors and comrades-in-arms, racing, suffering and struggling for four months on the great oceans of the world, and now shared a unique experience.

How unique? I was told that I had been the 46th in history to have sailed solo, non-stop, around the world, compared to 500 astronauts and 3000 who had climbed Everest. Ours was a small and kindred group.

With Norbert's finish, the provocative statistic was complete: 100% of the women had finished, yet only 1/3 of the men.

I presented a *GA3* daily flag to Denis Horeau and to Sophie Verceletto, President of the Vendée Globe organizing body who were both moved by this living memorabilia from their race, and to Directeur du Port Olonna (Harbormaster of Les Sables d'Olonne) Jacques Archambaud, who presented me with a book on the first Vendée Globe. He inscribed it:

> *Nous avons beaucoup apprécié votre aventure, votre humanisme, nos rencontres et votre gentillesse. Grand BRAVO pour votre performance dans ce Vendée Globe 2008/9.*
>
> *[English: We much appreciated your adventure, your humanism, our meetings, and your kindness. A big BRAVO for your performance in this Vendée Globe 2008/9.]*

He invited me to leave *GA3* at the Vendée Globe pontoon for as long as we liked.

I was spent from the race. My knees hurt, my fingers hurt, my wrists, elbows and shoulders hurt. My neck hurt from when I had fallen on my head. I was tired beyond description, worn out in every dimension. I'd been stressed, and apprehensive for a very long time. I couldn't imagine ever racing the Vendée Globe again.

In fact, I thought that I might never go sailing again. Although it would have been good for Americans to have seen a boat that completed this most arduous race, I planned neither to sail *GA3* home to Marblehead, nor to sail her offshore again. But *GA3* should be offshore, offshore was her home, so we would put her up for sale in France, where most shorthanded sailors lived.

If I were to sail again, it would likely be a small boat, like the bright red Haven 12½ footer *Flash* that my friend Bob Metcalfe had. *Flash* gave the joy of sailing, but so much more simply. Hoist the mainsail with one hand, the jib with one hand, cast off the mooring line, and sail. For anything else in sailing, this race had finished me.

Yet throughout that week one question surfaced often from the amazing French: *"Deux mille douze?"* Would I return for Vendée Globe 2012? I deflected the question with a smile: "*Merci pour votre confiance, mais une fois par vie, je pense.*" People accepted that, understanding the hardship that I had endured, physically, mentally, emotionally.

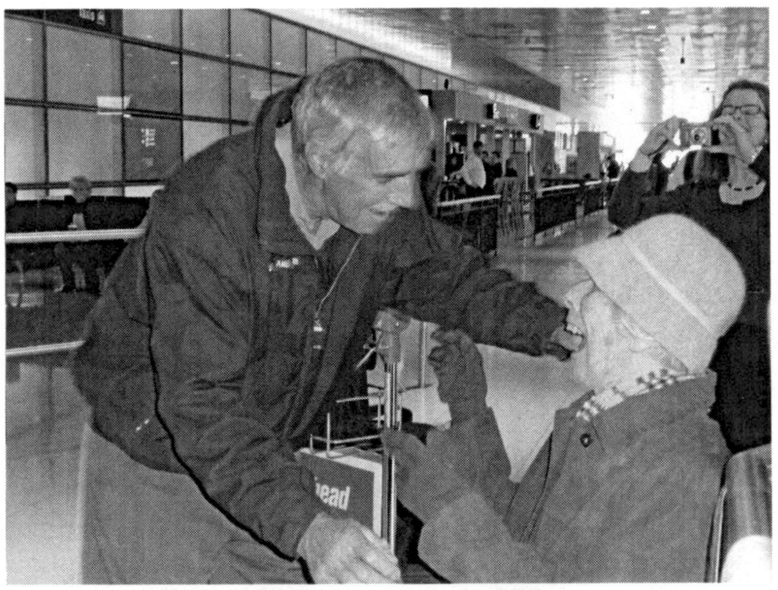

"Hi Mom, I Made It!"

Ten days after our finish, I returned to Boston. Exiting Customs & Immigration at Logan Airport, a cheer and applause startled me. I knew Ellen would be there, but not the other dozen friends who had followed our voyage daily. And there in the front row, in a wheelchair for ease of access, looking happy, proud, elegant and stalwart, was the original adventurer in our Wilson family, and my greatest inspiration, my Mother. My eyes welled up, I gave her a lingering big hug and kiss, and said, "I made it Mom, I'm home."

After a month of decompression, I returned to Les Sables d'Olonne to sail *GA3* to Port la Foret. Before leaving, a class of chattering schoolkids walked down the nearly empty dock. I waved. One student saw me, did a double-take, then shouted to the others and the teacher. They stopped, stared, then reversed course, and streamed down the finger pier to our cockpit. They had followed the Vendée Globe every day, each student following a specific skipper. The one who waved back had followed me and *GA3*. We took photos and I answered questions. What a delight!

The Prize-giving was scheduled for late May, 10 weeks after the fleet had finished. On a Saturday afternoon, the skippers were invited to a signing of the official Vendée Globe book at the central bookstore in Les Sables d'Olonne. What a heartfelt reunion! A limping Yann Eliès nevertheless looked refreshed. A smiling Dee Caffari looking happy in achieving her goals. A competitor's *preparateur* flattered me saying that he thought my performance was the most outstanding in the fleet.

That evening, we were treated to a formal dinner for all the teams and guests. I found Philippe de Villiers, President of the Vendée Department, and Louis Guédon, Mayor of Les Sables d'Olonne, to give each a *GA3* daily flag. Both serious politicians, when they realized what I was presenting to them, a living memento flown from a foreign boat on the far side of the world in their race, both teared up, grabbed my shoulders in both hands, and kissed me on both cheeks.

Our *GA3* table included Fabienne Mollé from the U.S. Embassy in Paris, Thierry Dubois, other friends from HBS who lived in Berlin, and close friends of Denis Horeau who had become friends of *GA3*. Sadly, Ellen couldn't come as her son's college graduation took understandable preference.

After dinner, the teams moved outside to the prize-giving ceremony.

The Oscars' organizers should go to Les Sables d'Olonne to learn how to put on a show. 120,000 people jammed the beach at low tide, the only venue in the city that could handle the crowd. Above a huge stage, backdrop, spotlights and speakers, spectacular fireworks lit the sky. The TV host from the finish stage emcee'ed the event. People had come to salute the race, skippers, boats and themselves, and to participate one final time in Vendée Globe 2008-9.

I wore my best suit for the occasion, the only skipper to do so, out of my respect for the French, the race, my competitors, and the public. Also, I felt I was representing the USA.

An Honor & Privilege to Stand with this Group

Seated in a special section in front, the thirty skippers were invited onto the stage. By accident, walking up last, I ended up front row, center, between Unai Basurko and Dominique Wavre. Michel Desjoyeaux was at one end with Jean Le Cam, and at the far end was Jean's rescuer Vincent Riou. The crowd cheered the group that had gone to sea, had told them en route about their lives at sea, and had come safely home, one way or another. For me, standing with that group was the pinnacle of my sailing career.

The group returned to their seats. One by one, each abandoning skipper was brought to the stage to receive a memento. And then more formally, the finishing skippers were taken behind the huge screen, up onto scaffolding, then to descend individually a spotlit curving staircase to receive their trophy and be interviewed. I spoke my French as best I could, repeating my anecdote about Thomas Jefferson that "all men have two countries, their own and France", and thanking the French again for their warm welcome and encouragement. After the ceremony concluded, I walked the barricade, and shook hands with everyone I could reach, to thank them personally.

The next day I returned to the bookstore for the second signing session. Working my way through the assembled crowd, several exclaimed their appreciation for my suit the night before - *"Très chic!"* At the bookstore table sat only one skipper – Michel Desjoyeaux! *Le Professeur! Mon Professeur! Le vainqueur du Vendée Globe 2008-9*! His Coureur des Océans was already published. So I sat with Michel and asked him how he came from behind to win after returning for repairs at the start. He said that although the lead pack was sailing fast, he thought they were in a "false rhythm", taking speed cues from each other. Re-starting separately, he found his own rhythm, it was a bit faster, and he was able to sustain it, catch up, and sail through them.

9th & 1st

He'd sign a Vendée Globe book, then push it to me, I'd sign it, and give it to the customer. If a customer wanted Michel's book, he'd sign it and give it to the customer. After a few, Michel began to push his book to me to sign my name under his name in his book – what an honor! Before the session was over, I slipped into the queue to buy his book, which he inscribed:

À Rich,
Pour la vie, la bonne humeur, et la force!
...Mich Desj

I was unaware at that time that Michel had written kindly about our email exchange in his book:

J'ai une relation particulière avec Rich. Nous avons beaucoup échangé par mail avant le Vendée, nos discussions essentiellement technique. Il me posait des questions en Français, je lui répondais en Anglais. J'aime bien son côté humaniste, son ouverture au monde et aux autres, aux jeunes surtout, pas si fréquent chez un habitant du Nouveau Monde.

[English: I have a particular relationship with Rich. We emailed a great deal before the Vendée, our discussions essentially technical. He asked me questions in French, I responded to him in English. I like his human side, his openness to the world and to others, especially to young people, not so frequently found from an inhabitant of the New World.]

Passing through Paris a few days later, Fabienne arranged a meeting with Mark Pekala, Acting Ambassador of the U.S. Embassy. I presented him with one of our daily *GA3* flags; he had followed the race, was honored to receive the salt-encrusted living memento from an American's participation in a great French sporting event, and would frame it for official display.

The French never ceased to amaze. En route to Charles de Gaulle to fly home, the French taxi-driver asked me for an autograph for his son! And at the airport, going through security, my bronze Vendée Globe trophy bubble-wrapped in a carry-on bag alarmed the inspector. The pointed masthead of the sailboat protruding from within a graceful globe appeared weapon-like on the scan. Explaining, and unwrapping it for inspection, the customs agent immediately called her colleagues over to see what they had never seen before. With smiles, they each shook my hand warmly, congratulated me on finishing the Vendée Globe, re-wrapped the trophy, and let me through to go home.

"Dream dreams, then write them, aye, but live them first!"
...Samuel Eliot Morison

Epilogue: 2012 or 2016?

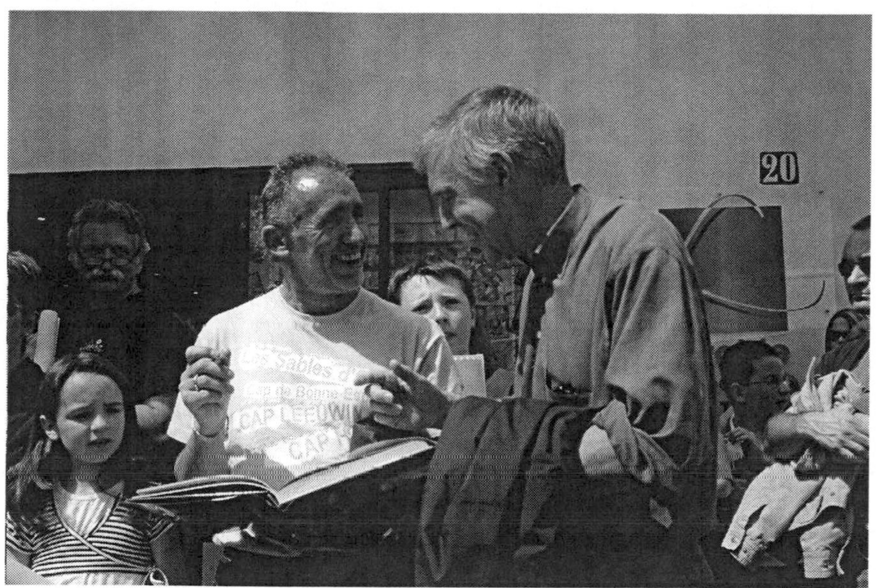

During my visits to France after the race, to sail *GA3* to Port la Foret, and for the Prize-Giving, one question continued to surface: "2012?" The question was asked with such sincerity that I realized that it demanded a more thoughtful response than my original *"une fois par vie."* Healing slowly, I considered what it would take to get me back to Les Sables d'Olonne for Vendée Globe 2012.

When the French asked "2012?", it showed their acceptance that if I was good at this, and that if this is what I wanted to do with my life, and even more so if we had good onshore purposes, then I should do it. In the French view, that was the role for hopes and dreams and purpose within being human and alive for our short time on this planet.

The American view was different. Back home, although there were sincere congratulations, they were nearly always followed by "You're not going to do THAT again, are you?" There was a risk-aversion in America that I did not find in France.

In this view of life, I subscribe to the French view over the American view.

§

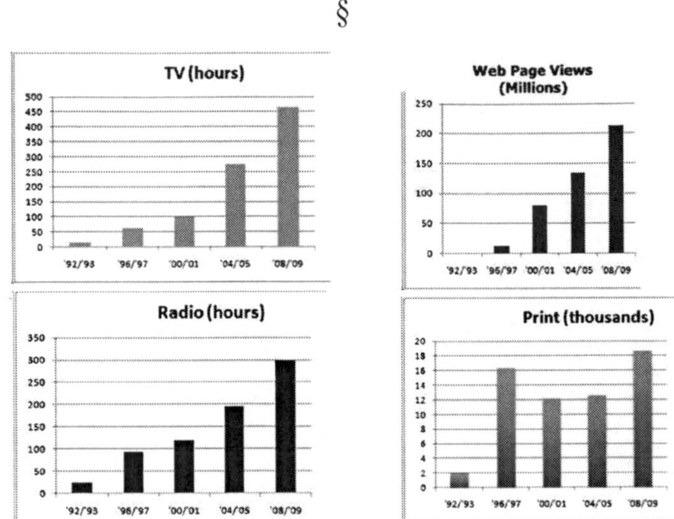

Media Up 50% From 2004

Turning 60 in April 2010, combined with seeing my Mom's slow decline in her 90s, reinforced the notion that whatever one could do to make the biggest contribution to society, one must do, now, while you have the chance. Clearly, the biggest contribution I could make would be to sail Vendée Globe 2012 or 2016, with globally expanded programs onshore to our three natural constituencies of K12, asthma, and seniors.

After reviewing our 2008-9 effort, four requirements emerged, three onshore, one offshore, toward Vendée Globe 2012 or 2016:

a. K12: Globally committed and contracted content distribution, via newspaper, online, and private sector distribution, to know absolutely that we were reaching students globally. Partner target: Pearson Education, Scholastic.

b. Asthma: Globally committed and contracted content distribution, to know absolutely that we were reaching asthmatics globally. Partner targets: Novartis, Glaxo, AstraZeneca, Merck.

c. Seniors: Globally committed and contracted content distribution, to know absolutely that we were reaching seniors globally. Partner targets: in the USA, AARP.

d. Open 60: 2008 generation Open 60 that would be faster for the same physical effort, so that the last two weeks of the exponential accumulated fatigue curve, both of boat and skipper, would be eliminated by generational advances in design and engineering.

We made progress on our onshore requirements, with international companies in pharmaceuticals, healthcare, and technology, and national advocacy groups for asthma and seniors, all wanting to participate.

Yet we did not made adequate progress in corporate sponsorship funding for our offshore need to access a 2008 boat, about a $2 million net project, small by American professional sports standards, so the chance for 2012 faded in the spring.

So I will press on to explore 2016, because the potential benefits onshore more than offset the personal risk offshore.

Vendée Globe 2008-9 was the most amazing experience in my life. No other experience has been so stretching, in mind, body, and spirit combined, as Vendée Globe 2008. To race the Vendée Globe again would stretch it further, and that would be a GOOD thing.

I will go to the start of Vendée Globe 2012 on November 10 in Les Sables d'Olonne to see many friends, and to feel the vigor of that amazing race.

And perhaps the publication of this book will trigger an interest in corporate or private circles to be partners in a truly unique and extraordinary global event. *Je crois mes doigts!*

§

Great American III was sold to Derek Hatfield in spring 2010. He had relinquished *Spirit of Canada* to a debt holder after his abandonment to Tasmania. In September 2010, he entered the Velux 5 Oceans race, the solo, round-the-world race, with four port stops and five legs. He finished third of four finishers of five starters. Thierry's terrific boat has now circumnavigated five times.

§

In fall 2009, we moved Mom from her retirement community to a harborside condo in Marblehead where she could see the water and boats. She had joked once, after seeing an exhibit at the Peabody Essex Museum on the Mayans and Water, that she thought maybe she was Mayan.

I had the inestimable privilege of visiting with her every day for the next year. Sadly, though not unexpectedly, in December 2010 she died. Throughout my life, she had been my biggest supporter, always encouraging, never questioning. She was truly the original adventurer in our family. I will miss her always.

§

Twice yearly Jean-Jacques Le Goff, our dockside friend who found our landlady's telephone number, calls out of the blue. Honored that I, a Vendée Globe finisher, have him programmed into my mobile, he will take off at high linguistic speed to tell me the news of Port la Foret. *"Plus lentement, Jean-Jacques!"* I will say, trying to get him to slow his excited French so that I can understand. These chats are a joy.

When returning to Port la Foret for the *GA3* sale to Derek, I called Jean-Jacques for coffee. He met me in his finest Sunday suit, and presented me with a copy of the official Vendée Globe Globe book that he inscribed upon my request. Another lifelong French friend.

§

Writing in the library one Friday in May 2011, just before closing I checked Facebook. Horrible, horrible news, Hubert Desjoyeaux had died of pancreatic cancer. I started crying. I hadn't known he was sick. He had helped us and me so much.

Hubert Desjoyeaux
1959-2011

After a flurry of messages, I learned that the next night the community was gathering at CDK for a remembrance. There was no way for me to get there in time, so I wrote an email to Michel to express my sorrow and appreciation of Hubert:

"Quand nous aurons une probleme avec le bateau, toujours Hubert aura un solution, avec un grand sourire et un bon mot."

[English: "When we will have a problem with the boat, always Hubert will have a solution, with a big smile and a good word."]

Married to Jean Le Cam's sister Monique, Hubert had four children.

My last memory of Hubert was when *GA3* was sold to Derek. We had found a hull delamination. In defining the boundaries for the needed repair, Hubert was on the outside of the boat, and a French surveyor was on the inside, both tapping and shining flashlights through the hull to find the edges. Occasionally, Hubert would turn to me and ask: *"Baleine?"* - did we hit a whale? No. Then some time later, *"Un arbre?"* A tree? No, I don't think so. Finally, he turned to me, put his arm around me in his kindest, most grandfatherly, most sympathetic way, and with his biggest, friendliest smile said *"Rich, what have you done?!"*

I will miss him, a lot.

§

Tragedy struck Port la Foret again when Hubert's wife Monique died a month after Hubert, leaving the Desjoyeaux and Le Cam families devastated.

§

The Daily Sentinel of Grand Junction, Colorado called: were we planning to do another Vendée Globe? If so, they'd like to sign up now.

§

Admiral Gurnon, Senator Kerry, me, General Dishner

The Massachusetts Maritime Academy, one of the seven American maritime colleges, awarded me an honorary Doctorate in Public Administration, the citation reading:

For his distinguished sailing career and his dedication to the education of schoolchildren worldwide.

As Senator John Kerry, an accomplished sailor himself, was also receiving an honorary Doctorate that day, I had the chance to give him one of our daily flags, and as well pass along for delivery through his good offices the daily flag that I had reserved for President Obama on his Inauguration Day.

Four months later, a stunning and humbling document arrived in the mail: a U.S. Senate – "Tribute to Rich Wilson" (see Appendix A). Mom and Dad would have been so proud.

§

Along with writing this book, one of my great pleasures since the race has been to give presentations about it to corporations, museums, conferences, schools, and clubs. Most in the audiences are stunned that an event like this – a solo, non-stop, race around the world – even exists, let alone that someone finished it. I love to give these talks, as the experience was the most extraordinary in my life. The race, the sailors, the south, the French, the schools, my friends and our team, the story just pours out of me.

I've attached as Appendix B comments from some of these talks.

§

After our finish, the diver inspected the bottom of *GA3*. It was perfect. Not a scratch. And both keel fairings were still there.

From page 275, English translation of my speech at the finish:

For me, this Vendée Globe was two Vendée Globes [a wondering murmur from the crowd].

One Vendée Globe at sea, very hard, very difficult, the most challenging course in the world, and with incredible sailors – [pause] – many incredible French sailors [with a big smile on my face eliciting an appreciative chuckle] – and several from other countries also.

[Big exhale of relief and fatigue from me] The Bay of Biscay, the North Atlantic, South Atlantic, Indian Ocean, the Pacific, Cape of Good Hope, Cape Horn [I shook my head at the thought, evoking sympathetic laughter], the Atlantic again…without end [shaking my head at the thought, and murmurs of understanding from the crowd].

But also, the Vendée Globe on land is the other Vendée Globe. Our… [I stumbled].

On my approach to Cape Horn, in the United States, we have had a new President…this is good [a cheer for our new President and the departure of our old]. Yet many, many years ago, our third President, Mr. Thomas Jefferson, who wrote our Declaration of Independence, before he was our President, he was our Ambassador to France, [knowing nod from the interviewer] and in Paris he said: 'All men have two countries: their own, and France. [Big cheer, the French love Thomas Jefferson]. And I think that he was absolutely correct [intrigued smile from the interviewer]. Because for me, this experience in France was incredible. Always, always, you have given me your encouragement, for three months in Port la Foret, and one month here in Les Sables d'Olonne, and I appreciate it very much.

In the future, when the things very difficult at sea – the storms, the gales, the fatigue, no sleeping – are lost from my memory [interviewer nods for my correct grammar], I will remember this other Vendée Globe, here, on land, in France, with you. Thank you. [Huge roar of approval and applause.]

Appendices

United States of America

Congressional Record

PROCEEDINGS AND DEBATES OF THE 112th CONGRESS, FIRST SESSION

Vol. 157 WASHINGTON, WEDNESDAY, SEPTEMBER 21, 2011 *No. 141*

Senate

TRIBUTE TO RICH WILSON

Mr. KERRY. Mr. President, just a few days ago I received a special gift from a consummate mariner, Rich Wilson of Marblehead, MA, the skipper of the *Great American III*. The gift was a U.S. Yacht Ensign, the red, white and blue flag used to identify American licensed yachts since 1848. What made this particular Ensign so special is that Rich flew it aboard the *Great American III* on December 10, 2008, in the solo, nonstop, around-the-world sailing race known as the Vendee Globe.

Rich flew the Ensign on his 31st day at sea from France, just as he was entering the Indian Ocean bound for Cape Horn. Ninety days later, Rich and the 60-foot *Great American III* completed their 28,000-mile global trek from France to France, ninth among the 11 finishers of a race that began with 30 boats. Rich was the only American entry, the oldest skipper in the fleet at 58 years of age, and only the second American ever to finish the Vendee Globe in its six quadrennial runnings.

The Vendee Globe is widely regarded as the Mount Everest of the seas. But, in fact, it is even a greater challenge than climbing Mount Everest. Consider the fact that while 3,000 people have climbed Mount Everest, Rich was only the 46th person ever to sail alone around the world nonstop. Consider, too, the fact that some 500 astronauts have flown in space, and that further underscores just how rare and special Rich's accomplishment in the Vendee Globe truly is.

The Vendee Globe is like no other event on this earth. It is a grueling contest largely unsullied by hype and commerce, a competition of men and women against each other but mostly against the ceaselessly moving sea, sometimes playful, sometimes terrifying, an immense power inspiring admiration, caution and, above all, respect.

But in the hands of Rich Wilson, the Vendee Globe also became a learning experience for students and newspaper readers throughout the world. As with his earlier long-distance ocean voyages, Rich shared his Vendee Globe experience through the online company he founded, www.sitesalive.com, a nonprofit that has produced 75 live, interactive, full-semester programs linking K-12 classrooms to adventures and expeditions worldwide. During the 2008-2009 Vendee Globe, sitesalive.com shared Rich's 15-part weekly series, written at sea from the *Great American*, with 250,000 students and 7 million readers.

Rich's goal was to excite students and engage students by connecting them to a live ocean expedition. As Rich explains it the reasoning behind sitesalive.com: "Excite a kid with dolphins, flying fish, and gales at sea, or with snakes, bugs, and bats in the rainforest, and they will pay attention, not knowing what will happen next. Then the science, geography, and math flow freely."

Anyone who enjoyed high seas adventure novels like Moby-Dick and Treasure Island or anyone who marveled at National Geographic expeditions or the adventures of Jacques Cousteau on the *Calypso* can understand how Rich is making the world come alive for students. And anyone who has sailed, even within sight of the shore, or who has run a marathon or has hiked a mountain range can appreciate the skill, conditioning, and discipline it took for Rich to complete Vendee Globe.

I thank Rich for the Ensign, the memento from his great adventure, and I congratulate him, not only for completing his great voyage but also for sharing it online with millions of people around the world. And as he considers whether to enter the Vendee Globe again in 2012, I urge him to once again climb aboard the *Great American III* and set sail.

With great respect and gratitude. — John Kerry

Lectures & Comments

To Book a Talk:
Visit **www.sitesalive.com or www.racefrancetofrance.com** .

Past Talks:
Facebook, Advanced Micro Devices, Fidelity, Novartis (France), Innovent Technologies, Salisbury Forum, Entertainment Gathering, MIT Museum, MIT Club of Boston, HBS Club of Boston, Mystic Seaport, Peabody Essex Museum, New York Yacht Club, + 50 more venues.

Comments:
"That was a riveting, inspiring hour. When is his book coming out?" ...Aileen, Facebook

"That was incredible. Bring him again anytime. I'll call in sick to listen to him all day." ...Pierre, Facebook

"Your talk was incredible! I'm a climbing speaker junkie, so I've heard all the Boston locals do their Everest and K2 stories but the Vendée Globe makes them all look like slackers!" ...Alice

"I have gotten extraordinary feedback on your talk. It was amazing!" ...Jon, Fidelity Investments

"Our faculty and trustees are saying that it is the best Commencement Speech that has been delivered here at the college." ...Gretchen, Marian Court College

"The Vendée Globe is a race that is beyond imagination; it is simply impossible, just like landing on the moon is beyond imagination." ...Dr. Robinson

"On a scale of 1 to 10, his talk was a 12." ...Dennis, Marion Music Hall

"The audience was clearly mesmerized by your story." ...Bonny, MIT Club of Boston

"We had just heard a world class sailor and a world class human being describe one of the most remarkable accomplishments I have heard. The standing ovation recognized this." ...John

"That was the most interesting, riveting, Vendée Globe talk that I've heard, and I've heard a few. That was brilliant, I was enthralled all the way. It was wonderful, wonderful." ...Merfyn O.

"What a remarkable presentation you made at the Annual Meeting. You said some very big things in a very understated way. Many thanks, it was awesome...I'm at a loss for words." ...Bill., S.E.A.

"THANK YOU in the name of our team, for your very impactful and emotional talk. Our [asthma] physicians, reps and team members really appreciated your testimony and were quite amazed by your exploit. I think you made them even more proud of working on such a product!" ...Anne, Novartis (France, my talk delivered in French)

"What an amazing presentation. You were informative, dynamic, funny, and inspirational. Despite thinking I knew something about what you did I was clueless! I was so impressed, even more moved by it. It really brought it to life and reality for me." ...Mike

"Rich's talk is one I shall never forget. There aren't many people in the world with that degree of knowledge, skill, determination and above all courage, who would undertake such an endeavor. We both felt exhausted just experiencing it vicariously through his lecture! What also impressed me was his motivation for this voyage – the children of the world who would not only learn about geography, etc., but also be inspired to undertake something really difficult for a good cause. I for one will never forget that talk." ...Anne

Newspaper in Education (NIE)

Participating Newspapers

San Francisco Chronicle (CA)
Denver Post (CO)
Seattle Times (WA)
The (Bergen) Record (NJ)
The News & Observer (NC)
Hartford Courant (CT)
Worcester Telegram (MA)
Arlington Heights Daily Herald (IL)
Winston-Salem Journal (NC)
Flint Journal (MI)
Jacksonville Daily News (NC)
Kalamazoo Gazette (MI)
New Bern Sun Journal (NC)
Grand Junction Daily Sentinel (CO)
Jackson Citizen Patriot (MI)
Joplin Globe (MO)
Monroe Evening News (MI)
Kinston Free Press (NC)
Cherokee Scout (NC)
Eagle Tribune Papers (MA)
- Lawrence Tribune
- Salem News
- Gloucester Daily News
- Newburyport Daily News

<u>Missouri:</u>

Adrian Journal
Branson Daily News
Boone County Journal
Cuba Free Press
The Current Local
Eldon Advertiser
Gasconade Cedar County Republican
Independence Examiner
The Kearney Courier

Lebanon Daily Record
Marshfield Mail
Marshall Democrat News
St. Joseph News-Press
South County Mail
Steelville Star-Crawford Mirror
Summersville Beacon
Trenton Republican-Times
Versailles Leader Statesman
Washington Missourian
Webb City Sentinel
Houston Herald
The Republic Monitor
Portageville Missourian News
Daily Dunklin Democrat
Warren County Record

sitesALIVE! Teacher's Guide

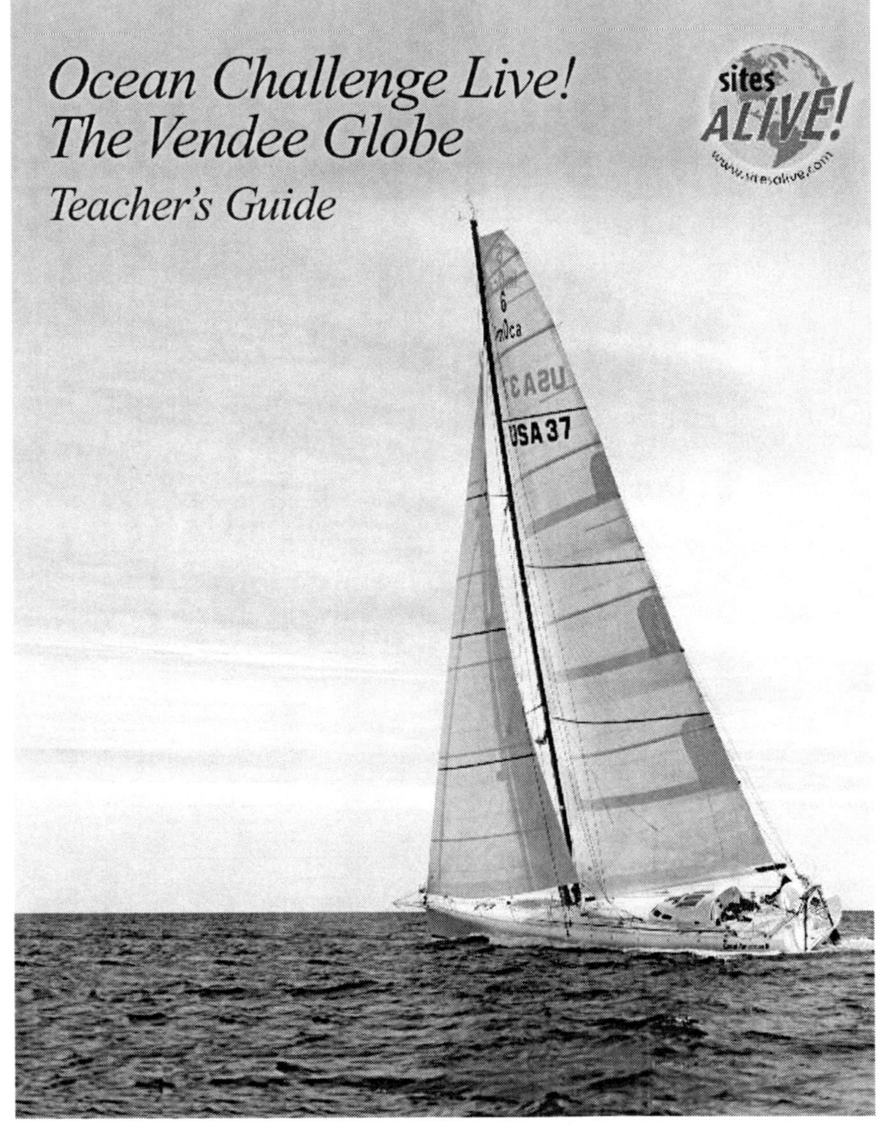

Teacher's Guide

Table of Contents

sitesALIVE! Team of Experts

Mr. Sean Connaughton
Maritime Administrator
U.S. Government

Prof. Dava Newman
MIT

Dr. Brien Barnewolt
Emergency Medicine
Tufts Medical Center

Capt. Murray Lister
M/V Cape York

Ms. Marti Shea
Select Fitness

Ms. Laura Mirabella
Shipbroker
C. R. Weber

Dr. Chris Fanta
Partners Asthma Ctr.

Dr. Ambrose Jearld
NOAA

Ms. Dava Sobel
Author, Longitude

Ms. Lorraine Leo
Jackson School

Dr. Ioannis Miaoulis
Museum of Science

Capt. Eric Wallischecke
Acting Superintendent
U.S.M.M.A

Dr. Chuck Czeisler
Sleep Medicine
Brigham & Women's Hospital

Dr. Jan Witting
SEA

Mr. Sam Scott
PEM

Mr. Scott Hamilton
Mt. Everest

Mr. Rich DuMoulin
Intrepid Shipping

sitesALIVE! NIE Series

Ocean Challenge Live!–The Vendee Globe
Solo, non-stop, around-the-world race

WEEK

1 Following Your Dreams

Race Online at **Sitesalive.com**

Team of Experts • Q&A • Ship's Log
Photos • Podcasts • Videos • Essays

By Rich Wilson, Skipper Aboard *Great American III*

The Vendée Globe race instructions state simply: start at Les Sables d'Olonne (France), leave Cape of Good Hope (South Africa) to port, leave Cape Leeuwin (Australia) to port, leave Cape Horn (Chile) to port, leave Antarctica to starboard, finish at Les Sables d'Olonne; 26,000 miles, 100 days, solo, non-stop, without assistance, in 60' sailboats.

Thirty sailors—men and women—are entered from seven countries. The fleet includes the best and toughest sailors in the world. They are friendly with and respectful of each other, perhaps because they know that if they have a problem deep in the Southern Ocean, thousands of miles from land, a rescuer will likely be a competitor, as has happened before.

I have followed this race in the past, but always shied away; it was too hard, too long, and too dangerous. What changed? My attitude. A young boy, in the crowd of thousands on the dock, put it best by simply saying in French "C'est important a participer." It is important to participate. And that's why I'm here even though I'm the only American, the oldest skipper at 58, and not one of the favorites to win.

Equally important to me is the chance to connect with students and families around the world with this Newspapers In Education program and our website. For me at sea, the science, geography, math, and history will all be living topics. It will be a great adventure. Welcome Aboard!

Love, Act, Discover and Innovate

By Dr. Dava Newman, Professor of Aeronautics and Astronautics and Engineering Systems, MIT

My motto for teaching aerospace biomedical engineering at MIT is "Love, Act, Discover, and Innovate", and this motto has guided me in my own life.

I grew up in Helena, Montana, and I LOVED learning, sports, and nature. After watching the Apollo astronauts, I dreamt that one day I would explore the world. I ACTED by attending Notre Dame and majoring in aerospace engineering. Afterwards, I went to graduate school at MIT and became a professor. Now I have the dream job of teaching engineering, I have trained astronauts and cosmonauts, and I have flown four space-flight experiments in space.

In our latest INNOVATION at MIT, I have helped create a spacesuit for Mars exploration, a second skin called BioSuit™, which, remarkably, is inspired by giraffes and armadillos.

Regarding the Vendée Globe, I have DISCOVERED that space flight and sailing have much in common. Both activities take place in extreme environments, and as an astronaut or sailor you need to have all of your food, spare parts, navigation, and communications onboard. You must keep your heart, bones, muscles, and senses healthy, and you have to be creative, resourceful and find unique solutions during emergencies.

My dreams have come true. I hope you will dream, love, act, discover and innovate, too!

---

sitesALIVE Foundation 

Massachusetts Institute of Technology • U.S. Merchant Marine Academy • Sea Education Association
Brigham & Women's Hospital • Tufts Medical Center • Peabody Essex Museum • U.S. Maritime Administration
Connecticut Maritime Association • Museum of Science • National Marine Fisheries Service • Select Fitness

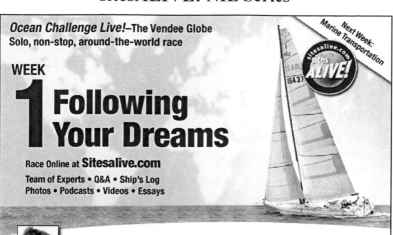

By Rich Wilson, Skipper Aboard *Great American III*

Looking at our chart explains the parade of ships that I saw last night by their lights, and heard the night before on our radar alarm. The Vendée Globe fleet intersected, and then joined, the sea route from the northwest corner of France (the entrance to the English Channel) to the northwest corner of Spain.

This sea route connects ports in northern Europe with ports in the Mediterranean Sea (via the Straits of Gibraltar), Africa, and South America. The sea's commerce is the unseen commerce of the world. A large containership may hold 3,000 containers, each container the size of a tractor-trailer on a land highway. A modern tanker may hold 250,000 tons of oil. Smaller, older, general cargo ships are out here too, carrying a wide variety of goods and resources.

I spoke to the *SEAROSE G*, an 80,000-ton-capacity OBO (oil/bulk/ore) ship, in ballast (no cargo), with 26 Philippinos in her crew. She crossed my stern, bound from Gijón, Spain to Gibraltar for bunkers (fuel) then on to Turkey for dry dock for a month. She appeared on our radar detector first, then on AIS (automatic identification system), then visually.

The Captain was pleasant and I informed him that there were 20 sailboats in his path. I can only imagine the amazing places and peoples that he and his crew have seen in their lives. These tankers and cargo ships connect the nations of the world.

Proper Preparation is Everything

By Dr. Brien Barnewolt, Chief, Emergency Medicine, Tufts Medical Center

Proper preparation is everything. On board *Great American III* Rich has an extensive first aid kit, and he knows how to use it. We added to the kit medications that Rich might need if he gets sick or injured: medications for infections, seasickness and his asthma. We can communicate by email or even satellite phone, so if something happens I know exactly what he has on board and can best advise him on his situation.

Rich also took an advanced first aid course, which is a great idea for everyone. He learned how to take care of wounds and burns, splint broken bones, and how to recognize and treat hypothermia. We also practiced many of these techniques, because you would not want to attempt them for the very first time in the middle of the Southern Ocean on a cold, wet, tossing boat.

Lastly, Rich is a big promoter of preventive medicine. He is in excellent physical condition, watches his nutrition, and has a great plan to get the proper amount of sleep during the race. When conditions are rough, he will wear protective clothing and pads, much like a BMX motocross rider. He even has a helmet! With prevention strategies like these, Rich should rarely need to make a trip to the "virtual" ER.

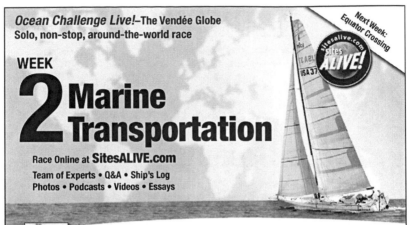

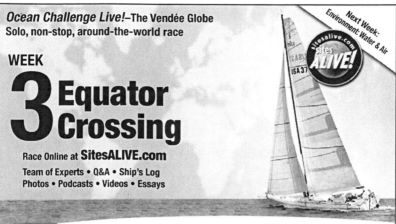

Ocean Challenge Live!–The Vendée Globe
Solo, non-stop, around-the-world race

WEEK 3 Equator Crossing

Race Online at **SitesALIVE.com**

Team of Experts • Q&A • Ship's Log
Photos • Podcasts • Videos • Essays

By Rich Wilson, Skipper Aboard *Great American III*

For a mariner, crossing the equator – the Line – is a major event. The tradition for a first-timer is an on-board ceremony where the initiate is degraded before King Neptune, who must pass judgment upon the initiate's worthiness to come into his new hemisphere. Typically, a shipmate will dress as King Neptune, with royal scepter, a crown, and beard, and act as judge, jury, and prosecutor prosecutor on the worthiness of the supplicant.

The tradition is taken seriously by mariners and aboard commercial vessels, too. When I was aboard the huge containership *New Zealand Pacific* (after our rescue by them off Cape Horn, Thanksgiving Day, 1990), and en route to Europe, those merchant mariners in their crew who had not crossed the Line before were smeared with bilge oil and grease in their hair. In our 2003 Hong Kong-New York passage, my shipmate Rich du Moulin, an initiate, ended up with a more modern version, granola and milk in his hair!

Either way, the intent is serious: to give King Neptune, who rules the seas, his due respect. And it is a way for us at sea to remind ourselves that we are not in control out here – it is King Neptune, with his winds and waves and currents, who rules. For us to be safe, we must respect the sea, and an equator-crossing ceremony is a symbol of that respect.

Dead Reckoning

by Dava Sobel, Author of *Longitude*

Skipper Rich will soon cross the Equator, 0° latitude, the great dividing line between Earth's northern and southern hemispheres. Having traveled from 46°30′N at the start, he will go as far as 56° south, below the tip of Cape Horn. As he circumnavigates the globe, he will also travel through the full 360° of longitude.

Fortunately for Rich, his navigational equipment keeps him constantly informed of his precise position. Earlier sailors had to rely on a mixture of guesswork and hope to do that, and only rarely figured out exactly where they were.

They could tell their latitude easily enough by the height of the sun or known guide stars above the horizon – in clear weather, at least. But longitude always posed serious problems. The most popular means, known as dead reckoning, called for a log on a knotted line to be thrown overboard. The navigator, using a sand glass to time how quickly the line paid out, gauged the ship's speed along its course. Then he factored in the effects of ocean currents and winds on their progress, to estimate a position east or west of homeport.

Not until the end of the 18th century were the necessary instruments – the sextant and the chronometer – invented to determine longitude at sea.

---

sitesALIVE Foundation 

Massachusetts Institute of Technology • U.S. Merchant Marine Academy • Sea Education Association
Brigham & Women's Hospital • Tufts Medical Center • Peabody Essex Museum • U.S. Maritime Administration
Connecticut Maritime Association • Museum of Science • National Marine Fisheries Service • Select Fitness

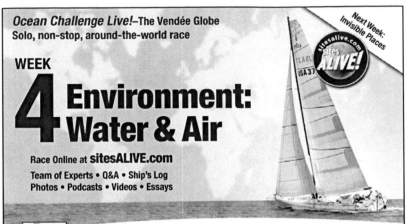

Ocean Challenge Live!–The Vendée Globe
Solo, non-stop, around-the-world race

Next Week: Invisible Places

sitesALIVE.com sites ALIVE!

WEEK 4 Environment: Water & Air

Race Online at sitesALIVE.com
Team of Experts • Q&A • Ship's Log
Photos • Podcasts • Videos • Essays

By Rich Wilson, Skipper
Aboard *Great American III*

What better symbol could there be for the interconnectedness of the world than the Vendée Globe, a non-stop around-the-world sailing event? As a skipper in the race, I can see that each salty wave is connected to the next in the Atlantic, Indian, and Pacific Oceans. The same interconnectedness is true for every breath we breathe.

These global connections show that pollution from one place, whether it is water or air pollution, can end up in any other place. We are all responsible for the environment of our neighbors—be they next door or around the world—and we should be aware of the waste we create and how it might affect other people (and other life) on the planet. With awareness comes understanding and action.

My friend and rival Raphael Dinelli, sailing *Ocean Vital Foundation*, has an intriguing wind charger aboard his vessel and new thin solar panels covering his boat. These may allow him to sail around the world without ever turning on his gas-powered generator, thus using no fossil fuel at all. It is a worthwhile goal.

In the Vendée Globe there is a race rule requiring the competitors to keep all their garbage aboard their boats for proper disposal at the finish. In the absence of universal morality, regulation is needed for our common good.

Asthma at Sea

By Dr. Chris Fanta
Brigham & Women's Hospital

While the challenges that Rich Wilson and the skippers of Vendée Globe face are enormous—managing a large sailing vessel by yourself, day after day, without break, and without a "time out" for bad weather—Rich Wilson has another obstacle to overcome that may not be shared by other skippers. Rich has asthma.

Asthma is a very common disease. In the United States approximately seven million children under age 18 have asthma, and an additional 16 million adults have the disease. In asthma, the breathing tubes in the lungs can become narrowed in two ways: (1) the bands of muscle that encircle the tubes squeeze down on the tubes, and (2) the tube walls can swell and fill with mucus. The result can be difficulty breathing (like breathing through a narrow straw), tightness in the chest, and wheezing.

So how can Rich Wilson, who needs to be capable of peak performance at any moment, avoid an asthma attack while circumnavigating the globe? The key is prevention. Rich takes several asthma medicines every day to prevent asthmatic reactions in his airways. Periodically, Rich will take additional medicine (a bronchodilator inhaler) before strenuous exertion. This medicine keeps the muscles from contracting in response to exertion.

Lastly, since Rich is far out to sea, it is unlikely that he will experience asthma attacks caused by pets, cigarette smoke or air pollution.

sitesALIVE Foundation 

Massachusetts Institute of Technology • U.S. Merchant Marine Academy • Sea Education Association
Brigham & Women's Hospital • Tufts Medical Center • Peabody Essex Museum • U.S. Maritime Administration
Connecticut Maritime Association • Museum of Science • National Marine Fisheries Service • Select Fitness

Ocean Challenge Live!–The Vendée Globe
Solo, non-stop, around-the-world race

WEEK 5 Invisible Places

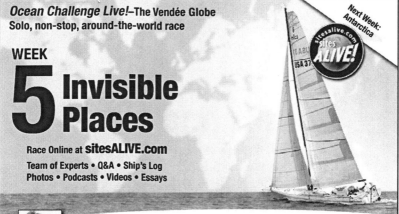

Race Online at sitesALIVE.com
Team of Experts • Q&A • Ship's Log
Photos • Podcasts • Videos • Essays

By Rich Wilson, Skipper
Aboard *Great American III*

In this race around the world, we will pass many places and peoples. Some will be nearby, as were Spain, Morocco, and the Cape Verde Islands. Others will be very distant and far over the horizon, as will be South Africa, Madagascar, Australia and New Zealand.

In spite of their distances from *Great American III*, these places stimulate my imagination. What are the people like? What are the places like? What is the terrain of each country? What kind of weather is dominant? What variety of natural resources do these places hold? What forms of government do they have? What styles of food do they eat?

In the United States, one can identify regions with distinct differences: the northeast, south, southwest, west, mid-west, northwest, etc. In spite of the differences between regions we are all Americans, and we embrace and honor these differences within our society.

On a larger scale, we are also citizens of Planet Earth, and we should embrace and honor the differences among peoples, cultures and places worldwide. As we have come to travel extensively within the US, so should we try to travel extensively outside the US to learn firsthand about the rest of the world.

Out here, we are always sailing past invisible places. Although glad to be in the race, I know that I am missing a lot, and vow to visit many more countries afterward.

Invisible Places

By Captain Eric Wallischeckc
US Merchant Marine Academy

Although Skipper Rich refers to the land that he is passing as "invisible", I think it really is the ocean that is invisible. A whopping 360 million square kilometers of the earth's surface is covered with seawater, yet at most we can see 2.4% of the oceans from all the world's shorelines. Thus, with so little of the ocean being visible from the shore, it seems like it is the ocean that is invisible; not the land. And since we cannot see Rich from the shore, maybe it is he that is invisible, too.

It's not easy being "invisible" to others, since humans are social beings. We like to spend time with our family and friends. Spending long periods of time away from others can make you lonely and sad. In the early days of ocean travel, voyagers spent months, even years, away from their homes, communicating only by mail. Babies were born, and people died, while their family members were isolated in the middle of the ocean.

Fortunately, Rich has access to the Internet, so he can stay "visible" to us. We can ask him questions, and follow his progress. He can talk to family and friends, follow the news, and get football scores. So, while he may be in an invisible place to us, we can see him and he can see us.

sitesALIVE Foundation 

Massachusetts Institute of Technology • U.S. Merchant Marine Academy • Sea Education Association
Brigham & Women's Hospital • Tufts Medical Center • Peabody Essex Museum • U.S. Maritime Administration
Connecticut Maritime Association • Museum of Science • National Marine Fisheries Service • Select Fitness

Ocean Challenge Live!–The Vendée Globe
Solo, non-stop, around-the-world race

WEEK 6 Antarctica

Race Online at **sitesALIVE.com**

Team of Experts • Q&A • Ship's Log
Photos • Podcasts • Videos • Essays

By Rich Wilson, Skipper
Aboard *Great American III*

The turning mark in the Vendée Globe is Antarctica. We will not see this cold continent as we circumnavigate it, but we will be affected by it.

Already we have passed Ice Gate #1, located to keep the fleet north of icebergs drifting out of the Weddell Sea. Six more ice gates across the Indian and Pacific Oceans serve a similar purpose. When the Southern Ocean's low-pressure systems hammer the fleet, they will do so with strong winds, big seas, and with frigid air spinning clockwise and north from Antarctica.

Many failed expeditions to the South Pole have proved it a brutal, inhospitable place. Yet it is also a place that reveals great courage and leadership, as with Sir Ernest Shackleton's legendary expedition.

Diplomatically, the Antarctic Treaty, which reserves the continent for scientific research and prohibits mineral exploitation, is a fantastic example of how people can cooperate internationally when they act as planetary citizens. Research conducted on this massive continent revealed the ozone hole in the earth's atmosphere; information on global warming and the planet's past climate comes from studying Antarctica's ice cores; and the seas surrounding the continent are teeming with penguins, birds, krill, and phytoplankton used for scientific study.

Although sailing past this time, I want to visit Antarctica some day, to see the white, to feel the cold, to experience the bottom of the world.

The Southern Ocean

By Sam Scott, Associate Curator
Peabody Essex Museum

Turn your globe on its head so that the continent of Antarctica is at the top. Notice the ring of ocean that encircles the continent. These waters are known as the Southern Ocean, and they have earned the deep respect of mariners for generations. Wind and wave move unimpeded all the way around the globe causing sailors to name the regions south of 70 degrees latitude the Shrieking Sixties, Furious Fifties and Roaring Forties. In addition to strong winds and massive waves, there are also icebergs with which to contend. Rich will be sailing into these waters as he rounds the Cape of Good Hope and turns the bow of *Great American III* for the long run eastward.

For much of the long passage toward Cape Horn, the closest continental land mass to Rich and *Great American III* will be Antarctica itself—the coldest, windiest and driest place on earth. Human contact with Antarctica began in the 19th century, and the long difficult journey across the Southern Ocean to this cold continent delayed a sustained human presence there until the 20th century.

The Antarctica Treaty System, begun in 1959, prevents any nation from claiming territory on the continent and promotes international scientific research. Long thought to be far beyond the reach of human impact, Antarctica is now seen as one of our best barometers for measuring the pace and magnitude of global climate change.

sitesALIVE Foundation 

Massachusetts Institute of Technology • U.S. Merchant Marine Academy • Sea Education Association
Brigham & Women's Hospital • Tufts Medical Center • Peabody Essex Museum • U.S. Maritime Administration
Connecticut Maritime Association • Museum of Science • National Marine Fisheries Service • Select Fitness

Ocean Challenge Live!–The Vendée Globe

Solo, non-stop, around-the-world race

WEEK 7 Climate Change

Race Online at sitesALIVE.com

Team of Experts • Q&A • Ship's Log
Photos • Podcasts • Videos • Essays

By Rich Wilson, Skipper
Aboard *Great American III*

In the last two days here in the Indian Ocean, we have been hammered by two severe storms with near-hurricane-force winds and mountainous seas. I'm tired, cold, and scared. But it was my choice to enter the Vendée Globe, and it is my responsibility therefore to deal with Mother Nature as she is.

In an analogous, moral way it is up to humankind to deal with the Earth's climate as it is, and not to allow our activities to change it. Sadly, we have violated that moral truth by causing global warming.

Since we are on a path of climate change, what is our responsibility now? I believe that it is to say, "OK. We caused this problem, and we must do something to fix it." Now we must have enough strength of character to make sacrifices for the betterment of the planet and of the 6 billion humans on it. We must slow and then stop this manmade climate change.

We in advanced economies and developed nations can often buy our way out of problems. We tend to think, "It's going to get hotter? Turn on more air conditioning!" Unfortunately that approach will only worsen the problem. And the underdeveloped nations of the world, who live more closely than we to nature, and therefore depend on nature staying consistent, will suffer the most. And it is simply not fair for us to change their environment.

Antarctic Ice Shelves

By Jan Witting, Faculty
Sea Education Association

Rich is alone in an endless landscape of waves, traveling the world's oceans with occasional sightings of seabirds, flying fish, and whales. For me, as a sea-going oceanographer, the ocean always looks so much bigger than we humans that it is difficult to believe that we could somehow change it. But we can, and we are.

So what kind of changes can be felt out there on the high seas? Well, global climate change and warming temperatures have done some things that are quite visible. Let's take the Southern Ocean, where Rich is now, as an example.

The big ice shelves surrounding Antarctica have started to break up during the past few years. These huge plates of thick, floating ice are hundreds of years old, and they are big enough to see from satellites. The most recent shelf to break up is the Wilkins Ice Shelf, and it broke up just this past spring. As big as the state of Connecticut, this shelf broke apart into smaller bits and is floating away slowly out to sea.

There are many other changes oceanographers worldwide are keeping an eye on. Some examples are the rise of sea level, changes in the ocean currents, and ocean acidification.

Earth really is the ocean planet, so if you think about it, global climate change will be felt in the oceans, too.

***Ocean Challenge Live!*–The Vendée Globe**
Solo, non-stop, around-the-world race

WEEK 8 Teamwork & Perseverance

Race Online at sitesALIVE.com

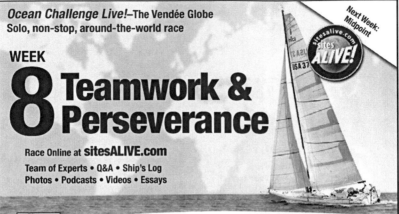

Team of Experts • Q&A • Ship's Log
Photos • Podcasts • Videos • Essays

By Rich Wilson, Skipper
Aboard *Great American III*

Because of Yann Elies' serious injury and remarkable rescue by the skippers of *Safran, Roxy* and the Australian Navy, we've decided to make this week's topic Teamwork & Perseverance and next week's topic Midpoint.

The day before the start of the Vendée Globe I saw Yann Eliès riding on his bike, standing on the pedals, with his young daughter on the seat behind him. Kind and cordial as always, he introduced me to her.

A few days ago, the physicality of this race came home to the fleet in a horrible way when Yann was swept down the foredeck of *Generali* by a wall of water, fetched up on some piece of equipment, and broke his thighbone. Somehow he crawled back into the cabin and alerted race officials and the race doctor.

Race officials alerted Australian Rescue Services. They immediately detailed a frigate to depart Perth for Yann's position with a medical team aboard. Race officials also alerted *Safran*/Marc Guillemot and *Roxy*/Samantha Davies, both competitors, to divert from the race and to head for Yann's position. They diverted immediately, as it is the unquestioned tradition of the sea to go to the aid of a mariner in distress.

Marc arrived first, circling *Generali,* trying to throw water and medicine down the hatch, and talking constantly with his friend Yann by VHF. The race doctor had specifically detailed the purpose of Marc's proximity to be emotional support.

Two days later, the frigate arrived and within hours had Yann stabilized, off *Generali,* and onto the frigate where the medical team awaited. All the players worked together, fulfilled their roles, and a good outcome was achieved.

Overcoming Physical Limitations

By Marti Shea, Select Fitness

When Rich started the race, he had a fitness plan in place to maintain his physical strength. When he broke his rib early in the race that plan evaporated. Instead, it was replaced by a plan to limit Rich's movement to allow the rib to heal quickly. Will the residual affects of the broken rib be a loss in overall strength and compromise his performance on the boat? The answer to this question, I believe, is no.

High-level athletic achievers like Rich Wilson have certain traits that make them successful. These traits include tenacity, perseverance, focus, dedication and the ability to make sacrifices to reach their goals. Rich has endured excruciating rib and back pain. He has not quit. He has not given up in the face of immense adversity.

The lesson we can all learn from Rich is that success can be achieved by having a dream, setting goals, working hard to achieve those goals, being confidant, and not giving up. He has prepared himself for the race mentally, physically and emotionally. When his body broke down, his mind took over.

As the race continues, Rich will find the physical strength to continue on because of his mental and emotional strength. Rich is enjoying this remarkable voyage, and he is equally enjoying sharing with all of us his dream. Rich now is leading by example, and this example will give others the courage and faith to strive to achieve their dreams.

sitesALIVE Foundation 

Massachusetts Institute of Technology • U.S. Merchant Marine Academy • Sea Education Association
Brigham & Women's Hospital • Tufts Medical Center • Peabody Essex Museum • U.S. Maritime Administration
Connecticut Maritime Association • Museum of Science • National Marine Fisheries Service • Select Fitness

Ocean Challenge Live!–The Vendée Globe
Solo, non-stop, around-the-world race

WEEK 9 Midpoint

Race Online at **sitesALIVE.com**
Team of Experts • Q&A • Ship's Log
Photos • Podcasts • Videos • Essays

By Rich Wilson, Skipper
Aboard *Great American III*

The midpoint of the voyage, estimated by time or mileage or geography, offers a symbolic chance for reflection on what we have accomplished, or not, and what we have still to do.

Our goals are two: on land, to create a global school program off this global event; and at sea, to finish the Vendée Globe.

Internationally, we were not able to turn initial interest by Newspaper in Education (NIE) programs in 25 countries to their publishing this series. In the United States, however, we have a record 50 newspapers, from large to small, publishing our NIE series and distributing it to schools. Via personal teacher networks, we have schools in over a dozen countries using the program, and in the United States via an online content partnership with Thinkfinity.org we have a broader reach on the web for sitesALIVE.com than ever before.

At sea, we are still in the race, although back in the pack. We knew this latter would occur, because *Great American III* is an older boat and she has an older skipper. We are not at all disappointed in our placement in the fleet. We have solved problems, and not, and we have made good and bad sail maneuvers and weather-routing decisions.

From the midpoint, emotionally, we'll be sailing home, but Cape Horn still lies ahead, and the Horn may be the real emotional midpoint.

Women in the Maritime Industry

By Laura Mirabella
Shipping Broker

The maritime industry can be a challenging and rewarding field for women.

Thirty years ago it was difficult for women to break into this industry. In today's world more and more woman are moving into principal positions. As a female broker, while I see that many women work in this business, especially in Texas, I believe that the industry still has much to do to recruit and involve more women. If you are a woman and work in this industry, it is important to be tough and to understand the phrase "It's business; it's nothing personal." This business is a difficult, challenging, 24/7/365 profession. The hours are long, and you have to be available at any time—even during Christmas dinner.

Women in every industry are working hard to "make it to the top" and to be treated as equals regarding salary, responsibility, and career advancement, and the maritime industry is no exception. As Rich Wilson and the rest of the skippers are demonstrating in the Vendée Globe, it is important to not let people discourage you from pursuing your goals, even though they may seem scary and uncertain. It is good, and often important, to try a position that you know will be challenging. Just remember that your mind and body are strong, and persistence will pay off—just keep trying.

sitesALIVE Foundation 

Massachusetts Institute of Technology • U.S. Merchant Marine Academy • Sea Education Association
Brigham & Women's Hospital • Tufts Medical Center • Peabody Essex Museum • U.S. Maritime Administration
Connecticut Maritime Association • Museum of Science • National Marine Fisheries Service • Select Fitness

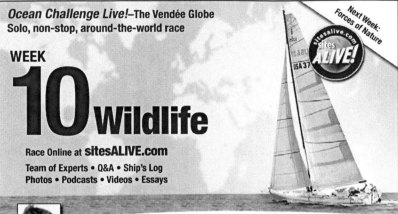

Ocean Challenge Live!–The Vendée Globe
Solo, non-stop, around-the-world race

WEEK 10 Wildlife

Race Online at **sitesALIVE.com**

Team of Experts • Q&A • Ship's Log
Photos • Podcasts • Videos • Essays

By Rich Wilson, Skipper Aboard *Great American III*

Halfway around the world, through the Atlantic, Indian, and now Pacific Oceans, we have seen a diverse array of wildlife.

Porpoises have played in the bow wave, flying fish have leapt onto the boat, and unlucky squid have been washed onto the deck by errant waves. Birds are everywhere; we've seen petrels, terns, and now the inspiring albatross of the Southern Ocean. With a wingspan of 9-10 feet, they glide effortlessly, almost never flapping their wings, and are the royalty of the air.

On previous voyages, we've seen whales off South Africa, and sharks in the tropics. And here now, when a wave sweeps the deck, it leaves behind dozens of minuscule shrimp, each about 1 centimeter long. Last night, a small gray animal made a hasty exit from the surface as we approached, leaving only a whirlpool.

Each species we see at the surface is amazing in its own way. Beneath the surface more species are being discovered to add to the thousands known. Sadly, all are threatened by pollution, global warming, and overfishing.

What an embarrassing legacy. Still, as we did with the ozone hole and CFCs, perhaps we can organize globally to save the oceans and make them vibrant again. Individually, we can join a group, make a donation, or write a congressman. As the young boy said to me in Les Sables d'Olonne, "C'est important a participer."

Learning from Animals

By Ioannis Miaoulis, Director and President, Museum of Science

Rich's Ship Logs reveal an extraordinary variety of marine life including sea birds, porpoises, flying fish, tiny shrimp, and squid. As Rich mentions, the aerodynamics of the albatross and the agility of porpoises are amazing.

We can learn a lot from these animals about science, engineering, and our world. Animals have already solved some of their own engineering problems through evolution. For example, I learned while on a snorkeling trip to the Great Barrier Reef that the sea anemone has evolved into an ideal shape and size for filter feeding. It is engineered to retrieve its food without being swept away by the current.

When the Museum's visitor attends one of our animal presentations, and they explore an alligator, a great horned owl, or a hedgehog, they are engaged; they are learning. They observe, experiment, and conclude as scientists do. The Museum's 3-D Digital Cinema lets visitors swim with a whale shark, a great white shark, and more. In the upcoming *Frogs: A Chorus of Colors* exhibit (February 13-May 25, 2009), visitors will learn about the remarkable diversity among frog species.

So while we can't all sail the world's oceans to see wildlife like Rich, observing wildlife at home or at a museum can teach you a lot about your world.

sitesALIVE Foundation 

Massachusetts Institute of Technology • U.S. Merchant Marine Academy • Sea Education Association
Brigham & Women's Hospital • Tufts Medical Center • Peabody Essex Museum • U.S. Maritime Administration
Connecticut Maritime Association • Museum of Science • National Marine Fisheries Service • Select Fitness

Ocean Challenge Live!–The Vendée Globe
Solo, non-stop, around-the-world race

WEEK 11 Forces of Nature

Race Online at sitesALIVE.com

Team of Experts • Q&A • Ship's Log
Photos • Podcasts • Videos • Essays

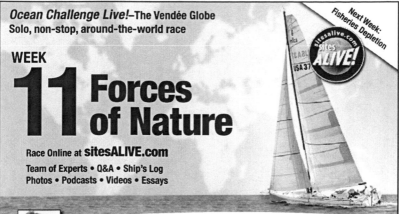

By Rich Wilson, Skipper
Aboard *Great American III*

Take a globe. Center it in your gaze at 15° South latitude, 155° West longitude. Look at all that Pacific Ocean!

The Pacific is huge, and down here in the southern part powerful low pressure weather systems keep marching along, circling Antarctica like beads on a necklace, pushing big waves, winds and currents in front of them.

A different, but similarly huge, oceanic force is in the North Atlantic, where the Gulf Stream moves massive volumes of warm water from the Gulf of Mexico, around Florida, up the east coast, and across the Atlantic, heating northern Europe to temperatures far more moderate than we have at the same latitude in North America.

Volcanoes are powerful forces of nature, too. In the Pacific, the volcanic islands of Hawaii rose up from a "hot spot" in the tectonic plates. On the sea charts, one can see a string of sub-surface mountains that didn't quite make it to the ocean's surface to become islands – these are called seamounts. In 15,000 feet of water, we passed a seamount a few days ago that rose to within 25 feet of the surface – now that's a mountain!

It's logical to feel very small in the face of nature's enormity, but mankind still has an effect on nature. We should minimize our impact so that our relationship can remain in the realm of awe.

The Gulf Stream

By Captain Murray Lister

Nature gives the world so many variations of force and climate. Think of the tides, rain, snow, wind, ice, hurricanes and typhoons. Let us now consider the forces involved in those of the ocean currents.

For the United States there are two main currents: the Gulf Stream coming from the Gulf of Mexico, and the California Current in the vicinity of San Francisco and Los Angeles. These ocean currents are created by the rotation of the earth.

The better known of the two is the Gulf Stream which flows westward through the Caribbean Sea, thence northeast past Florida, up the east coast of the US, and eventually completes a full circle of the Atlantic Ocean, returning to the Caribbean.

The forces involved allow this initially warm water to drift thousands of miles, to the extent that because the water temperature is still above freezing, even around the United Kingdom and the coastal regions of Europe in winter, there is no sea ice and thus all the ports in those regions are able to remain open year-round.

In the sailing ship days, once sea current forces were recognized, mariners used them to their advantage when making passage. Even today in motor ships, captains may utilize currents to allow quicker passage time to the next port so they can arrive earlier than scheduled and reduce the consumption of expensive fuel.

sitesALIVE Foundation 

Massachusetts Institute of Technology • U.S. Merchant Marine Academy • Sea Education Association
Brigham & Women's Hospital • Tufts Medical Center • Peabody Essex Museum • U.S. Maritime Administration
Connecticut Maritime Association • Museum of Science • National Marine Fisheries Service • Select Fitness

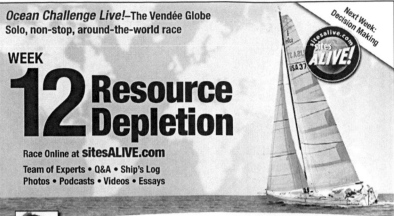

Ocean Challenge Live!–The Vendée Globe
Solo, non-stop, around-the-world race

WEEK 12 Resource Depletion

Race Online at **sitesALIVE.com**

Team of Experts • Q&A • Ship's Log
Photos • Podcasts • Videos • Essays

By Rich Wilson, Skipper
Aboard *Great American III*

Each boat in the Vendée Globe is an example of resource management and depletion. We bring food, fuel, spare sails, spare electronics, extra epoxy and fiberglass, spare rope, etc. Gradually, over the course of the race, these resources are consumed. Food levels decrease; repairs use up epoxy; electronics fail; ropes fray from chafing; and solar panels yellow and produce less electricity. Every skipper has to carefully manage his or her resources to last.

Planet earth has depletion issues, too, and we must carefully manage our resources. The fossil fuels (oil, gas, coal) are being used up, and fuel emissions are depleting our fresh air and increasing global warming. Many fresh water lakes and rivers have been polluted, thus depleting their availability. Forests have been depleted either to provide wood for building, or in some cases, the land is cleared to provide space for building. In the oceans, fisheries have been over-fished, and only rarely are there adequate resource management programs put in place to allow replenishment.

All of these circumstances boil down to the same thing: we've over-used many of our resources, and now we need to change our way of living. Ultimately, this will be a good thing, as it will push us toward more renewable living. That will be good for future generations, and it's our moral duty to think of those generations and not just our own.

Sustaining Our Fisheries

By Dr. Ambrose Jearld, Jr.
Fisheries Biologist, National Marine Fisheries Service, NOAA

As Rich sails across the world's oceans he may see occasional sharks or whales, but he will not see the thousands of fish species living in the waters far beneath his boat — many of them species that you and I eat for dinner. Fish is a growing source of food for people around the world, but as more people eat fish and the technology to locate and catch them improves, many species have been depleted (or are being depleted) by overfishing, climate change, and other factors.

We want to be able to keep eating fish, but we won't have enough for the future unless we allow depleted fish populations to rebuild and grow, and unless we keep other populations at healthy levels.

The good news is that fish are a renewable resource, and they can naturally replenish their populations if the right management measures are put in place. As scientists we try to understand basic biological questions like how does each species of fish grow and reproduce, but we also need to know how the environment or ecosystem in which the fish live affects its behavior and life cycle. This way of looking at the whole picture (and not just the fish) is called ecosystem-based management, and it is being put into practice in many parts of the world. A number of depleted fish populations are recovering, but we have a lot more work to do.

Ocean Challenge Live!–The Vendée Globe
Solo, non-stop, around-the-world race

WEEK 13 Decision Making

Race Online at **sitesALIVE.com**
Team of Experts • Q&A • Ship's Log
Photos • Podcasts • Videos • Essays

By Rich Wilson, Skipper
Aboard *Great American III*

Prior to the start of the Vendée Globe race, there were hundreds of decisions made: which boat to use, which qualifying race to sail, what to refit on the boat, what equipment to install, which vendors to use, etc. The notes on which our decisions were made fill a dozen thick 3-ring binders.

At-sea decisions include what route to take, what sails to set, how fast to go, what repairs to make, and much more. These decisions are made based on our own experience at sea, logic, input from experts where our own expertise is limited, and by doing research. Once we collect all possible information, there is a discussion within the group by email or phone, and I make the final choice.

A big challenge for me has been the tradeoff between speed and risk. To sail faster risks breaking things, but it also gets me across the finish line sooner. Events like climbing the mast to carry out a repair hold their own set of risks: I could get hurt, or, if I decide not to perform the repair, something might break. Sometimes I review my logic for hours. In the end I may turn to my gut feeling, which is really a measure of my confidence one way or the other.

Hopefully, we can make enough correct decisions from here on to get us safely to the finish.

Decisions At Sea

By Rich du Moulin, Owner
Intrepid Shipping

We all have to make decisions in our lives, many of them important to our friends, families, and ourselves. Rich has had to make decisions during the Vendée Globe to maintain the safety of *Great American III;* to produce articles, photos, podcasts and videos for sitesALIVE; and to balance sailing fast with preserving his physical and mental strength.

Rich is the oldest competitor with a seven-year-old boat that is not the newest or fastest design. He knows that many of the competitors are sailors who are aggressively pushing their newer boats. Knowing that he cannot win on pure boat speed or physical strength, Rich is using his experience to make decisions that keep himself and the boat in the race, with the goal of crossing the finish line through experience and endurance.

Decision-making at sea is very hard because you are tired, alone, and sometimes scared. Very often you do not have much time to act. Making a good decision relies on experience and judgment for sure, but planning and preparation are also very important. If you can anticipate a problem, then you can plan ahead and not have to make a last-second decision which might be too late. Good luck and good decision-making, Rich Wilson!

Rich du Moulin raced with Rich Wilson on Great American II *from Hong Kong to New York in 2003.*

---

sitesALIVE Foundation 

Massachusetts Institute of Technology • U.S. Merchant Marine Academy • Sea Education Association
Brigham & Women's Hospital • Tufts Medical Center • Peabody Essex Museum • U.S. Maritime Administration
Connecticut Maritime Association • Museum of Science • National Marine Fisheries Service • Select Fitness

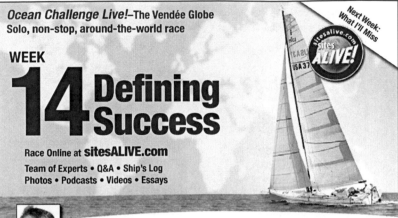

Ocean Challenge Live!–The Vendée Globe
Solo, non-stop, around-the-world race

Next Week: What I'll Miss

WEEK 14 Defining Success

Race Online at sitesALIVE.com
Team of Experts • Q&A • Ship's Log
Photos • Podcasts • Videos • Essays

By Rich Wilson, Skipper
Aboard *Great American III*

For Michel Desjoyeaux, success in the Vendée Globe is winning the race, which he has just done for the second time with an extraordinary effort. He is a professional sailor, and this is his proving ground.

For many of the other skippers in the race, the goal is to finish. They may have older boats or be amateur sailors. For them, winning is out of reach—their goal is to finish.

For me, there are two goals. One goal is to produce a great school program within sitesALIVE, both via newspapers and the web, and with significant contribution from our Team of Experts. The other goal is to complete the race.

On our school program, now 14 weeks along, feedback suggests that we have been successful in exciting and engaging students, mostly in the US, but also with classrooms from a dozen countries worldwide. Additionally, we have 50 newspapers publishing our series in the US.

If I can keep going and reach Les Sables d'Olonne, we will also meet our second goal. We won't know that outcome for several weeks from now.

In defining success, one must set realistic and specific goals. And then, at the finish of the project, be very honest about whether they were reached or not. For us, except for our desire to have had overseas newspapers participate, we are close to having a successful project.

A successful education program

By Lorraine Leo, Technology Teacher, Newton, Massachusetts, USA

Rich entered the Vendée Globe race in part for the challenge of the race, but mainly for the opportunity to create an education program designed to excite and engage students and families. As Rich says, "Once you've hooked kids with excitement, you can feed them whatever content you want—math, science, geography, teamwork, goal-setting, and more."

Was his education program a success? YES! Rich wrote articles, maintained a ship's log, called in audio podcasts via satellite, and answered questions throughout his voyage. With help from his shore team, he also published a weekly print series that has appeared in many national, regional and local newspapers. Rich did this all while sailing *Great American III* in severe weather conditions, on dangerously high seas, in the heat and cold, and over the course of more than 25,000 nautical miles.

Rich was followed online by thousands of teachers and students from around the world. To date, he has received a great deal of positive feedback and support from his followers. These point to the success of the education program.

Now we wait for Rich to cross the finish line and complete the Vendée Globe. Thank you Skipper Rich Wilson for your inspiration and perseverance. On behalf of all, we salute you!

sitesALIVE Foundation 

Massachusetts Institute of Technology • U.S. Merchant Marine Academy • Sea Education Association
Brigham & Women's Hospital • Tufts Medical Center • Peabody Essex Museum • U.S. Maritime Administration
Connecticut Maritime Association • Museum of Science • National Marine Fisheries Service • Select Fitness

WEEK 15 What I'll Miss

Race Online at **sitesALIVE.com**

Team of Experts • Q&A • Ship's Log
Photos • Podcasts • Videos • Essays

By Rich Wilson, Skipper
Aboard *Great American III*

Surrounded by 360 degrees of horizon, you are totally immersed in nature. You see every sunrise, every sunset, the stars, the clouds, and the waves. Last week the full moon rose just after sunset, demonstrating the geometry of its fullness.

The wildlife, what one can see at the surface, is fascinating. From whales to albatross, from flying fish to squid, from porpoises to tuna to the myriad of bird species unknown to me, all of this wildlife is captivating.

Aboard the boat one is constantly challenged by the changing weather and its analysis, by the immense physical exertion of sail maneuvers, by hanging on for safety in bad weather, and by problem solving applied to mechanical and electrical systems that stop working, break, or are just plain finicky.

In this solo race, solitude is not an issue due to the satellite telephone connections that can be made, but being alone aboard *Great American III* when the conditions are difficult is incredibly physically demanding, and it would surely help to have another one, two, or three crew members aboard.

A great teacher of mine, Dr. Ray Pariser of MIT, told me once, "You need to stretch your mind." Surely that is a great prescription for many pursuits in life. For me, being at sea does that exactly.

The next expedition

By Scott Hamilton
Investment Advisor, Explorer

When an expedition comes to an end, I don't really miss much except for my comrades. There is a huge sense of relief when I arrive back in a place that is warm, safe, dry, and where I no longer feel a constant element of great danger. And, of course, I enjoy the many conveniences we take for granted like hot water, flush toilets, a clean bed with sheets, electricity, heat, and stores filled with fresh foods.

But after a period of rest and recovery, life back in civilization starts to seem a little dull and boring compared to the excitement of being on an expedition. When you are on an expedition, all your senses are alive and each and every day is an adventure. You get to experience encounters with nature that most people can only dream about: spectacular sunrises, huge storms, wild creatures in their natural habitat, and majestic peaks sticking up like islands above the clouds.

Being on an expedition is a mental challenge because you have to rely on your experience and judgment to solve the problems that inevitably arise. It is challenging indeed, but it is also very rewarding. After a while, life back in civilization starts to seem too easy, and I find myself craving the adventure, excitement, learning, and camaraderie that come with exploring. That is when I start planning the next expedition.

---

sitesALIVE Foundation 

Massachusetts Institute of Technology • U.S. Merchant Marine Academy • Sea Education Association
Brigham & Women's Hospital • Tufts Medical Center • Peabody Essex Museum • U.S. Maritime Administration
Connecticut Maritime Association • Museum of Science • National Marine Fisheries Service • Select Fitness

List of Photos, Credits & Cover Design

Front & Back Cover: *Great American III (Jacques Vapillon)*

Front Matter:
Dorothy Ann (Simpson) Wilson; Race Route; 30 Skippers (*Vincent Curutchet*); *GA3* Sailplan, Spinnaker, Hull

Prologue:
Everest of the Seas?

1. Les Sables d'Olonne:
"Yes U Can"; Crowd on Dock; Skippers' Ages; Michel Desjoyeaux; Fleet Starts

2. Battling the Bay of Biscay:
GA3 Starts (*Jacques Vapillon*); Marti Shea (*Lee Krohn*)*; Groupe Bel* broken mast

3. Respect in the North Atlantic:
Map; Dr. Brien Barnewolt; *Radio Vacances* - Andi Robertson; Flying Fish; Double Rainbow; Dolphins; Cindy's Chanel Scarf

4. My Path to the Vendée Globe:
Swimming with Model Boat; *Holger Danske*

5. sitesALIVE!:
Logo; *GA2* Departs NY; Neal Skorka

6. Asthma at Sea
Lung Function Test; Asthma Medications; Dr. Chris Fanta

7. South Atlantic in Missouri:
Map; Jean-Yves Bernot; MaxSea; Prayer Flags; BowSplash; Missourian

8. Gales of the Indian Ocean:
Map; Jonny Malbon & Dame Ellen MacArthur (*Mark Lloyd*); Sea Gets Up; Barograph Double Low; Helmet & Visor; Yann Eliès Rescue (*HMS Arunta*); Albatross; Eye Gash

9. Halfway Home aboard *GA3*:
Cockpit (*Billy Black*); Broken Rudderpost; Broken Daggerboard;

Brian Harris; Keel; Chart Table; 90 Degree Test; Mike Birch; Hugues Riousse; Rick Williams

10. Pacific Ocean:
Map; Balaclava & BandAid; Yves Parlier (*Jean-Marie Liot*); International Date Line; Samantha Davies; *VM Matériaux* capsized (*Vincent Riou*); Moonlight; Foot Ascender

11. Cape Horn:
Cape Horn; *New Zealand Pacific*; Chief Mate Murray Lister

12. The South Atlantic...Again:
Map; Storm Weathermap; Storm Wave Height Forecast; Barograph Dives; Never-Give-Up; Sleep Data Example from Transat 2004

13. Northern North Atlantic:
Map; Wave Height Forecast; Weathermap

14. Finishing Among the Amazing French:
GA3 Surfing Home (*Olivier Blanchet*); Thierry Dubois (*Patrice Bodin*); In the Channel; Denis Horeau; On Stage

15. Prize-Giving Ceremony:
Emotional Man on Dock; Raphaël, Norbert, and me; Mom's Welcome Home; Prize-Giving Ceremony (*Jean-Marie Liot*); With Michel Desjoyeaux

Epilogue: 2012 or 2016?
Signing man's book; 2008-9 Media Graphs; Hubert Desjoyeaux; Massachusetts Maritime Academy

Appendices:
U.S. Senate Tribute; Lectures & Comments: Team of Experts; Participating Newspapers; NIE Features (15 weeks)

Front & Back Cover Design:

Bob Santosuosso

Acknowledgments:

The Vendée Globe is solo only at sea. Ashore, a vast group of friends, advisors, vendors, workers and race managers, surround the project, all with goodwill and expertise, with the goal being that the skipper comes home safely, and project objectives are attained.

To my Mom, to whom this book is dedicated, and my Dad, the best I ever saw at preparing a boat to go to sea, you gave me the inspiration and grounding to undertake the voyage.

My sisters who came to the start and finish: Eleanor, Anne, and Sarah, thanks. And Cousin Rick Simpson, for wowing the French on the dock at the start with your inspired renditions of *"La Marseillaise"* from the cabin top of *Great American III.*

To my inner circle, Ellen Stone, George Gibson, Doug Borg, Trip Lowell, you were always willing to listen, and I could not have done it without you.

To my friends who encouraged, yet kept their fears to themselves, Carrie Snyder, Bill Griffen, Paul Tamburello, Rick & Nonnie Burnes, thanks. Thanks to the Big Boys who encouraged, and especially those who came to France to see a fellow Big Boy off on a great adventure: Bob Metcalfe, Bob Shotwell, John Sculley, Scott Hamilton.

Thanks to sailing friends and former shipmates who encouraged and advised: John Kiley, Bill Biewenga, Steve Pettengill, Rich du Moulin, Mike Birch, Ed Sisk, Wayne Colahan, Pierre Jean, and my two mentors, Phil Steggall and Walter Greene, it's been an honor to know and sail with you all, you taught me a lot along the way.

To Clarke Smith, you insured *GA3* when no one else in the USA would, thanks for your confidence, it allowed us to start the project.

To Bob & Kate Niehaus, and Michael & Dorothy Hintze, your early generosity allowed us to know absolutely that we could fund our sitesALIVE! K12 program. We reached 250,000 students because of you, and I and they thank you.

Thanks to Bernard Nivelt for designing a great boat and to Thierry Dubois for building her so well, to Benoit Lequin who helped assemble her, and to Bernard Gallay for managing her purchase and later sale.

To Drew Lyman, Steve Tofield, and the crew at Lyman-Morse, thanks for the good repair on short notice after our boat-breaking collision with the submerged object south of Iceland.

To Maine Yacht Center: Brian Harris, Will Rooks, Nate Andrews, Zach Kane, Fred Dodge, and Julie Ferris, for the amazing re-fit, all with a smile, *GA3* became your boat too, and she sailed the world.

To Mark Wylie, electronics guru from England, I've no idea how you know what you know, but your wiring worked and we made it!

To Robbie Doyle (Doyle Sailmakers), Moose McClintock (Dimension Polyant), and Hugues Destremeau (Incidences Voiles), you made the sails right, and they went all the way with no problems, thanks hugely.

À Michel Desjoyeaux, Le (et Mon) Professeur, merci pour notre échange par email avant la course, tu m'as aidé beaucoup.

À Hubert Desjoyeaux, et toute l'equipe de CDK Technologies, you treated *Great American III* as if she were French and helped me reach my dream. And to Patrice, always there with a big smile, a strong hand, and to teach me more French.

To Hugues Riousse and Rick Williams, *GA3 preparateurs* extraordinaire: thanks for your skill, hard work, seamanship expertise, and dedication. As only two, you did the same workload as the fully-sponsored teams, and we finished, and some of them didn't. *Bien fait.*

In Port la Foret et Les Sables d'Olonne, to the welders, electricians, diesel mechanics, sailmakers, divers, port authorities and customs agents, you were all on my side, merci.

To my Doctors, Dr. Beverly Woo who has kept me healthy, Dr. Chris Fanta who has managed my asthma so skillfully, Dr. Brien Barnewolt who managed my injuries at sea from afar in Boston, and Dr. Jean-Yves Chauve, the official Race Doctor: in combination you helped me become only the second American, and the second oldest finisher ever, in this harshest endurance event in the world.

To Marti Shea, you got me into the best physical condition of my life, irrespective of age. It's impossible to overstate how demanding this race was physically. I, and my friends, hug you in thanks.

To Jean-Yves Bernot, you taught me about the weather on the great oceans of the world, theoretically and pragmatically, an immense thanks to you.

To Neal Skorka, long-time sitesALIVE! veteran, knowing you were CAPCOM for our big and complex K12 program gave me comfort offshore. Amazingly well done, you achieved our primary goal in the classrooms of the world as much as I achieved our goal at sea. To Lorraine Leo, technology teacher extraordinaire, thanks for bringing in your global network of teachers to this live global ocean expedition; our nation needs another million of you. To Bob Graham, thanks for writing a terrific Teacher's Guide. To Dianna Fletcher, thanks for help on PR.

To our Team of Experts, what an honor to have you all aboard with sitesALIVE! And how fortunate for all the students to read your essays and to send you questions, a completely unique experience in K12 globally. Thanks to: Prof. Dava Newman, Dr. Brien Barnewolt, Ms. Dava Sobel, Dr. Chris Fanta, Capt. Eric Wallischecke, Mr. Sam Scott, Dr. Jan Witting, Ms. Marti Shea, Ms. Laura Mirabella, Dr. Ioannis Miaoulis, Capt. Murray Lister, Dr. Ambrose Jearld, Mr. Rich du Moulin, Ms. Lorraine Leo, Mr. Scott Hamilton, Mr. Sean Connaughton, and Dr. Chuck Czeisler.

To the Vendée Globe management and Race Officers, especially Sophie Vercelleto, Denis Horeau, Julian Hocken, Eve Loyola, and Joël Gâté: the regulations were detailed and intelligent, the inspections and paperwork were done cordially and helpfully, an efficient effort by you. Your emotional task may be more challenging, as the skippers feared for themselves individually, yet you feared for us all, until the fleet was home or at least accounted for.

To Andi Robertson of *Radio Vacances*, you were a friend through the airwaves, always remembering *GA3*'s challenges and encouraging us ever onward, thanks.

Thanks always to the Riousse family, Hugues, Flo, Benjamin and Sylvain, my family in France, et j'aime La Maison Vague! And to Benjamin especially, your quiet tackling of your own big challenge inspired me in the south.

To Myles Jessel, long-time friend and French translator, you always had a smile and a quip, and it always helped!

To new friends in Port la Foret, Willy at Mer de Glace, Jean-Jacques Le Goff, and to restaurants and boulangeries, your welcome made me feel completely at home there.

To my friends at the Buffalo Grill, you stabilized my nutrition before this big adventure, thanks for your encouragement and my nightly Pony Express!

To Christophe and Patricia Jean in Paris, thanks for your kind and continual encouragement, and for your generous hospitality when I passed through Paris to or from the boat.

To Fabienne Mollé of the American Embassy in Paris, thanks for your encouragement, and for helping us represent the USA well in this amazing French sports event.

To Senator John Kerry, your U.S. Senate Tribute took my breath away, thank you.

To all the Open 60 skippers who welcomed me into the Class, and into their amazing races.

To George Gibson, Michael Carlisle, Sarah Flynn, Sarah Twombly, Rosalyn Schanzer, William Callahan, Bob Santosuosso: you helped me complete this this book, and thanks mightily.

Lastly, thanks to the French public. Your attitudes about life, and living it to its utmost, are a lesson to us all. You welcomed me and our American team into your race and your hearts. As I said after my finish, there were two Vendée Globes, one offshore, the hardest sailboat race in the world, and one onshore, with you and your warmth and welcome, and in the future, when the trials and pains and fears of being offshore alone are lost from my memory, what I will always remember is the race on land, with you and your warmth and friendship. Thank you.

CPSIA information can be obtained at www.ICGtesting.com
Printed in the USA
LVOW081421111112

306810LV00002B/136/P